December '88
Best Wishes for you
from J

GREEVES

OSPREY
COLLECTOR'S
LIBRARY

GREEVES

All off-road, road and road-racing motorcycles

Rob Carrick
Mick Walker

Published in 1988 by Osprey Publishing Limited
59 Grosvenor Street, London W1X 9DA

British Library Cataloguing in Publication Data
Carrick, Rob
Greeves: all off-road, road and road-racing motorcycles.
1. Greeves motorcycles, history
I. Title II. Walker, Mick
629.2'275
ISBN 0-85045-882-X

Editor Nick Collins
Design Gwyn Lewis

Printed by BAS Printers Limited
Over Wallop, Hampshire
Great Britain

Contents

FIM
FEDERATION INTERNATIONALE
MOTOCYCLISTE
Dave Bickers
CHAMPION D'EUROPE
MOTOCROSS
250cc
1960

Foreword by Dave Bickers

The eight years I spent with the Greeves factory were probably some of the happiest, if not most hectic, years of my life. I often sit down and wonder how on earth I survived the rigours of racing every weekend, month in and month out, in order to complete the season's schedule. Thinking of my time riding for Greeves brings back fond memories of the riders, mechanics and officials met on the numerous jaunts to the various British and continental rounds whilst contesting the European and World Championships.

The factory's design staff, led by Mr Greeves, together with the technical back-up staff and fitters, were a very enthusiastic bunch, just like a big, close-knit, happy family. We each did our respective jobs, as well as helping each other out, for understanding each other's problems made life a little easier and achieved the end results we all wanted. The design team and technical staff were not unapproachable, as was the case with some employees of the other sporting factories, and would listen intently to any constructive criticisms I may have made about their masterpieces. Discussions were always polite, but sometimes a little heated until a compromise was reached. These discussions brought about the logical development of the motocross model, the results which were obtained justifying any changes we may have made.

Because I had been associated with the Greeves factory for such a long time by modern standards, readers may be forgiven for thinking that I rode the Essex marque from the onset of my career. Not a bit of it. As a kid, my first machine was an old Norton 16H, which I used in the field behind my father's garage. Living so close to the Shrublands Park circuit, I used to watch riders there and on returning home would mimic their antics on the old Norton. Being so enthusiastic about scrambling, at the age of 16 I joined the local Ipswich club and took part in my first Eastern Centre scramble in 1954. Prior to my Greeves days, I raced a home-tuned Dot 197, which attracted the attention of Brian Stonebridge, and he signed me up in 1958.

Dave Bickers (left) and British motocross chief Harold Taylor with the 1960 FIM *Champion d'Europe* **award**

For a year Brian Stonebridge was my friend and master. We shared the driving on the Grand Prix circuit, although it always seemed to be me who finished up in the driving seat. But I never dared complain.

He used a Morris Oxford van with an engine he had tuned himself, but unfortunately it wasn't very powerful. I was always getting into trouble for taking my foot off the accelerator on corners, as it took miles to build up speed again. When he was driving he would never let me sleep. He would slam on the brakes, hoot the hooter and bang his fist on the roof if I happened to doze off. I tried to catch him out in the same way many times, but never succeeded. He always knew what I was doing.

Brian never told me anything; I learned from just being with him. He taught me to think for myself, as well as making me a better rider. At my first Grand Prix in Belgium I hit a tree during practice, the Greeves finishing up in the branches above. I waited for Brian to come along, thinking he would give me a hand. He stopped, looked at the bike in the tree, turned to me and said, 'You silly bugger', and rode off!

I soon learned about Stonebridge the practical joker, too. Often when I went to the factory he would ask me to test new ideas on the bikes he had been experimenting with. He wouldn't tell me what he had done, but simply ask for my comments. One day he asked me to take a bike up the road and get it going flat out. By the time I reached 40 mph the bike was jumping up and down like a pogo stick—he had built a pair of

wheels with the hubs 6 in. off centre!

I found the news of his death hard to believe. I had lost my teacher and my friend, and I was on my own. Luckily some of his skill and knowledge had rubbed off on me.

The highlight of my career must have been the European Championships of 1960 and 1961, which were not gained lightly, much energy and midnight oil being expended. The effort was not all my own, for the back-up needed for these achievements in terms of spares and expertise was enormous. In contrast, I must say that at times things were quite the opposite and nothing would seem to go right. The disastrous 1963 season, and the gear-selection problems of 1964, illustrate the fact that we did not have it all our own way.

Leaving the Greeves factory in 1966, I did not sever all links but kept in touch, albeit from afar. The pressure of work from my various business interests now consumes a lot of my time, but by way of relaxation, when time permits, I like nothing more than a gallop on one of my old machines to try to keep my hand in for the all-too-few pre-'65 scrambles events which I enter. You never know, I might even be Greeves-mounted in the near future and shake up a few pre-'65 riders.

Bickers in characteristic forceful style, which made him feared throughout the dirt-bike racing world, and the most photographed rider of the era

Dave Bickers
European Motocross Champion 1960 and 1961
Nine-times British Motocross Champion

CODDENHAM, SUFFOLK

Acknowledgements

This book evolved from an unpublished manuscript, written by Rob Carrick, on Greeves trials bikes. Unfortunately, at the time (1986), it proved too specialized a subject to tempt a publisher. It was also Rob's first attempt at compiling a book, so he sought advice from his near neighbour, Mick Walker (well 14 miles is counted as next door in rural East Anglia), who had had a number of titles successfully published. Mick proffered the same view as the publishers, saying, 'It's too specialized, why not do a Greeves history?' Rob replied that although he could cover the dirt-bike side—trials, motocross and the ISDT—he was not sure about attempting the roadsters and road racers.

Having raced a Silverstone in the classic era (his brother-in-law's RCS model) and having competed against not only the Silverstone, but the 350 Oulton too, on a variety of machines, Mick *knew* he could cope with the racing chapter. This left the roadsters, so becoming ever more enthusiastic about the project, he came up with a synopsis one evening, scribbling it out while watching the television. This proved to be the blueprint for the book you are now reading—even down to the chapter titles.

It was agreed that each author would write half of the chapters, with Rob compiling the appendices, and Mick taking responsibility for the picture captions—and that's exactly what happened. In the meantime, the two became firm friends—respecting each other's ability and enthusiasm—a true team effort.

This is also a story of East Anglia. Not only do Rob and Mick both reside in that part of the British Isles but, in addition, the Greeves factory was based there, and even today many of the marque's most famous names live there, including Bert Greeves himself, Dave Bickers and Reg Everett to name but a few.

A large proportion of the people who make up the Greeves story were consulted in person, ensuring maximum authenticity, and enabling the marque's amazing success in sporting events to be fully uncovered and documented for the first time in so much detail. This had the added advantage of bringing to light many previously unpublished photographs, the majority being from private collections.

So just where do we start in an attempt to say thank you to all those who assisted? For example, Dave Bickers, for not only kindly agreeing to compile the foreword, but for providing much useful background information on the scrambles and motocross scene in general. And O. B. 'Bert' Greeves OBE, without whom there would not be a story to write in the first place and who was particularly helpful in revealing his early history, answering many questions (some very difficult!) and generally providing encouragement with the project.

Don Smith shared his fund of knowledge, enthusiasm and photographs in the compilation of the Scottish and Anglian chapters. Further help came from Mike Jackson, now the managing director of the leading accessory company Andover Norton, but formally the South Eastern area Greeves representative and a trials and scrambles rider of some note; Gordon Swift, early Greeves scrambler, ex-motorcycle dealer and currently gentleman farmer and sailing-barge skipper; John Oliver, another ex-scrambler, now working for British Aerospace; and Mick Noyce, who competed in the Valli Bergamasche three-day and ISDT events.

Sammy Miller supplied various photographs, details of his 1960 ISDT ride and much valuable information from the Miller Motorcycle Museum. Two-stroke specialist Barry Hickmott assisted in both technical and competition research on the marque, while Reg Everett—seen by many as the rider who first put Greeves on the road-racing map—not only helped compile the early racing details, but also loaned many photographs. Bob Stevenson provided photographs and information on his very special 350 and other Greeves-based road-racing projects, and Brian Woolley not only gave much valuable assistance in his position as chief archivist at EMAP, but also related his personal experiences of entering several Greeves road racers in the 1960s, including Reg Everett and Trevor Burgess.

Reg Orpin kindly read through the road-racing chapter and made valuable comments, while Tony Plumridge (Mick Walker's brother-in-law) lent his complete collection of Greeves photographs and recalled past experiences. Bob Mills, the loyal factory road-race mechanic, helped in many ways. In the opinion of the authors, Bob was *the* lynchpin of the Silverstone saga and was the man who did much of the day-to-day work on the tarmac racers at the Thundersley works.

There were also several others who provided great help: Dave Street, Doug Jackson, Philip Tooth and Frank Ball in particular, and many GRA (Greeves Riders Association) members, especially John Collard, whose help with the technical side was invaluable. John's pet subject is the ISDT, and

Right **Ducati-mounted Mick Walker leads Charles Mortimer's Greeves Silverstone RDS at Snetterton in May 1966**

Below **Co-authors Rob Carrick (left), on a 1965 246 cc TFS, and Mick Walker, with a 1971 169 cc Pathfinder**

the information and pictures in his collection must be seen to be appreciated.

Several of the photographs used carried the imprint of professionals: Cecil Bailey, Jon Davis, W. Emberton, Gordon Francis, Brian Holder, Angela Knight, Michael Marriott, Charles Marston, B. R. Nicholls, Donald Page, Ken Price, D. Rowe, Len Thorpe and Dan Upshaw. If anyone has been overlooked, we can but apologise and assure them that it was unintentional.

The manuscript was typed by Joan Carrick (Rob's mother) and Carol Green (Mick's secretary)—a big thanks to both. Finally, thanks to the Osprey editorial team—Caroline, Catherine, Ian and editor Nick Collins—for the usual very professional assistance in helping bring our work to life.

Rob Carrick
DOWNHAM MARKET, NORFOLK

Mick Walker
WISBECH, CAMBRIDGESHIRE

1 Invalid carriages to Earls Court

Oscar Bertrum 'Bert' Greeves was born in Lyon, France, on 5 June 1906, of English parents. His father was a tanner—a European export consultant in all aspects of leather manufacture for a leading Northampton company. Greeves senior was also the inventor and developer of the now famous chrome tanning process. The family remained on the other side of the Channel until 1913, when they returned to England. This was to make Greeves Junior a true Anglo-Saxon, being able to speak both French and English fluently.

Not old enough for military service in World War 1, young Bert's first employment came as an apprentice with the Austin car company, which he joined in 1922. However, he left the following year to become an improver apprentice with the Worcester firm Heenan and Froude, the legendary dynamometer manufacturers. After serving his apprenticeship, he was involved in the production and testing of small dynos and acted as a detail draughtsman. His career with Heenan and Froude ended in late 1930 when he left to become the senior partner, with his brother, in a garage business in Surbiton, Surrey—during the throes of the Great Depression when the industrialized world, including Britain, was on its knees.

During the war years (from 1940 onwards), the partnership acted as small subcontractors, doing machinery work for various government ministries. The business came to a sudden end at the beginning of 1945, when the building was blown up by a German V1 rocket. Luckily, this happened outside working hours!

Soon afterwards, Bert Greeves founded Invacar Ltd, to design and manufacture invalid carriages. The idea for this venture had come from his modification of a Villiers lawn-mower engine, which he had fitted into a wheelchair belonging to his cousin, Derry Preston-Cobb, who had been paralysed from birth, and who was almost totally paraplegic, having only a small amount of voluntary movement in his right hand and arm. Without doubt, one of Bert Greeves' greatest achievements was to devise a system of controls which could cope with this level of disability. Though obviously not planned that way, this proved to be a classic instance of the right invention at the right time.

The immediate post-war period had witnessed thousands of severely disabled and limbless ex-servicemen in Britain—victims of the carnage which had just ended. These unfortunate people had become the responsibility of the Ministry of Pensions, and with a newly-elected socialist government in power, a strong voice in authority decreed that they had a right to be independently mobile. To meet this need, Bert Greeves conceived Invacar, a company that would build the necessary vehicles, which he felt could be achieved following the work on his cousin's prototype.

A location for the company was found at West Road, Westcliff-on-Sea, Essex, and production began in early 1946. This site, since redeveloped by the Ford Motor Company, was vacated in May 1950 when the sheer demand for its products meant that Invacar needed larger premises. These were found in Church Road, Thundersley, a short distance away.

Shortly after the move, the works produced its first motorcycle. If this seems strange, it should be remembered that Bert Greeves had gained his licence in 1919 and, after first borrowing his father's 225 cc James, he purchased a side-valve 350 from the same company. He related recently that his father's machine was 'too slow, and could easily be overtaken by cyclists and mad dogs!'

Following the James experiences had come a variety of two-wheelers, including an ohc Norton CSI 500 single which he rode in trials during the late 1920s, gaining several awards. The Norton was purchased new in 1928, and he paid £1.00 extra for works tuning—it would do 85 mph and, at the time, was the fastest machine he had owned. It was not reliable if thrashed, but if used at 70 mph it was okay. When *towing* a car back from Cornwall, the piston of the CSI disintegrated in Bridgewater, Somerset. Bert wired his mother to send another one, which arrived within 16 hours. The motor was rebuilt at the side of the road and the journey continued.

Bert Greeves managed a best time of 33.2 seconds for the standing kilometre (with a 10 yard run in) with his CSI. He could complete the journey from Richmond, Surrey, to Worcester, to see his uncle, in two hours and five minutes. Eventually, the faithful Norton suffered a fractured down-tube (which was rewelded), and, finally, in 1936 the engine had a terminal blow-up when the con-rod broke. The latter ended the machine's life, as it was not practical to rebuild it.

Post-war, Bert owned a couple of Vincent V-twins, and several other machines, including one with the registration OLD 1! Even today, aged over 80, his enthusiasm has hardly waned, and there are six Greeves motorcycles of various types in his garage.

Back in the early 1950s he had the chance of actually producing his own motorcycle. Invacar had needed to carry out an experiment on a new suspension system for the company's invalid cars. This was based on rubber in torsion. But how to test the theory? Together with draughtsman Jack Collins, Bert Greeves came up with an ideal solution. With his great enthusiasm for bikes, the Invacar boss used the opportunity to fulfil a long-held dream—that of creating his own motorcycle.

Following an abortive first venture with a modified pre-war Norton, he decided to construct a purpose-built machine from scratch. To make life easier and utilize existing materials, including a Villiers two-stroke engine, it was decided to make the prototype a lightweight. A little known fact is that four-stroke engines were considered. Bert Greeves wanted to use the 250 JAP motor, but JAP would not, as he put it, 'play ball'. He did, however,

Bert Greeves with his Norton CS1 at Madresfield during the Worcestershire Speed Trials in July 1928

By 1950 the Invacar looked like this. Bert Greeves' cousin, Derry Preston-Cobb, himself incapacitated, is shown in the vehicle

manage to obtain three 35 cc two-strokes from the same concern. One was used to drive a dynamo, one to charge boat batteries, and the third was lost. But the Invacar boss was not impressed, saying, 'Horrible little things, let down by an unreliable magneto.'

The first hint that the Greeves machine existed was carried by the magazine *Motor Cycle* in their issue of 10 May 1951. In fact, there were *two* prototypes. One, a roadster, was the bike sampled by *Motor Cycle*, but the other, perhaps more significantly for the future, was a scrambles version.

In their report, *Motor Cycle* commented that at a later date—perhaps towards the end of the year—Invacar hoped to market a production version of the roadster. But the original 'official' purpose of the design had not been forgotten. The Greeves lightweight employed a new type of frame, which used rubber bushes in torsion as part of an ingenious suspension system. The frame had no lugs in its construction and was nickel-bronze welded throughout. The front down-tubes of the duplex cradle frame were brought up to the top of the steering head, and an exceptionally large-diameter top frame tube was welded to the bottom of the steering-head support. At the rear of the cradle frame were two rubber bushes, which acted as a pivot for the fork of the rear suspension. The rubber bushes in torsion, which constituted the suspension medium, were mounted under the saddle at the rear of the top tube, and the load was transmitted to them by links running from pivots above the rear wheel spindle.

Rubber bushes in torsion were also used for the trailing-link fork which carried the front wheel. The various tubes of the frame were of a light gauge and, in spite of the frame's apparent size, the complete machine, which had a 197 cc Villiers engine, weighed only 200 lb.

Among the advantages claimed at the time for the system were that the rubber-bushed pivots were unaffected by grit and moisture, requiring no maintenance, and that no shock absorbers were needed, as the rubber was self-damping. The frame also had the advantage of possessing great lateral rigidity. The front suspension provided 6 in. of movement, the rear 4 in. Bottoming of the rear end was virtually impossible, owing to the leverage on the rubber bushes decreasing with large deflections, and the rubber stops for the front forks were found necessary only for serious off-road work.

A week after the *Motor Cycle* report, their rivals, *Motor Cycling*, of 17 May, carried out a track test of the Greeves scrambles prototype. As the well-known journalist C. P. Read reported; 'Wadered and coated, Mr Greeves was in attendance to give a personal demonstration.' The scrambler closely followed the basic design of the roadster which *Motor Cycle* had featured, and it is interesting to note that Bert Greeves himself had not only done much of the design work, but *personally* tested his theories into the bargain!

Without doubt, it was the appearance of the Greeves that caused the most comment. Witness, for example, C. P. Read's comments; 'We tend to become rather hidebound in our conceptions of what a motorcycle should look like and I must confess that the appearance of the front end of the Greeves somewhat shook my rather conventional outlook'—yes, it did (and still does) look weird! But the most interesting extract from the test of that very first competition model was the final comment; 'I should very much like to see this model handled by an expert trials man or scrambler over tough going when I feel sure it would be well worth watching.' I wonder if the *Motor Cycling* tester had a crystal ball handy—or some other means of looking into the future—when making that statement?

Soon, Greeves' draughtsman and development engineer Frank Byford began to campaign that very same prototype, modifying it in the light of experience gained in local Eastern Centre scrambles. As the machine became faster so more faults would appear in the steel-tube frame. Then one day at a scrambles event, Bert Greeves watched Francis Barnett's top rider and competition manager, Ernie Smith (destined to join Greeves in January 1960), weld a length of solid $1\frac{1}{4}$ in. steel shafting into the frame in place of the front down-tube, and came up with the answer—and with it a design feature which was to remain a hallmark of the Essex company for many years afterwards.

Although, at first, Bert Greeves had found the incident with the shafting extremely funny, he had to admit that it actually worked. When he returned to base, it set him thinking that there just might be something to be gained from the idea—the result was the legendary alloy beam. Cast around the welded-up area of the main frame loop and the steering head, the beam proved

The original Greeves roadster prototype, as illustrated in *Motor Cycle*, **10 May 1951**

GREEVES

GREEVES

Above left **The 1951 off-road prototype**

Left **Off-road prototype frame and fork details—production models differed considerably**

Above **Features of the Greeves sidecar chassis, which went on sale in the summer of 1952**

exceptionally strong and light. In testing, it proved unbreakable.

Even so, there were to be no production Greeves for almost two and a half years after that initial burst of press reaction in the spring of 1951. The next piece of news did not concern a motorcycle, but a sidecar chassis, reported by *Motor Cycling* in their issue dated 7 August 1952. This also utilized rubber in torsion for its body suspension. The main frame was formed of a single $1\frac{3}{4}$ in. o.d., 16-gauge steel tube, bent into a hairpin shape and carrying on the rearward ends the main rubber units. These were coupled together by a tubular suspension bar, which prevented independent movement developing. To provide a degree of flexibility in roll for the body, four bonded rubber units were used for the actual body mounting. A rubber bush was also incorporated in the drop arm of the rear connection. This acted as a shock absorber, providing controlled support for the chassis.

Designed for single-seater and child-adult bodies, the Greeves chassis, which weighed only 91 lb complete with all fittings, could be supplied with an alternative harder suspension for use when a double-adult chair was to be fitted. Priced at £39 18*s* 0*d*, few were actually sold.

However, this did not mean that either Bert Greeves or, for that matter, any of the Invacar team had lost interest during the two years since the two motorcycle prototypes had first appeared in public. This was borne out in no uncertain terms when a trio of production models burst on to the world (or, at least, British) stage in September 1953, a few weeks prior to the prestigious London Earls Court Motorcycle Show to be held in mid-November.

Not only had much useful prototype development taken place while competing in sporting events in East Anglia and the Home Counties, but during the interim period after the original press stories, much further experimental work and tooling up had been undertaken as a prelude to the autumn 1953 launch.

Obviously, Bert Greeves, company chairman and both managing and technical director, was largely responsible for the creation of the machines, but it is worth recording the efforts of

An early 1950s photograph showing a section of the Invacar works

his co-director on the sales side, Derry Preston-Cobb. Although restricted to a wheelchair—or his specially-adapted (and tuned!) Invacar, Preston-Cobb proved in no uncertain terms that there was a world of difference between 'incapacitated' and 'invalid', for he was certainly not the latter, being a very active businessman whose ability in this direction quickly earned him the respect of all his friends *and* rivals in the trade. He acted as company secretary and chief buyer, in addition to appointing dealers. He and his Invacar were also a familiar sight at weekend scrambles, often many miles from home, having driven there himself. But perhaps his biggest asset was his cheerfulness which, considering his disability, was truly outstanding.

When the first production line-up was announced in September 1953, the range consisted of three Villiers-engined models, all of which used rubber in torsion throughout as a suspension medium. This meant that there were no sliding telescopic parts, no metal-to-metal pivot bushes and no springs in the conventional sense. Further, Greeves probably made history, at least in the early post-war period, by dispensing with journal-type wheel bearings and employing, in the case of one model, plain phosphor-bronze bushes front and rear. In addition, the conventional tubular frame had been largely superseded by one consisting of cast-alloy members as a result of the experience gained on the scrambles circuit.

The main front down-member of the frame was of tough, H-section alloy, embodying a fabricated and cast-in steel head lug and top frame tube. The steering-head race seatings, which were of Greeves' own design and manufacture, were machined on centres before the casting process. Each race accommodated 17 steel balls.

The alloy engine carrier-members also supported a platform for the battery, which had the advantage of not being affected by acid corrosion in the same way as a conventional steel battery support. Another practical aspect of the design was that after slackening the various control cables and fuel lines, and detaching the final-drive chain, the engine and gearbox assembly, complete with cradle members, could be dropped down by the removal of six locating bolts.

A single $\frac{7}{8}$ in. diameter, 14-gauge tube, the ends of which carried bronze-welded fixing lugs for the engine cradle plates, was swept upwards and then looped to accommodate circular housings for the rubber-in-torsion units and to provide a cross brace and anchorage for the end of the top frame tube.

Rear suspension was by a swinging-fork, taper-tube structure, which was conventional save for the use of rubber as a springing medium, while movement of the swinging-fork frame assembly was limited by the progressive torsional resistance of two heavy-duty Metalastik bushes, plus supplementary hand friction dampers controlled by the rider. Bushes with the same damping qualities were used at the frame pivot and as bearings at the extremities to rear strut members. Thus the need for greasing and adjustment, and the risk of accelerated wear due to friction between the metal bearing surfaces or exposure to

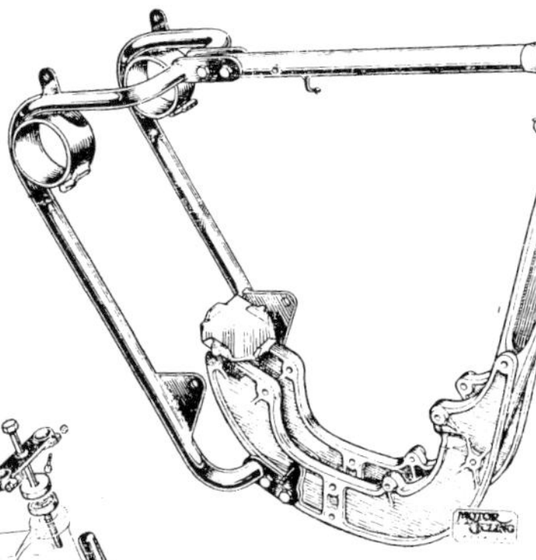

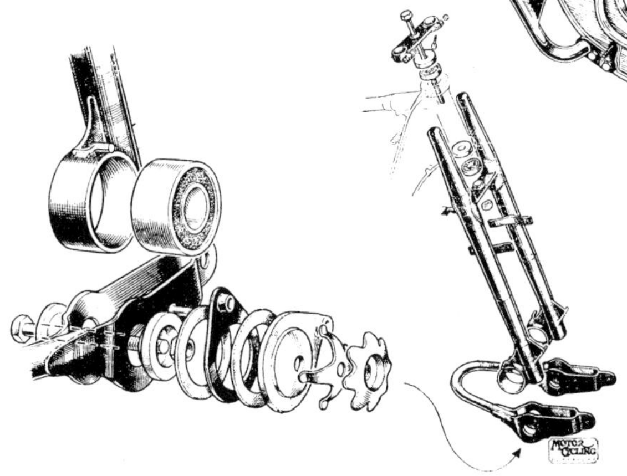

Left **The first Greeves production motorcycles were announced in September 1953. These drawings show frame and fork details**

Below **Greeves advertisement for the 1953 Earls Court Show**

the weather, were avoided.

Similarly unconventional were the Greeves leading-link front forks—now forward rather than trailing as on the prototypes—which pivoted on rubber bushes with external hand-controlled dampers. Rigidity achieved by a short connecting loop, plus minimum unsprung weight, were two obvious advantages of the design. A less obvious feature of the Greeves forks, which were made of bronze-welded, double-taper, Grade-A steel tubing, was flexibility. That is to say, while essential rigidity had been preserved in the direction of steering, the lower fork yoke was not, in this case, the elaborate casting or forging used in conventional telescopic forks to clamp the main tubes and so permit flexing under impact only from that point downwards to wheel-spindle level. Such limitation, needed where slider members are an

1954 model 20S scrambler—as it appeared at Earls Court in 1953

all-important part of the design, was not called for in the Greeves component, which absorbed stresses by a degree of 'bending' (to use a basic term) below and above the main fork yoke. Both sets of head bearings, it was claimed, thereby took a share of the impact loading.

It had been found, whilst subjecting the Greeves forks to destruction tests, that although performance was impaired, they were still usable, whereas conventional teles had become completely unserviceable due to highly localized stresses built up in the fork yokes.

The specifications so far described were standard on the model 20R, a roadster fitted with a three-speed, 197 cc Villers unit with 6-volt electrics, Dunlop 19 in. tyres—3.00 ribbed front, 3.25 section studded rear—and finished in overall black. They applied also to the 20D, a de luxe version of the standard model, which had a four-speed box, Avon tyres, pillion footrests, rectified lighting and a finish in an attractive shade of blue (later to become a feature of Greeves machinery). These two machines employed journal wheel bearings and had deeply-valanced mudguards—the rear guard, together with the dualseat and number-plate assembly, lifted clear for easy wheel removal and other related maintenance tasks, following the removal of only four nuts and bolts. The 6-volt battery, with a Westalite rectifier clipped neatly behind it, was anchored by a single strap, which also acted as the horn mounting.

The third machine, announced at the same time, was the 20S, a pukka scrambler. This used the same unorthodox frame and suspension as the roadsters, but had lightweight alloy mudguards, knobbly tyres (still 19 in.), integral number plates and *plain* wheel bearings.

At the centre of the brake hub, used on both the front and rear wheels of the 20S, was a flanged, $\frac{7}{8}$ in. diameter, hollow shaft, which was precision ground from hardened steel and was carried on a $\frac{1}{2}$ in. diameter knock-out spindle. This shaft carried two $1\frac{1}{2}$ in. long, high-density, oil-impregnated Compo bronze bushes, which ran free on the shaft when fitted, but which were an interference fit in the light-alloy hub body. The spoke flange and 6 in. diameter brake drums were pressed on to the hub body and located by shoulders. The bush assembly was protected at each end by Weston seals retained by circlips, and at the extremities by laminated cork washers. On the roadsters the function of the seals was to retain grease in the hub, but on the 20S Scrambler the seals were reversed to exclude mud and water.

Other items of interest in the design were the internal speedometer drive (the only component, except the steering-head bearings, calling for the use of a grease gun), which was taken from a pinion on the hub boss; the robust design of the footrests, which bolted directly on to the lower cradle frame-members; a substantial centre stand; and the use of self-locking nuts throughout.

One of the few criticisms from the press of the day was that a larger-capacity, deeper fuel tank would have served not only to usefully increase the range, but also, from an aesthetic point of

Close-up of the rear frame design, taken during the 1953 show—this is a roadster model with cast-alloy battery carrier

view, to reduce the amount of open space between the engine and top frame tube.

When launched, prices were: 20R, £141 *7s 6d*, 20D £151 *0s 10d*, and 20S, £152 *5s 0d*. The only extras listed were plain-bearing brake hubs on the 20D.

When the Rt Hon Anthony Eden MP performed the official opening ceremony at Earls Court to inaugurate the 1953 Cycle and Motorcycle Show, the 28th in the series, on Saturday 14 November, to all intents and purposes, it was also the launch of the Greeves motorcycle marque. Visitors were able to witness at first hand the many novel features on the three recently-announced 197 cc models—plus a brand-new model displaying the same original thought. This surprise was the Model 25D Fleetwing, and its power unit was an entirely new engine, the twin-cylinder, 250 cc, two-stroke, four-speed unit manufactured by British Anzani and incorporating a rotary induction valve by means of a ported crankshaft. This engine and other roadster developments for 1954, and beyond, are fully described in Chapter 4. A trials version based on the other 197 cc singles and known as the 20T, also made its debut at Earls Court. It cost slightly less than the 20S dirt racer.

Proof of the friendly nature of that first public exhibit by the Essex concern was the fact that Cliff Lewis, the man who had revived the BMCRC (British Motor Cycle Racing Club), or 'Bemsee' as it was more well known, was acting as one of the sales staff—he was on holiday from his tractor business in Hereford!

Although the Earls Court appearance got the fledgling marque off to a reasonable start in a wave of publicity, Bert Greeves and his staff could have hardly visualized that within a few short years the Greeves name would be held in high regard, not just in Britain, but by enthusiasts around the globe—humbling in the process many larger, long-established makes. That success, and the men and machines which made it all possible, are recounted in great detail over the succeeding chapters. It is a story of how a small East Anglian company took on the world, and came out on top more times than not—a real 'David and Goliath' performance.

2 Early competition

From the advent of competitive motorcycling, the sport was dominated by four-stroke machines, riders preferring to place their faith in the low rpm, brute power provided by these early dirt dinosaurs. The reasoning behind the choice of a four-stroke machine was based on the traditional use of this type of engine, not because it had been developed especially for competitions work, but because it was the only engine available that was powerful enough to do the job. Two-stroke powerplants had been around for years, but they were seriously under-developed, and their use as competition engines was not even considered, due to their low power output.

Looking at the sporting scene today, one cannot help noticing the two-stroke domination—the emphasis has gone full circle. When did this supremacy begin and why should the two-stroke engine suddenly gain favour?

The Villiers 125 cc motor had been in production since pre-war days, but its power output was dismally low, more suited to the job of propelling ultra-lightweight commuting machines for which it was originally intended. The first manufacturer to take advantage of the Villiers power unit to contest the 125 cc scrambling class was Dot, as far back as the early 1950s. Dot continued to dominate the 125 cc class until the mid-1950s when the class was dropped in favour of a 200 cc upper limit. The mid-1950s can be seen as the beginning of the two-stroke invasion, when Greeves and Dot began to make inroads into the prestigious unlimited events, and started beating the giants at their own game.

The engine in general, ultra-lightweight use was the 7 or 8E Villiers unit, which developed 7 bhp in standard form, but with factory tuning could be made to produce nearly 12 bhp. This motor was the mainstay of the class, until superseded by the purpose-built 9E competition unit used by Greeves from 1956. As more riders began to use the Villiers engine, expertise in its tuning was gained, and it was developed into the top runner in its class. With the gradual development of the two-stroke, more and more riders turned their attention to it, and success followed; with success came the motivation for further development.

During this era, motorcycle manufacturers began to realize the potential of the Villiers 197 cc powerplant as motive power for a competitions mount. The lower power output did not demand a frame and cycle parts being built to 'Forth Bridge' standards, as the heavyweight four-stroke unit required. Manufacturers became weight watchers when it was realized that a low-powered lightweight was capable of the same sort of speed as a heavyweight four-stroke. The added advantage of the smaller machine was its ability to virtually fly over obstacles, rather than plough through them, together with a higher degree of controllability. The lightness and ready availability of the Villiers unit swayed many manufacturers of the mid-1950s to design and produce a complementary lightweight chassis to contest the competition formulae of the day. One factory, above all others, hit the right compromise and produced a functional-looking mount, finished in blue and natural alloy, which was destined to be a world beater—that factory was Greeves.

First shown at the 1953 Earls Court show, the newly-introduced Greeves competition machines aroused a lot of interest. They were, in the eyes of the staid rider of the day, radical in design, but not unproven in capability. The designs were a logical progression and an updating of the original machine which Bert Greeves had shown to the press some two years previously. Even the original machine, a 125 cc scrambler, was viewed by the press with some reservations. The tester, being polite, called it unorthodox, but was pleasantly surprised by the capabilities and handling.

The prototype scrambler reflected its creator's

advanced ideas in motorcycle suspension design, for it used rubber as a springing medium, an adaption of the Invacar suspension system, which he had also designed. Some ten years later, this system was hailed as a major breakthrough in suspension design, but the credit did not go to the Greeves factory—it went to the makers of the Austin Mini.

The original front fork of the prototype was an ungainly-looking, trailing-link affair, using Metalastik bushes as the springing medium, augmented by progressive rubber bump stops. The trailing-link configuration was probably chosen as a direct result of the old axiom that it was easier to pull a wheelbarrow over a kerb than to push it. The rear suspension employed a swinging arm supported by vertical links which were attached to a pair of Metalastik-bushed arms, rather than hydraulic spring units. The rear units, being smaller in size than the fronts, were again backed up by rubber bump stops.

Greeves motorcycles did not always have a cast-alloy head stock and down-beam, for the frame of the prototype was an all-tubular affair. It gained its strength from the use of two large-diameter top tubes, which ran from the steering head down to the rear subframe. Joined together at the rear, they formed a triangle, to which the engine cradle rails and subframe were attached. This configuration was faintly reminiscent of the Vincent oil tank, and being a Shadow owner, Bert Greeves knew how strong that was. The engine cradle rails, which also carried the swinging-arm pivots, were widely spaced to give the frame extra rigidity.

Having served its purpose, the prototype scrambler was put to one side and work began on the second prototype. Trailing-link forks now became leading-link. The frame down-beam was cast in alloy—a design that was to be the Greeves trademark for the next 18 years. As related in Chapter 1, Bert hit on the idea of using a cast-alloy member after witnessing numerous frame breakages under competition conditions. The failures were caused by poor-quality tube, for this was all that was available in the early post-war period. The twin, triangulated top tubes were now reduced to one, as the frame gained its strength from the alloy beam bolted to a pair of cast-alloy engine plates which formed the lower frame loops. The rear suspension remained the same as that of the first prototype, but now the machine was fitted with a Villiers 197 to compete in the 200 cc class. The

Sammy Miller with a nicely restored 1955 20T trials model outside his museum at New Milton, Hampshire

extensive use of aluminium, and the redesign of the forks, brought the overall weight down to only 210 lb.

The time was now right to test the machine under competition conditions, this job being entrusted to Frank Byford, a factory draughtsman and a keen trials and scrambles rider. Frank raced the new Greeves in most of the Essex events during the latter part of 1951, and every event of the following season. Development continued, the machine gradually being refined into a first-class racer. By 1953 the suspension sported friction dampers fore and aft, damping being achieved by the application of pressure via large cast-alloy hand wheels to friction rings on the Metalastik housings. Initially, it was thought that additional dampers would not be required, as the Metalastik units possessed inherent damping characteristics, but competition highlighted their inadequacy.

Peter Vine, another factory employee, joined Frank in 1953 to form the first works team, and

Above **1955 20S scrambler—last of the original 8E-powered models, but already sporting hydraulic rear dampers**

Right **Works rider Peter Hammond in action with his 1956 Villiers 9E-powered 20T mud-plugger**

together they continued to develop the scrambler. A lot of interest was shown in the machine, and to this end a dozen or so Byford replicas were sold. This was an inspiration to Bert, but it was Frank's third place at an earlier Shrublands Park national meeting which finally persuaded him to go into production.

The general public was given the chance to examine the new Greeves range at the Earls Court show of 1953. Together with the roadsters, there was the new 20S scrambler, which was a refined version of the Byford and Vine machine, offered for the princely sum of £152. The scrambler, together with the new 20T trials machine, had the same frame, forks and cycle parts as the roadster, but the specifications were tailored to suit the job in hand. The scrambler was fitted with close-ratio gears, stub exhaust and knobbly tyres, whereas the trials machine received wide-ratio gears, a full exhaust with upswept silencer and sports tyres. Extra to the trials 20T were, of course, the speedo, number plates and tool box.

A factory-fresh 1956 model 20T

Shortcomings in the suspension friction dampers led the factory to fit Armstrong units to the rear of the scrambler for the 1955 season. The fitting of friction dampers to control the suspension began as a necessity but ended up as a nightmare on the track, since it was impossible to adjust all four units to the same pressure. Under racing conditions, the friction dampers tended to have a will of their own, sometimes tightening up and locking the suspension, and at other times, slackening off altogether.

Also new that season was the use of ball-bearing wheel hubs. Surprisingly enough, the original models were fitted with oil-impregnated, full-width wheel bearing bushes, for in practice, they stood up to wet and dirty conditions better than inefficiently-sealed ball bearings. With the advent of a better grease seal, this problem was alleviated and the change was made. A further minor cosmetic change to all models for that season involved the fitting of cast-alloy tank badges, another item made in the factory's own foundry. They were made to the same design as the earlier chromed items, each one bearing a facsimile of Bert's signature.

Sometime previously, the Villiers concern had noted that the 197 cc 7/8E unit used in competition left a lot to be desired in terms of power and reliability. However, these shortcomings were never admitted by the factory, as they maintained that their engine units were adequate for the job in hand. When the 9E variant was produced, it represented a major step forward in engine design, as the whole of the engine unit was beefed up. Villiers took the opportunity during the redesign to strengthen any items which had proved troublesome in the 8E, and this included the crank, crankcases, cylinder, primary drive, magneto and gearbox.

The 9E motor was pressed into use on the Greeves competition machines during 1956. As the crankcases were different to the old 8E, a new set of engine cradle plates had to be made, being constructed from 10-gauge sheet steel. In order to regain frame strength lost by the phasing out of the cast-alloy engine cradle plates, twin seat-pillar stays were added, running from the top subframe mounts down to the swinging-arm pivot bolt.

Seating arrangements were revised that season, with the scrambler getting a new dualseat and the trials machine being fitted with a Dunlop rubber saddle. To bring the competition machines into line, the 20T received Armstrong rear hydraulic dampers, as had the 20S in the previous year. Another, less obvious, change was the redesigned

Barry Greep keeps his 197 cc Greeves in front of Gordon Swift's 500 Triumph twin during a late 1950s Eastern Centre scrambles meet

exhaust system—brought about by the increase in size of the exhaust-pipe fitting on the 9E engine. The scrambler still retained the very short, tuned pipe, but this was increased in diameter, whereas the trials bike received a new silencer and a slight change of routeing under the primary-drive case.

Birmingham rider, Sammy Peters, was given the use of a works scrambler during 1956. All he got was a machine and a bit of factory backing in the way of spares, but he had to provide his own transport and crew. Such was the tight budget the Greeves factory were running to in the early days.

Another rider who enjoyed himself during the 1956 season was John Pizzey, who put up some creditable rides on a 1955 ex-works scrambler. John liked to test his own products, for he was a director of the British Hub Company, which supplied Greeves with wheel hubs for their entire range.

By the end of the 1956 season, scrambler production had reached some 14 units, not a very impressive figure if one compares it with the other competitions manufacturers of the day. Although this figure represented some 10 per cent of total factory production, Bert wanted a bigger slice of the action. What was he to do? The only answer was publicity via track successes. To this end, he showed great forethought by enticing Brian Stonebridge away from the giant BSA company, not only to be the factory front runner, but also, the competitions department development engineer. Bert had had his eye on Stonebridge for some time, and noted his brand of individuality and enterprise. Bert liked Brian's somewhat unorthodox approach to solving engineering problems, an approach similar to his own style. Together, the pair made a formidable team.

The 28-year-old Stonebridge, a Cambridgeshire man born and bred, was no stranger to the attributes of the Greeves scrambler, having sampled one in 1952 at the invitation of Derry Preston-Cobb. He had enjoyed the test session, but his commitments to the Matchless works team prevented him from actually racing one of the Frank Byford-developed machines.

Stonebridge joined the factory in January 1957, setting up his development workshop in a suitably tidied, redundant chicken shed, and being helped by Bob Mills, a young mechanic borrowed from the Invacar line. The experience he had gained by working closely with Hermann Meier in the development of his ultra-quick 150 cc BSA Bantam was soon put to good use in the tuning and refining of the Villiers 9E unit. Brian was soon extracting nearly double the original 9 bhp from the motor, which was tested on a home-brewed dynamometer manufactured from an axle and brake unit which originally saw service in an old Ford lorry. This crude, but effective, piece of apparatus was designed by Bert himself, who (as already related) had learned his trade as a draughtsman with Heenan and Froude many years previously.

Brian was not content with engine modifications alone, but also turned his attention to frame development. The friction-damped front forks, which caused so many problems, were replaced by a completely new design utilizing a pair of partially-enclosed Girling units to control the fork loop movement. The design and development expertise of this great man was soon felt, his genius reflected in the factory works mounts, giving them a new lease of life.

The march for competitions supremacy was on. Factory fortunes began to take a turn for the better almost instantly, for that year Stonebridge took both the 250 and 350 cc experts' Grand Nationals—beating the works BSAs—and, in addition, won the 350 race and finished second to John Draper in the early-season Hawkstone unlimited event. Before the year was out, he had also taken the 250 cc Sunbeam Point-to-Point, the Lancashire, the Shrublands Park, and the second Hawkstone Park Grand National! And history was in the making when he beat BSA team leader Jeff Smith to become the first-ever 200 cc mounted winner of the Hawkstone Park unlimited invitation race. These results were the tonic Bert had been waiting for—the publicity gained by Brian in knocking arch rivals Dot off their lightweight perch had the desired effect. Sales of the scrambler rocketed that year by over 50 per cent more than the last three years' production combined.

The other side of the competitions department had to take a back seat during the hectic 1957 scrambles season, but it was not forgotten. Between races and the scrambling seasons, Stonebridge liked nothing more than to relax at a good weekend trial. Lessons learned on the scrambles track were passed on to the trials mounts, the 20T receiving the Girling-damped front fork that year.

My (*Rob Carrick*) earliest recollection of Brian Stonebridge was during his hectic 1957 season,

An early shot of the maestro, Brian 'Strawberry' Stonebridge, in action on one of the Thundersley machines

when I was still at school. I would cycle the ten or so miles to Wansford, the venue for the Peterborough club scrambles meetings, solely to see the maestro perform, for his name on the programme was the only one to attract me there.

The sights, sounds and smells which greeted the spectator were unrivalled by any other pastime. In those days, the battle still raged between those riders who thought they would go faster with a lighter and more manageable machine, and those who demanded brute power. The two-strokes offered good handling, but with fragile reliability, whereas the four-strokes, being more powerful, needed a higher degree of riding precision to cope with the power. Gold Stars, Matchless G80s, and various Triumph-engined machines did battle with the growing numbers of Villiers-powered bikes, manufactured by Greeves, Dot, James, Francis-Barnett and DMW. But one man and machine outshone the lot. The lanky Stonebridge, aboard his 197, could outride anyone, and frequently did so, much to the delight of the crowd. The racing was always fast and furious, resulting in some very exciting duels with other established aces of the day. His riding style always seemed so relaxed, even the exit from the 'hole', but he always managed to make the highest leap, which had the spectators applauding his every move.

Silencing rules did not exist in the early days, and no one seemed to care, least of all the spectators, for the noise was all part of the overall scrambling scene. The four-strokes universally used an open pipe, which was positively quiet compared to the raucous din emitted by the short stub exhaust of the Villiers 'stroker'. The fearsomely-noisy, open megga was becoming popular on the 197 during this period, not for cosmetic reasons, but because the system actually produced a couple of extra bhp. Any increase in power output was gladly accepted by the two-stroke rider in an effort to put one over on the four-stroke brigade, even though it meant extra noise.

The scrambles tracks of the 1950s cannot be compared to the motocross circuits of today—the obstacles were all natural, and the spectators were nearer the action, standing behind a single rope barrier. Yes, racing was slower by today's standards, but not that much slower, and certainly just as enthusiastically ridden. The original off-road meetings of the 1950s could not be repeated today, as the rules and regulations have changed significantly. Standards of rider protection, crowd safety and, above all, noise levels would not allow it. We, as spectators at those early events, can only reminisce over the thunderous roar at the start line, the apparent disregard for personal safety shown by the scantily-dressed (by modern standards) riders and, above all, the clouds of sweet-smelling Castrol 'R' smoke which hung over the track.

The 1957 season showed the potential of the Greeves factory and its riders, but better things were to come. When the factory announced its new range of models for the following season, its intention to take on all comers was apparent, for this new era would be fought on the battlefields of Europe.

TRIALS

Model 20T

ENGINE: Villiers Mk. 9E 197 c.c. (A tuned engine can be supplied at extra cost).

GEARBOX: 4-speed, foot change, wide ratio. Overall ratios: Top 7·45, 3rd 9·99, 2nd 17·89, 1st 26·83 to 1. (Alternative overall ratios can be supplied to special order. Details on request).

TYRES: DUNLOP TRIALS UNIVERSAL Front: 2·75" x 21" Rear: 4·00" x 18"

DIMENSIONS: Wheel Base, 52". Handlebar width 30¾". Seat Height 31½". Ground clearance 8½". Weight 233 lbs.

ACCESSORIES: 75 m.p.h. speedo, bulb horn and front and rear number plates.

Factory brochure showing a 1957 model 20T with 9E powerplant

3 European Champions

The dawning of the 1958 motocross season saw the factory poised ready for action once again, but now the horizons had widened with the commencement of a European race series for machines up to 250 cc. The series, instigated by the *Fédération Internationale Motorcycliste,* and entitled *Coupe d'Europe,* supplemented the 500 cc series which had been upgraded to World status. Because of the interest being shown in the 250 class, together with the capacity's increasing potential and development by various factories, the FIM saw a need to include this category, replacing the old 200 cc class. To contest a 250 cc class championship on a machine giving away some 20 per cent in capacity did not worry Greeves, for the 197 cc scramblers were now in a high state of tune, thanks to the efforts of Brian Stonebridge and his 'chicken shack' gang. Light weight and an increased power output more than made up for the capacity handicap, a combination proved time and time again throughout the previous season.

The gauntlet had been thrown down, and Greeves took up the challenge, with Stonebridge contesting the European Championship on his 197. The Greeves had been proved in competition on home ground, snapping at the heels of the mighty BSA works team and, at times, beating them. If it was possible to embarrass the works 500 riders at home, then it should be no problem to tackle the continental Europeans on their 250s. So with this idea in mind, the factory embarked on its cross-channel, giant-killing crusade. Stonebridge contested the season's ten events, accompanied by Bert Greeves, and put up a creditable performance, beating many of his old rivals.

As prophesied, the Greeves factory did indeed make its mark, fending off most of its rivals—ESO, Dot, Maico and Monark all fell victim to the aggressive riding of Brian Stonebridge. But one man was hard to beat, and he was Jaromir Cizek on his Jawa. All season long the pair battled it out and, in the end, it was the Czech who took the Championship with Stonebridge in second place. This placing certainly gave a big boost to Greeves sales at home and abroad, for it was noted at the time that the British did not usually get on too well in the European motocross scene. They had always been regarded as the poor relations of the European sporting scene by their continental cousins, who thought that the Greeves success was just a stroke of luck. The factory had other ideas. They knew that the machine's development was paying off, and in the hands of Stonebridge, it had to be a winner—national pride was running high.

Alongside the official works team during these early days, ran a works B-team comprised of willing unpaid, but nevertheless enthusiastic, amateurs. The B-team followed the master, paying their own way to home and nearer continental events because they loved the sport and participated in it for the sheer enjoyment. This team, which included Mike Jackson, John Oliver and Gordon Swift, was looked after by the factory on a limited basis only. Receiving minimal expenses, they were expected to participate in as many events as possible to swell the number of Greeves machines on the starting line, possibly in an effort to make the name known more quickly. In return for this dedicated enthusiasm, the machines were looked after, serviced and updated by the factory. Gordon Swift recalls that his bike was regularly delivered to the factory for checking, and was returned serviced, ready to race, and bearing all the latest modifications. The invoices, which he expected for the work carried out, never materialized.

To illustrate the extent to which the competitions shop treated the B-team, on one occasion Gordon returned his machine to the factory for attention to a twisted frame sustained in a prang during his previous outing. A chance

Stonebridge leads Jawa rider Jaromir Cizek during the British round of the 1958 ***Coupe d'Europe*****, which was held at Beenham Park on 15 June**

remark to Brian Stonebridge, referring to the extra power required to propel a rider of Gordon's stature, resulted in the bike being given a special Stonebridge tune-up, which enabled him to win every race on the following weekend. Again, this work was carried out free of charge.

It was during the 1958 season that Stonebridge, intent on swelling the ranks of the official works team, noticed the talents of a regular Shrublands Park Dot rider. This young East Anglian, Dave Bickers, was a rider who had given Stonebridge a few good dices. He was taken under the master's wing and given a Greeves frame in which to house his home-tuned, much-used (and abused!) Villiers motor. The engine, tuned for dope fuel (then allowed for Eastern Centre events), did not like the reversion to petrol for national events, but with the help of Stonebridge it soon became a flyer. As an apprentice to Stonebridge, the young Bickers learned his trade well, picking up all sorts of hints and tips, and even showing the boss a thing or two at times. When the season finished, the pair retired to the workshop, for there was always something to do in the way of machine improvements for the following season.

During 1958 the factory staff had been working on a full 250 Villiers-based motor. The first conversion used on the factory machines had an all-cast-iron cylinder (of Vale Onslow manufacture) and alloy head. This combination utilized a brand-new 66 mm piston developed by Hepolite. The cylinder featured detachable transfer ports, and it first saw competition during the Welsh Three Day Trial, which was used as a selection event for the International Six Day Trial. Making the cylinder barrel from iron did not achieve the required result, for it still carried the weight penalty of the original Villiers item. The next logical step, therefore, was to cast an alloy cylinder, and head, in the factory's own foundry. So was born the famous Greeves square barrel. It also featured

Dave Bickers at the Sunbeam Point-to-Point in April 1958, when only 17 years old—one of his first events as a Greeves rider. Note the Hermann Meier exhaust system

detachable transfer ports, so that further development could be carried out on port shapes. This cylinder had a hard-chrome-plated bore, the process being carried out by the German firm Van Der Horst, mainly because no one in Britain was capable of doing the job to the standards required by the factory.

For many years the Greeves factory had been in the business of casting alloy components, a technique which they had pioneered and carried on as a commercial venture, specializing in a process called shell moulding. This necessitated the use of a hot metal pattern, which was strapped to the top of a box containing resin-coated sand. When the box was inverted, the coated sand that came into contact with the pattern would run and form a pastry-like coating which, when removed and cured in an oven, would form one half of the final mould. With the two halves of the mould clamped together, and buried in sand, high-silicon LM6 aluminium alloy, heated to 720–730 degrees Celsius was ladled in by hand. When the casting was cool enough, usually after ten minutes, the mould was removed with a large, well-aimed mallet, which shattered the resin shell.

To maintain a quality check on the cast components, especially frame members, a test bar was always incorporated in the pattern. The bar, which was stamped with the frame number, was always cut from the frame and given to the lab for checks to be carried out on ductility and grain size. If any specimen failed to come up to specification, its donor casting was scrapped.

The experience in this specialized art of alloy founding led to the design and manufacture of a radial-finned, alloy brake drum. This new drum, used initially only by the works riders, retained the steel hub centre onto which was cast the alloy muff, all hubs being skimmed to eliminate ovality after final wheel building. The original pressed-steel drum, which was quite adequate for the slower-moving side of the sport, did show its faults when used hard—it tended to swell under heavy application of the brakes, loosening the spokes and putting the rim out of true.

With the gradual improvements in power output putting a greater strain on the cycle parts, the original pressed-steel brakes soon showed their inability to cope. Fitting the new, heavily-finned alloy drums (sometimes referred to as cauliflower or pterodactyl hubs, due to the spiky appearance) solved the problems for a further five years until they were replaced by an entirely new hub.

Coincidental with the decision to contest the European Championship was the launch of a new breed of scrambler, designated the 20SA and bearing the name 'Hawkstone', in commemoration of the many wins by Stonebridge at that venue. The Hawkstone was built around a new frame which featured a stiffer cast down-beam and a slimmer rear subframe, the twin seat-pillar stays now being replaced by a single, thicker, T-shaped tie bar. Alongside the Hawkstone, the factory offered a Hawkstone Special, into which was fitted a specially-tuned 9E motor that produced some 14 bhp. To differentiate it from the standard Hawkstone, the Special was fitted with a dull-chromed fuel tank.

The factory was always aware of the fact that they were giving away 50 cc by only offering a

1958 20SAS production scrambler with a tuned 197 cc Villiers motor

197 cc scrambler to contest the almost universal 250 cc class. Some riders wanted a full 250, but a suitable engine was not available to the factory; all they could offer was a roadster-based, 2T twin-cylinder Hawkstone. The heavy, underpowered 2T motor was no problem to install in the scrambler frame, for the factory simply utilized the roadster twin engine plates. The major drawback with the twin was its power-delivery characteristics; though ideal for the road, they were completely wrong for the race track. With power coming in at the wrong time and fed through a gearbox which contained roadster ratios, it was doomed to failure. The Hawkstone twin, designated the 25SA, did not see much competition (only 32 were produced), but did find favour with the street-scrambler fraternity, for they wanted a roadster fitted out with scrambles equipment and a minimal off-road capability.

Brian Stonebridge also saw the need for a full 250 to contest the 1959 European series and retired to his workshop in the winter of 1958 to construct a secret weapon. The 2T engine, having shown no promise as a production scrambler in the hands of lesser mortals, was not considered this time, for Stonebridge had already built a twin scrambler and used it in anger during the latter part of the 1957 season.

Bench testing of racing engines was an art which Stonebridge perfected on the works home-brewed dyno, which allowed him to plot the power output. Looking at the shape of the curve told him more about the ability of the engine than did the peak. Often his tuning produced an engine which developed lower maximum power than his rivals, but had a healthier low- to mid-range power spread, and he often proved his point by being faster round the track. With this requirement in mind, he looked around for a full 250 engine to fit into his Hawkstone frame, and came up with a tuned German 247 cc NSU Max ohc unit.

The hybrid was not an official works machine, but it was constructed at the factory, hidden away from prying eyes in a corner of the competitions shop. Initially, Bert Greeves was not privy to the building of the beast, for he would probably have put his foot down and said no. When he did find out about it, and recovered from the shock of seeing such a motor in one of his frames, after some thought he grudgingly accepted the marriage. The final seal of approval came with the following statement: 'The higher power output of the Max unit will give the cycle parts more than the usual stress, and so will ensure a higher than ever safety factor for the private owner.' The project was safe and ready to be tested in action.

With the experience gained from the previous season's jaunts into Europe, winter development, and the backing of Dave Bickers, Stonebridge once again attacked the *Coupe d'Europe*. The 1959 season, staged between April and August, consisted of some 12 events, the schedule being so tight that the factory team did not contest them all, but certainly showed up the opposition when they did compete. Dave Bickers was by now a fully-fledged Greeves rider and joined Stonebridge for the onslaught, backed up by Bob Mills, the factory's travelling mechanic.

Above **Lovely period shot of both rider and machine being refuelled in the paddock. . .**

Below **. . .And period transport—the Austin belonging to Mike Jackson is pictured at Southampton docks**

In fact, there were at least *four* NSU-engined Greeves around in 1959. Two were built at the factory by Stonebridge—Bob Mills revealed recently that he 'nearly got the sack when the boss found out.' The other two were private efforts. One was a Sportmax-engined creation, built in Northern Ireland by NSU specialist Terry Hill. The other, using a roadster Max unit, like Stonebridge's machines, was constructed by Bridport, Dorset, enthusiast R. J. 'Ginger' Dunn.

Using the NSU-engined Greeves, Stonebridge won both the Swiss and Belgian legs, but reverted to the detachable-transfer-port, Greeves-cylindered Villiers engine to take the Italian round and the British event at Beenham Park. As the power output of the Greeves-modified Villiers motor increased, so did the problems. Villiers insisted that their motors were adequate for the job in hand and could not be bettered, but this insistance was based on feedback from users of standard production roadster engines. Increasing the swept volume to 246 cc, with the proportional increase in power, soon showed up weaknesses in the design, weaknesses which caused Stonebridge

Above **Villiers 2T-powered 25SA scrambler—only 32 were made**

Top **197 cc SA—produced during 1958–9**

to retire from both the Czech and Swedish events with gearbox trouble.

Towards the end of the season, old rival Cizek was being pushed further down the leader board, but the Swedish Husqvarna rider, Rolf Tibblin, was heading the field. Had it not been for an unfortunate start-line tangle during the Dutch event, in which Stonebridge badly dislocated his shoulder, this position might well have been modified, for the injury impeded his progress for the remainder of the season. Tibblin went on to win the Championship, but only three points behind was Stonebridge, with Dave Bickers in third position.

The 1959 season had seen a few changes in the production Hawkstone, for now a full 250 was on offer to the public to replace the ill-fated 2T twin device. This was the new 24SAS Hawkstone, which was based on the previous season's works machines and utilized the finned alloy hubs.

It was at about this time that the Villiers empire was beginning to change its attitude to the use of their motors in competition. Once proud of their specialization in the utility or general-purpose market, Villiers were now showing signs of a new and very welcome outlook with regard to sport.

For a long time, the old established Wolverhampton company had shrugged off the need to manufacture a 250, but due to user pressure and the upsurgence of the many 250 conversions for their 197 engine, they decided to jump on the bandwagon and produce their own motor, designated the 31A. The new motor, which powered the 24SAS, had the same size of bore (66 mm) that the Greeves factory had been experimenting with for the past year, but used a piston of Villiers manufacture. The 31A's power output was lower than the Greeves 250 conversion, but it was better than a 9E and enabled riders to sample the delights of a 250 without having to go to the trouble of purchasing a costly after-market conversion. The 31A only lasted one season, for it was produced as an interim measure until the new breed of Villiers competition motors was ready for the market.

The success of the 1959 European season was to be short lived, for in October of that year, Stonebridge was to lose his life under the most tragic circumstances. While returning from a visit to Hepolite's Bradford factory, the car in which he was travelling with Bert Greeves was involved in a horrific head-on collision. The factory boss was to receive only minor injuries, but Stonebridge was killed outright. The sorrow of the factory staff does not need reporting, for Brian was irreplaceable. With plans thwarted and dreams shattered, they somehow carried on, wondering what would happen during the following season. Could Bickers cope with the responsibility of being the front runner in Europe? Could he stand the pressure?

Above **Brian Stonebridge, with his unique NSU Max-powered scrambler, at a continental event in early 1959**

Top **Stonebridge with a more conventional Villiers-engined dirt racer in the same year**

Above **Factory advertisement proclaiming Bickers' success in the 1960 250 cc European Motocross Championship**

Below **Bickers at work in Czechoslovakia during August 1960**

Would he stand the pace? Only time would tell. With Ernie Smith pushed into taking over the development side of the scrambler, the young Bickers did not disgrace himself, allaying any doubts which may have been levelled against him.

Before the European series started, a special event was held at Hawkstone Park to commemorate the passing of 'perhaps the greatest character ever to grace the scrambles scene', for this was the Brian Stonebridge Memorial Scramble. All parties rallied to the call, not only the riders who came from far afield, but the organizing bodies and the public—all felt a need to pay homage to the great man. This unforgettable occasion was made even more memorable by the Park's owner, Sir Alexander Stainer, who waived his fee, the ACU who waived its $2\frac{1}{2}$ per cent gate money, and the riders, who declined any offer of prize money, all proceeds of the day going to Brian's widow, Janet. The event was sponsored by

the Daily Herald, who commissioned The Brian Stonebridge Memorial Trophy, which was to be competed for at the initial meeting and thereafter annually—the trophy is still awarded every year, but it has lost its original meaning, since the modern motocross rider regards it as just another pot to put in the trophy case.

The trophy commemorates an event which took place some 30 years ago, and is a lasting reminder to all of us who used to watch the great man in action. Now, many old timers, and even some younger elements, think it is time that the trophy be contested with a little more reverence to the man, and the era, which it proclaims. To this end, certain factions are demanding that the trophy be removed from the clutches of the modern motocross rider, and be awarded annually instead at one of the major pre-'65 events which abound in the British Isles. An event such as the British Bike Bonanza has been suggested, as this not only gives an airing to many old Greeves machines, but also attracts a few works riders out of retirement. This suggestion would, if adopted, certainly revitalize the importance of this historic trophy.

By July 1960, after installing a Heenan and Froude dynamometer, the factory design team finally perfected the transfer porting of the alloy cylinder, and began to cast the one-piece version which was to go on sale to the general public the following year. Bickers continued to use the detachable-port cylinder for the 1960 and 1961 seasons, but only because it was easier to get inside the transfer passages to apply the final polish, its optimum shape having already been finalized.

With a new and improved machine, which now used an Alpha full-circle flywheel assembly and streamlined conrod, Dave Bickers took on and beat the opposition to gain the European Championship for the Greeves factory. The title was assured at the penultimate event held at Vannas in Sweden, when Bickers (hard pressed by Jeff Smith) took the chequered flag. Wins in Switzerland and Poland, together with second placings in Luxembourg and France, gained enough points to ensure victory. This win was no fluke, for with a further refined mount, he took the Championship for the second time in 1961.

On his own for the first time, Bickers missed the organizational ability of the master, Stonebridge, for it was he who arranged the routes, accommodation, ferries and machine carnets, with Bickers being happy as chauffeur. Sometimes a trek was required to the Stonebridge home at the Cambridge University Farm, prior to heading for the weekend venue, the driving to be shared on a 50/50 basis, but usually being carried out by the eager apprentice.

Now Bickers had to fend for himself, making many slip-ups before perfecting travel arrangements for the successful 1960 season. The bike carnet was an unknown document to the youthful Bickers, but he soon found out about it at the first customs post. Luckily, his Suffolk sense of humour carried him through. His first trip to the Swiss event of 1960 nearly ended in disaster, for he turned up at the address of the meeting's organizer in Geneva, miles from the venue.

Bickers liked to travel, seeing new places, meeting new people, and visiting such countries as Switzerland, Sweden, and even Russia. It was on one such trip to Leningrad that he fell foul of the Russian agricultural import regulations, when he had a bag of his favourite Suffolk potatoes impounded at the border post. The spuds were taken into custody and kept under lock and key until he came back through the border post.

On the home front, a new model was announced for the 1960 season and designated the 24SCS. It featured a new frame with taper steering-head bearings. The frame altered the steering-head angle slightly and, coupled with a repositioned engine (moved forwards), it gave improved handling. The rear fork was widened to accommodate a 4.00 section rear tyre, which was becoming standard wear during that era. Further refinements included a new, one-piece, triangulated rear subframe, and a redesigned seat. The 24SCS was powered by a new, purpose-designed scrambles motor from the Villiers concern. Designated the 34A, it was derived from the earlier 33A scrambles unit which, in turn, came from the original 31A unit. The 34A would push out some 19 bhp in standard form, and could be tuned to produce even more power. Topped by a Greeves square cylinder barrel and head, it developed approximately 21 bhp.

The 1961 season saw a change of designation for the top competition model of the range. In line with the success of the factory in the European Motocross Championship, Greeves proudly presented the 24MCS motocross special, developed from the 1960 Bickers works machine. Being a virtual replica of the Bickers mount, it featured the factory alloy cylinder-barrel conversion, a special

Left Motor Cycling **journalist Mike Bashford testing a Greeves with Marcelle top-end conversion during the winter of 1961–2**

Right **Dave Bickers in action during the Two-Day TV Scramble on 27–8 October 1962**

Below right **Bickers at the Spanish GP in 1963**

Below **Early efforts at conceiving a more effective silencer for motocross events**

two-stage air filtration system and alloy fuel tank. The rear hub had also been modified, in that it now featured a larger left-hand spoke flange, which required the use of a sprocket with a bigger central mounting hole.

Although externally similar to the original factory item, the cylinder now used an iron liner, a step Bert Greeves had to take in order to meet a growing demand for the MCS model. The original chrome-lined cylinders were used to good effect by the works riders, but with mass-production in mind, a rethink was in order. The factory did not want to rely solely on foreign plating firms to apply the chrome, for there was no British firm capable of doing the job, so the decision was made to use an iron liner and to do the work in-house. This move was welcomed by many private owners, for now the cylinder had as many lives as there were oversize pistons. In the event of a blow-up, the cylinder could be rebored, instead of being consigned to the dustbin.

The MCS continued into the 1962 season, but was soon ousted from the top of the range by another Bickers replica, the 24MDS. When first produced, the MDS was the ultimate motocross machine, its production continuing for nearly four

years. During the latter part of its life, the MDS was to be fitted with a 36A-based motor instead of the original 34A-based unit, and a new pair of full-width alloy wheel hubs from the British Hub Company. In later years, although popular as a clubman's mount, it was overshadowed by further factory developments in the international sector.

The 1961 Bickers machine, bearing the frame number GWM/1 (Greeves Works Motorcycle Number 1), has recently come to life again. Found in a dilapidated state, it has been lovingly restored to its former glory by ex-factory employee, Chris Goodfellow, and can now be seen performing at numerous pre-'65 events. GWM/1 was the first motocross machine to use the new frame, which became a standard fitment to the 24MDS. The frame top tube was of a larger diameter and curved down to the engine cradle plates behind the gearbox. This stronger structure was complemented by the use of a rectangular-section swinging arm, a move deemed necessary because the original round-section arm had a tendency to bend on returning to earth after a mighty leap. Also stiffened was the front fork assembly, which featured a large-diameter fork loop and strengthened bush housings.

After winning the European Championship two years in a row, Greeves surprisingly withdrew from the 1962 series. Dave Bickers had declined the prospect of a third season in Europe, for he was heavily involved with his new motorcycle business in Ipswich. Bert Greeves was also thinking of the financial implications of putting a team into Europe again, for tearing about all over the continent had proved a very costly affair. The Greeves factory had made its point by doing the almost impossible, so they rested on their laurels and only contested British events during 1962, with Bickers winning just about every race in which he started. The only *Coupe d'Europe* round contested that year was on home ground, at Shrublands Park where, in front of 30,000 spectators, Bickers won both legs in convincing style.

The Greeves-modified 34A Villiers motor, as used by the factory riders, was beginning to show signs of fatigue by the end of the 1962 season. This situation was not surprising, as Greeves had increased the power output by some 25 per cent over the original Villiers figure. Problems arose in the gearbox, mainly due to the use of bronze bushes to support the layshaft and the right-hand end of the main shaft. Greeves had used specially-hardened gears to cope with the stress of racing, but even these proved to be inadequate. Even more serious, the clutch and primary drive were never man enough for even the mildest state of tune. The clutch drum splayed and cracked, and the single-row chain stretched at the slightest hint of rapid acceleration. The engine itself sheared drive shafts and wrecked main bearings, due to the enormous flywheel and a lack of external air cooling to the bearing housings.

Greeves now became concerned at the failure rate of the works machines, and set about the task of designing an all-new motor to power their next generation of motocross machines. In the meantime, Villiers were not oblivious to the fact that concerns like Greeves were modifying their motors, quite considerably, in an effort to stay ahead of the opposition—modifications which put undue stresses on all components and which eventually led to component failure. Not wishing to be blamed for a lack of enthusiasm within the competitions world, Villiers attacked the problem in two ways. By far the easiest way out was to redesign the 34A which, in turn, became the 36A. Basically similar to the 34A, the new engine featured a plain crankcase and gearbox shell, in an effort to keep the main bearings cool. The second and more difficult solution was to produce a completely new, purpose-designed, universal competition motor.

The Earls Court show of late 1962 was chosen for the unveiling of the new Villiers motor. Named the Starmaker, it was radically different to anything the concern had produced previously. With a strengthened crank, duplex primary chain, all-metal clutch and redesigned gearbox supported on needle-roller bearings, the unit showed considerable promise with its quoted output of 25 bhp at 6500 rpm. By far the most radical feature was the use of two Monobloc carburettors, flexibly mounted on a single inlet manifold. The carburettors were set to open progressively, first one, then the other. This set-up ensured good torque at low speeds from one instrument, and high power at high speeds when both units were open, a system often employed in the car world.

In September 1962, Greeves, in line with Dot and Cotton, were offered the free use of the new Starmaker engine for evaluation—a noble gesture, but the engine was only to be used by the works riders. As the motor was still top secret, all maintenance was done by a team of Villiers engineers, who would not even let the Greeves mechanics look inside the unit. Testing progressed well. Particularly liked was the use of a new 'quiet' expansion chamber developed by Greeves, for this was the beginning of an era in which noise was beginning to be classed as an environmental pollutant. The ACU (Auto Cycle Union) had been pushed into making new rules on noise—not by riders or spectators, but by landowners and nearby residents of motocross venues—and in an effort to make events less offensive felt it necessary to impose a maximum noise limit, with the introduction of the now familiar noise meter.

The Starmaker, with its quieter exhaust, fulfilled the requirements of the 1963 season, and so was evolved the 24ME Starmaker production motocross machine.

Bickers did contest a few early events during the 1963 season, but they were disastrous for him, a saga which he wants to forget. The episode led to him transferring his allegiance to Husqvarna for the remainder of the series, not as a works rider, but as a privateer, for he purchased the machine himself. Many stories abounded about why Bickers split with Greeves, the favourite being that Greeves would not fit telescopic forks to the motocross machines. To disprove the rumour and poke fun at the storytellers, Bickers actually fitted and rode the Husky equipped with a pair of Greeves leading-link forks. The combination worked well, for he went on to win the ACU Motocross Star again, for the fifth time.

By now, Greeves were becoming increasingly disenchanted with the products and policies of the Villiers company, and relationships became somewhat strained during 1963. The Starmaker powered 24ME motocrosser entered production, but ceased after only 89 units. Quite simply, it was a dismal failure with its under-developed power unit. It was time to go it alone, for an all-Greeves motor (well, nearly all) had been on the drawing board for some time.

With a little help from various firms, like Alpha Bearings, Albion Gearboxes, and Stefa Magnetos, the new engine was to become a reality, and with it the tiny Essex factory was to enter yet another phase in its domination of off-road sport.

Start-gate action—the machine getting a flyer in the foreground is a 24ME model

4 1950s roadsters

Following their debut at the 1953 Earls Court show, the Greeves roadsters were to play an important part in the progress of the Essex company throughout the 1950s, albeit living very much in the shadow of their more glamorous and publicity-grabbing off-road brothers, the trials and scrambles models.

The events leading up to the 1953 Earls Court appearance, and the show itself, have already been recounted in Chapter 1. For 1954, the new range was headed very much by the Fleetwing sports roadster, powered by the 242 cc British Anzani twin engine, which itself was very much one of the 1953 show's sensations. It was derived from a small marine unit featuring a crankshaft with a hollow, ported middle section which served as a primitive rotary inlet valve, and was built by The British Anzani Engineering Company, based at Hampton Hill, Middlesex.

British Anzani was a pioneer name in its own right within the British motorcycle scene, having been involved almost from the start of the fledgling industry at the turn of the century. More recently, the name British Anzani had been associated with power units for outboard marine craft. However, its chief designer, C. Harrison—a motorcyclist at heart, who had spent his early years with the famous JAP concern—had created a motorcycle version of the two-stroke, twin-cylinder engine.

Performance, then, was already a known factor, and earlier in 1953 *Motor Cycling* had carried out a brief road test of the engine in prototype form in what was described as 'a lashed up frame' which, incidentally, was nothing to do with Greeves.

In its design, the Anzani twin broke away entirely from British two-stroke motorcycle design practice of the era. The engine, a parallel, long-stroke (52 × 57 mm) twin, featured separate crankcases, an alternate firing order and the pre-mentioned rotary-valve induction. It offered striking acceleration, even though peak power was only 10 bhp at 4800 rpm.

The crankcases were split horizontally—not vertically, as on other British motorcycle engines. The lower casting was, in fact, a shell comprising two side-by-side crankcases separated by a central induction chest and space for a wide, plain, centre bearing. Mould-like, the lower shell was also shaped to take halves of a drive-side roller bearing and a ball race at the flywheel end, together with outer compression glands and composition washers for effective compression sealing purposes.

The components were assembled on a built-up crankshaft, which consisted of a pair of full flywheel webs with pressed-in crankpins and needle-roller-bearing big-ends for the two connecting rods. A special half bearing cap of phosphor bronze, which was a dowel fit in the central recess, was dropped in before the complete shaft assembly was laid in position. The top half of the bronze cap bearing, the next item to be assembled, was cut away.

The shaft which comprised the rotary induction valve had drillways extending obliquely into the webs of the adjacent flywheels. Moreover, it operated in what was, in effect, an intermediate induction chamber and, during the period of each engine revolution, when the drillways registered with the cut-away bearing shell, the shaft acted as a rotary inlet valve, passing petroil from the induction chamber through the flywheel webs to each crankcase alternately. By this process, the inlet timing could be used to more advantage than was possible with a conventional piston-ported cylinder. A secondary, but nonetheless important, advantage was the absence of fuel blow-back from the single Amal carburettor and, therefore, not only more silent induction, but also none of the messy remains of wasted petroil mix to be found on many other British 'strokers' at the time.

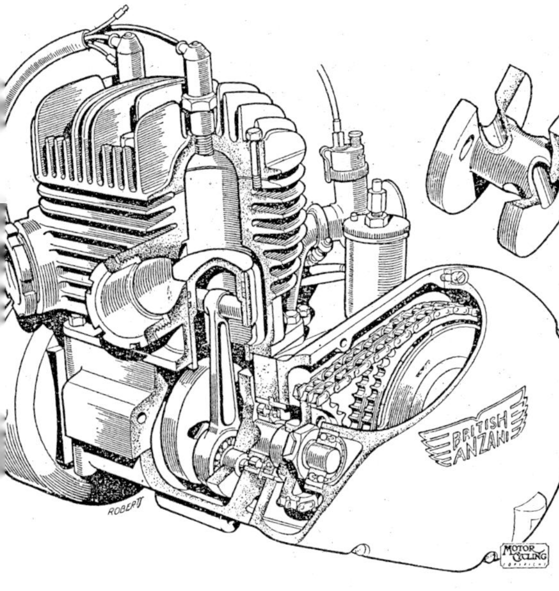

Above **Twin-cylinder Anzani model was displayed for the first time at Earls Court in November 1953**

Left **A cut-away drawing of the 244 cc Anzani engine with its unusual crankshaft rotary valve** (*top right*)

The upper crankcase, fashioned in a similar manner to the bottom section, save for the provision of top crankcase mouth openings and eight studs for final fitting, completed the assembly. This section, pressed over the crankshaft, was retained by eight nuts. Wide flanges and a sealing gasket ensured a gas-tight fit.

Originally water-cooled in its marine form, the Anzani motorcycle unit was air-cooled, having a finned, cast-iron barrel and finned, light-alloy cylinder head. Each cylinder had a single exhaust

New for 1955 was this tubular frame and hydraulically-controlled rear suspension system, shown here on the 197 cc Villiers-powered 20R

port, angled at 15 degrees, to take a $1\frac{3}{8}$ in. diameter exhaust pipe. The pistons, which were of the ported type, were slightly domed, and each carried two rings. The stub-fitting carburettor was connected to the crankcase by an unusually long downdraught induction pipe, flanged at the lower end and bolted to the upper crankcase, which was cored to provide a continued passage to the central induction chamber and crankshaft porting.

On the electrical side, power for both the ignition and lighting came from a Wico-Pacy generator suitable for 180-degree, twin-cylinder engines. The generator flywheel was keyed to the crankshaft taper and bolted in position. There was no taper at the opposite end of the crankshaft, which carried a dual engine sprocket for the duplex primary chain. The sprocket itself was keyed and retained by a large nut. Beyond the sprocket, the extremity of the shaft was supported by an outrigger, double-row ball race, housed in the primary-chaincase outer cover.

The primary chain was pre-stretched and transmitted its drive via a two-plate clutch and Albion four-speed, foot-operated gearbox. The latter component was bolted to the rear of the engine and offered internal reductions of 2.93:1, 1.82:1, 1.35:1 and 1:1. A 15-tooth, final-drive sprocket was provided to transmit the power via a $\frac{5}{16} \times \frac{1}{2}$ in. (428) size chain to the rear wheel.

The $\frac{1}{4}$-litre, Anzani-engined Fleetwing joined the 197 cc, Villiers-powered, single-cylinder 20D roadster (fully explained in Chapter 1) and, of course, the trials and scrambles machines powered by the same basic engine. All five of the 1954 model line (25D Fleetwing, 20R and D roadsters, the 20T trials and 20S scrambler) used the unique three-section, cast-light-alloy and tubular frame structure.

Throughout the spring and summer of 1954, the Greeves team toiled away, consolidating their initial toe-hold, which had been made at the end of the previous year. Based well away from the mainstream of the British bike empire in the industrial Midlands, the Essex marque would, no doubt, have found the going extremely difficult if it had chosen to produce purely roadsters. As it was, the trials and scrambles machines not only brought in useful revenue, but also did an excellent job of promoting the fledgling bike builder's name.

Four new Greeves models were announced for the 1955 season in late October. As *Motor Cycling* reported, the central position of the company's forthcoming display at the Earls Court show would undoubtably be occupied by one of these, the 32D. This incorporated the new, larger version of the twin-cylinder Anzani powerplant—with a capacity of 322 cc, achieved by boring out the cylinders to 60 mm. With the new dimensions, the unit was now considerably oversquare, rather than having the long stroke of the original.

Known as the Fleetmaster, the newcomer utilized the, by now, well-known cast-aluminium frame with pivoting fore and aft suspension controlled by rubber in torsion, but with additional friction damping. The front wheel, though, was a definite departure, with its twin 6 in. diameter brakes. The finish of the Fleetmaster, priced at £198, was in Moorland blue, a colour which was also used for the first time for the complete range, the black finish having been discontinued. Power was improved significantly over the smaller twin, with 15 bhp at 4800 rpm on tap. The gear ratios were also different: 5.38, 7.26, 9.68 and 15.75. Otherwise, except for an increase in weight from 262 to 276 lb, the two Anzani-powered machines were identical.

In *Motor Cycling's* Earls Court show number, dated 11 November 1954, Greeves took a large advertisement showing the new 325 Fleetmaster twin and stating it to be the 'Thrill of a lifetime!' The illustration showed one of the new models—with a charming model of the two-legged variety—posing on the nearby Southend promenade. The advertisement also highlighted the fact that a privately-entered Greeves, ridden by John Mallalieu, was the only 200 cc machine to be awarded a gold medal at the ISDT that year. Elsewhere in the same magazine, dealers advertising Greeves machines not only came from the capital but provincial centres, such as Cardiff, Chelmsford, Glasgow and Liverpool.

To meet a demand for more competitively-priced lightweights, a new, conventional steel-tube frame was introduced which had its rear swinging arm controlled by twin Armstrong shock absorbers. This chassis was employed for the newly-introduced R range of machines, the original D roadster (together with the trials and scrambles models) retaining the rubber-sprung, cast-aluminium version. Two of the R trio had the 197 cc Villiers single, the R3 and R4 (with three- or four-speed boxes), while the other, the 25R twin, utilized the 242 cc Anzani unit. At £134 8*s* 0*d*, the 20R3 was a full £15 12*s* 0*d* cheaper than its respective 20D model.

Features applicable to the entire 1955 range were a Vynide dualseat, cast-aluminium tank motifs and, as an optional extra costing £2 5*s* 0*d*, a tank cover in the same material as the new seat covering with a transparent-fronted map pocket.

In their issue of 10 February 1955, *Motor Cycling* carried a test of the new 20R3 and proclaimed it 'A Luxury Villiers Powered Lightweight with Many Unusual Features and a Mile-a-minute Maximum.' By a coincidence, the test machine's registration number, 197 AVW, matched the cubic capacity of the engine.

Tester John Griffiths began the appraisal with the words 'When a new manufacturer enters the highly competitive motorcycle industry, the machine to be launched must offer something "better-than-average"—if it is to succeed in overcoming the traditional conservatism of the motorcyclist!' He found that in the case of the Greeves, the machine's outstanding feature was 'quality', commenting; 'The finish of the model tested was of an extremely high standard', and 'that no deterioration occurred to either the paintwork or plating during the period of the test, even though the machine was left in the open for many nights—wet ones included—and remained uncleaned during the long spell of riding on filthy roads in the middle of winter.'

Out on the road, the front and rear suspension 'worked in harmony to provide a very comfortable ride even on the roughest going'. At first the friction dampers on the forks were adjusted so they were 'just biting', but after a few miles had been covered, a stop was made to slacken them completely—and so they remained for the rest of the test.

The fork movement was 'very light around the static load position and the springing absorbed all the road shock'. The rear suspension, though not quite so soft as the front springing, proved 'above average for this class of machine and gave a general air of "tautness" to the handling, which did not disappear at speed.'

Gaining particular praise were both mudguards which, being of generous proportions, proved 'very effective, damp roads making but little mark on the rider's feet and legs, whilst protection in the rain was well above average'. The rear mudguard was in semi-unit with the dualseat and was quickly detachable, making life easier in the event of a puncture in that tyre.

In a determined attempt to test the ubiquitous 197 cc Villiers motor to the limit, the machine was ridden from *Motor Cycling*'s London office to the Midlands: 'As hard as it would go—about 55–60 mph and the time taken for the 65 mile journey was only 10 minutes longer than when done on a 500—and at two thirds of the cost in

Top of the roadster line in 1956—the 32D Fleetmaster. This was the last full year in which Anzani engines were used. Note the dual front brakes

fuel.' This trip was undertaken at night and Griffiths lavished praise on the 6 in. headlamp, saying 'This gave enough light for maximum speed to be used with complete safety—the lights would have been good enough for speeds in the 70 mph region'.

When the engine's performance was used to the limit in the gears, a pleasant *lack* of vibration was experienced. Griffiths considered this due, at least in part, to 'the sensible steady from the frame to one of the rear cylinder-head fixing bolts'.

Overall fuel consumption throughout the test averaged 85–90 mpg.

So much for the good points, what of the criticisms? These were few, in the main centring around the 'personal fads of the tester'. Like footrests that, for greater comfort, could have been situated a few inches further back; a front brake which required more than normal hand pressure to make it really effective; and the exhaust silencing which was hardly adequate.

The 1956 model range, announced in September 1955, saw a rationalization of the roadsters, with only four models. However, the most noticeable change was that all models, including the competition bikes, now had conventional, hydraulically-damped rear suspension, rubber in torsion only being employed for the front forks. Much detail work had been carried out so that a more homogenous appearance was presented.

The latest Villiers 9E 197 cc engine assembly was used in the 20D (and the 20T and 20S dirt bikes), the 8E being retained for the sole remaining roadster single, the 20R3. In fact, the 20D had taken on the name Fleetstar. British Anzani twins continued to power the 25R Fleetwing (now referred to as the Standard) and the top-of-the-range 32D Fleetmaster.

Modifications applicable to the entire roadster line-up included a new dualseat, which had the Sentercel rectifier for the lighting set carried under its nose. Another feature, which won considerable praise from the press of the day, was a new toolbox which, located under the rear of the seat, could be readily detached and placed close at hand when needed—for example, when working on the machine at the roadside. On the opposite side of the seat, the tyre pump was carried in a position where it was protected from road grime and water.

To facilitate cleaning, the rear number plate was valanced, and on the more luxurious models—the 197 cc 20D and 322 cc 32D—the headlamp was supported by a curved steel cowl, which also housed the speedo and tax-disc licence holder. The horn was relocated underneath the headlamp on the deeply-valanced, sprung front mudguard.

Heavier-duty Varley 9 amp/hour batteries were now specified, fitted in a suitably-modified carrier positioned just above the rear of the gearbox; and with the transfer of the rectifier, toolbox and horn to other areas, a much neater appearance was achieved.

The fuel tanks ($2\frac{1}{2}$ gallons on the 20R3 and 25R Standard, and $3\frac{5}{8}$ gallons on the 20D Fleetstar and 32D Fleetmaster) were now mounted further forward. The increase in fuel capacity was not only a benefit for the touring rider, but it also silenced those who had viewed the original Greeves roadsters as having too much daylight between the engine and the base of the fuel tank. It should also be noted that the larger tank was new for 1956. On the 20D, this meant that Greeves could boast of offering the largest fuel capacity for any 200-class British roadster at the time.

The entire range, with the exception of the 20R3, had a new type of guard with deeper valances which afforded a greater degree of protection for the rear drive chain. The cast-alloy frame member, for several years an exclusive feature of the marque, was only continued on the

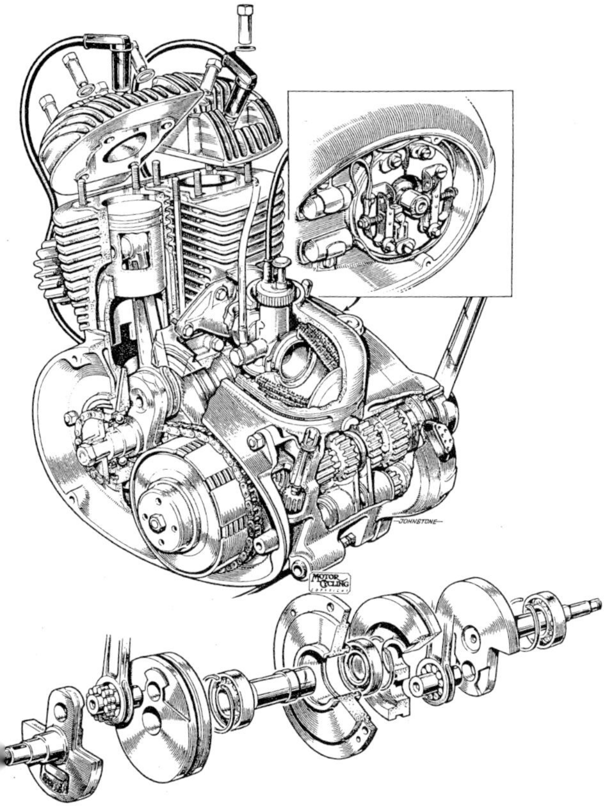

Above **1956 9E-engined 20D Fleetstar De Luxe, with plaid-covered seat, beam frame and 'ear'-type headlamp brackets**

Left **249 cc 2T engine assembly, showing in detail the pistons, carburettor, clutch, primary drive and crankshaft**

Above **1957 saw the debut of the Villiers twin-cylinder 2T-engined 25D**

de luxe D models for 1956, the tubular frame introduced for the 1955 season being employed on the remaining road machines.

The 242 cc twin engine featured new, deeper finning for both the head and barrels, although power remained unchanged at 10 bhp—compared to the pride-of-the-range 32D Fleetmaster, the $\frac{1}{4}$-litre, Anzani-powered model was a definite disappointment in terms of performance. *Motor Cycle*, for example, obtained a mere 61 mph (almost identical to the 200 single) in a May 1955 road test. Compared to this, the larger 322 cc Anzani gave a much superior turn of speed. In fact, its performance was on a par with many ohv 350s, despite sacrificing around 25 cc. A special feature of this model for 1956 was the provision of a full-width, alloy centre for the dual 6 in. front brakes, which cost an additional £5. Along with the smaller twin, the Fleetmaster also had the deeper cylinder barrel and head finning. Both Anzani engines now featured the newly-introduced Amal Monobloc carburettor, although the singles retained their Villiers instruments.

July 1956 saw the local Southend Police and Southend and District Motorcycle Club co-operate in running a training scheme in the town. Besides a BSA Bantam, which was donated by the RAC, Bert Greeves was on hand to present a shining new 20R3 model. Although rider training schemes are all the rage today, over 30 years ago this move was truly innovative.

Although the 242 cc Anzani had not proved much of a success for solo use, the factory considered that it might be suitable as a running mate for a lightweight, single-seat sidecar—and so emerged the Greeves and Watsonian Windsor combination. One of these was put through its paces by *Motor Cycling* for their issue dated 23 August 1956.

With the little Greeves attached to the Watsonian Windsor, the pairing managed to cover 65 miles on a gallon of petroil and could hold 50 mph. But perhaps even more amazing, at least compared to modern-day $\frac{1}{4}$-litre, two-stroke twins, the Anzani unit displayed excellent low-speed torque characteristics, providing exceedingly smooth power in a completely usable form. This, coupled with a very quiet exhaust, provided the pilot with a means of pleasant lane pottering and, if such was his desire, the ability to haul smoothly away from little over 15 mph in *top* gear.

Motor Cycling put it this way: 'In short, here is an outfit which behaves in a most gentlemanly manner, and when a downward change is required, the sweetness of the Albion clutch and gearbox make this in no way tedious operation'. However, as the test progressed, it noted that clutch drag had set in. Except for the better than expected flexibility, the biggest feature to attract the *Motor Cycling* tester's interest was the light handling.

The price of the Greeves/Watsonian combination came out at £239 0*s* 8*d* (£192 4*s* 0*d* for the motorcycle and £46 16*s* 8*d* for the chair).

However the Greeves/Anzani marriage was almost over, and a year later, when the 1958 range was announced, both Anzani-powered twins had been deleted from the list. In fact, so had all but one of the single-cylinder, Villiers-powered roadsters. There were now only two street machines—the 20D Fleetstar single and a brand-new twin, still called the 25D Fleetstar, but with the new Villiers 2T motor.

Producing 15.5 bhp at 5500 rpm, the 2T had a capacity of 249 cc (50 × 63.5 mm) and offered a substantial improvement over its predecessor. In fact, in many ways it was a direct replacement for not only the $\frac{1}{4}$-litre, Anzani-powered model, but also the larger 322—as the new Villiers twin Fleetwing utilized the twin 6 in. front brakes from this model—and boasted a similar power output. Not only did Villiers of Wolverhampton supply the engine and gearbox unit, but also the complete exhaust system and carburettor.

Both the 1958 roadsters had an unusual plaid seat covering and, together with the dirt bikes that year, 9-gauge spokes. The 20D Fleetstar sold at £172 3*s* 1*d*, and the new Villiers-2T-powered 25D Fleetwing twin at £217 1*s* 4*d*.

One could have been forgiven for thinking that, with the success of its Scottish trials and Hawkstone scrambler models, Greeves' roadsters would have been at best neglected or perhaps even phased out entirely. But no, when the usual new-model season came around again in the autumn of 1958, the Essex factory astounded the doubters by launching four new models. Two of these were trials and scrambles mounts, but there were also two new sports roadsters—one a twin. All four machines, including the competition models, were 250s. The roadsters were designated 24DB Sports Single and 25DB Sports Twin with respective capacities of 246 and 249 cc. These replaced the Fleetstar and Fleetwing. The new sports roadsters were identical except for their engines and gearbox assemblies.

A prototype only, this 349 cc twin-cylinder RCA machine was put through its paces by *Motor Cycle* **in the autumn of 1958**

The Sports Single's power unit was the four-speed Villiers 31A. This engine was a development of the 197 cc 9E unit, adopting 66 × 72 mm bore-and-stroke measurements and a toughening up of existing 9E bottom-end components and transmission. This provided a 'new' 246 cc single with a definite sporting bias. Gearbox was a four-speeder.

The Sports Twin utilized the Villiers 2T four-speeder employed in the 1958 model Fleetmaster—which it replaced. However, unlike the earlier model, it had a siamezed exhaust system leading into a single Villiers silencer on the nearside.

Tyre sizes on both the Sports Single and Sports Twin were 2.75 × 19 front and 3.25 × 18 rear. The tyres were exclusively Avons, fitted on chromium-plated rims. Again 9-gauge spokes were specified. Fuel-tank capacity was 2 gallons.

A 6 in. diameter Miller pre-focus light unit and a Smiths speedometer were mounted in a rounded steel moulding at the top of the leading-link front forks. The lighting switch and horn were set in the front of the battery and tool box under the dualseat. On the left-hand side a panel was removable simply by depressing a catch at the top.

Weight of the single was 245 lb and that of the twin 270 lb. Finish was in Moorland blue, except for the mudguards (which were of polished alloy) and the tank which had a two-tone scheme in Moorland blue and Essex grey.

The 247 cc 24DB Sports Single sold for £179 5*s* 0*d*, while the 249 cc 25DB Sports Twin cost £199 15*s* 0*d*. For an additional £4 10*s* 0*d* it was possible to specify the heavily-finned brake drums, as fitted to the 24SAS Hawkstone scrambler.

Motor Cycle soon carried out a full test of the Sports Twin, published in their 30 October 1958 issue. This began by commenting that normally one might be excused for thinking that there was no resemblance between the rigours of scrambling (the word 'motocross' was still only used in continental Europe) and main-road touring. However, as the test progressed, it soon became apparent that in the case of the Greeves, its competition development was a positive advantage, helping to elevate the machine so that its behaviour was 'wholly delightful and often exciting in terms of ordinary road use.'

On the open road one of its best features was its acceleration. The *Motor Cycle* tester stated: 'Up to a quarter throttle, acceleration was moderate, but above that setting the power really developed and the model surged forward in a most exhilarating manner'. It was found that, provided the gearbox was used, the Greeves could keep pace up to its 70 mph maximum speed with most machines of double its capacity. Vibration was only really felt once 60 mph had been exceeded.

The biggest advantages of the machine's competition development were the steering, roadholding and general handling, which were found to be of the highest order. *Motor Cycle* went as far as commenting: 'Indeed, so delightful was the handling that whenever a choice of route was offered, secondary roads were invariably chosen. Bend swinging at all speeds was sheer joy; without any conscious effort the model could be cranked over to either side until a footrest grounded.' With a passenger aboard, the handling was virtually unimpaired, although the centre-stand legs were prone to ground rather too easily.

The front and rear suspensions were adjudged to be perfectly matched, and road shocks went virtually unnoticed. This was summed up in the following manner: 'Proof that the front suspension was doing a fine job on rough surfaces was provided by the unsprung light alloy mudguard which could be seen bobbing up and down like a cork in choppy water.'

The model tested sported the optional finned drums. These too came in for praise, both at high and low speeds. In common with earlier Greeves roadsters, the headlight was found to offer safe night cruising, and with the Sports Twin, this meant any speed up to 55 mph.

However, as with any machine, some features could be criticized if one looked far enough. For instance, a certain amount of groping was necessary to locate the lighting switch, which was mounted underneath the seat. And the horn gave what the *Motor Cycle* man described as 'such a ridiculous squawk that it caused amusement to pedestrians!' (One wonders if this was before or after they had been savaged!)

Another failing was a lack of fuel reserve—this meant that a careful watch had to be kept of the level, and with only a 2-gallon tank this soon became a bind. At a constant 60 mph, consumption was 52 mpg.

The tool kit was said to be 'barely adequate for routine maintenance', and there was no spanner to fit the cylinder head bolts and the plug spanner, which also fitted the wheel spindle nuts, broke rather too easily when the rear wheel nuts were being tightened following chain adjustment.' It was also found that adjustment of the $\frac{1}{2} \times \frac{5}{16}$ (428) chain was required every 500-odd miles.

In 1958 a full 350 Greeves roadster appeared, although only as a prototype. This was powered by the new 349 cc (63 × 56 mm) RCA two-stroke twin designed by Peter Hogan. When the RCA Greeves was put through its paces by *Motor Cycle*'s Vic Willoughby, it showed a respectable turn of speed – over 75 mph. Equipped with twin Amal type 6 carburettors (a single Zenith 25 mm instrument was also tried), it utilized a Siba Dynastart with 12-volt ignition coils. Due, in no small part, to the availability of the Villiers 2T/3T engines, the RCA Greeves went no further.

November 1958 saw the entire Greeves range displayed at the Earls Court show. That year the company's advertising theme for the roadsters was: 'The Lightweight with the Heavyweight reputation!' which was backed up by a list of the major sporting events which the marque had taken that year. As will be revealed in other chapters, the Thundersley marque was by then in a purple patch of dirt-bike glory, with the roadsters living from now on very much in the shadow of their glamorous competition brothers and sisters. When the 1960 range was announced in October 1959, this was evident from the three new models all being off-road mounts. The two sporting roadsters remained unchanged.

So, as Greeves entered the new decade, all was very quiet on the roadster front, but not so in the worlds of scrambling and trials ...

1959 246 cc 24DB Sports Single, perhaps the most attractive Greeves roadster of the decade

5 Scottish—the event and machine

The Scottish Six Day Trial, or just plain Scottish (not to be confused with the Scott Trial), is Britain's premier trials event and is held annually in the Western Highlands based around Fort William. This event combines breathtaking scenery with some of the finest natural obstacles to be found anywhere in the British Isles, and it is the mecca of all true trials enthusiasts.

The Scottish used to be regarded as a holiday event by the many privateer clubmen who entered it, and they often went without the necessities of life just to compete in this classic event once a year. The dream of cleaning all sections was always there, and every entrant strived to gain a special first-class award (the equivalent of an ISDT gold medal). All riders knew that only one person could capture the outright winner's prize, but this situation did not bother 90 per cent of the entrants—for them, just to take part and finish the event was enough. On their return to everyday life after the Scottish, the stories that could be told and retold of the sections, the machines, and the stars encountered, could earn untold favours for the participating clubmen.

The event has altered somewhat from its initial conception in 1925, when it was a complicated event for three-man factory teams. Except for a break between 1939 and 1947, the event has been run annually. Individual capacity class awards were introduced in 1928, but it was not until 1933 that the present system of an overall winner was instigated. Between 1932 and 1948, and also in 1950, sidecar crews competed in their own right for the premier sidecar award.

The Scottish, with nearly 150 observed sections and a total length of some 800 miles, is so different to anything else staged worldwide. The Americans, and even the Spanish, have tried to upstage the event, but to no avail—it is the Scottish every year which attracts the crème de la crème of trials riders. Unfortunately, today the trial is viewed somewhat differently by the massively-supported works entrants, as results mean big money for both the rider and the machine manufacturer. To this end, the Scottish has been tailored to suit the modern trials rider. Observed sections have become harder and, in some cases, downright impossible, thus excluding the fainthearted and riders of older or traditional machines.

If one scans the outright winners' list, it will be seen that the big names feature quite prominently. Sammy Miller has taken the premier award on five occasions, twice on his legendary Ariel GOV 132, and three times on a Bultaco. Tying with Sam is Mick Andrews, also with five events to his credit on a mixture of Ossa and Yamaha machines. Hugh Vinney and Gordon Jackson have each taken the award on four occasions, both riders being AJS mounted. The only time the award was won by a Greeves rider was in 1969 when Billy Wilkinson, riding an Anglian, collected top honours. Unfortunately, this was the last time a British machine featured on the leader board.

Billy Wilkinson joined the Greeves team during the early Scottish days. At the tender age of 17, his presence was requested by the Greeves factory chiefs who invited him to Thundersley to talk a little business, his rise to fame in local Yorkshire events not having gone unnoticed. Once Greeves mounted, he justified the factory's faith in him by gaining the best first-time award in the 1959 Scottish, and a string of awards in many other major trials, notably the premier award in the British Experts held in the November of 1960. Other successes followed. After many misses, the Allan Jefferies trophy was finally won in 1966, but by far his crowning achievement was the 1969 Scottish win. Riding a Greeves for ten years, helped by the factory and pushed on by his father (who had ridden in 16 Scottish Six Days), Billy took the outright winner's award and finally put Greeves in the position that they had been trying to achieve for so long.

By far the biggest problem encountered by the young Wilkinson was the stigma of having to display learner plates on his trials machines, for it took him five attempts to pass his driving test. The Auto Cycle Union breathed a sigh of relief when the test was finally passed, for they had had to waive an ACU ruling which stated that learners could not hold a National Competition licence to compete in the major events so that Billy could ride.

Brian Stonebridge, himself a competent trials rider, also contested the Scottish, notably in 1959 on a 250 cc chair outfit. The outfit he rode, 220 ETW, was also used as a solo (or, at least, another bike with the same registration number) during his early years at the factory with good results, for he won the Folbigg Cup for the best 250 in the November 1958 Scott Trial, against considerable odds. The idea of using one registration number to cover more than one machine was not a new practice, and number swapping seemed to be fair game in this era. Brian probably borrowed the idea from the Royal Enfield factory, which practised this art regularly to avoid paying too much duty to the state coffers.

Don Smith was another regular contestant in the Scottish, always finishing in the first dozen or so, but never gaining the coveted premier award. The 1961 event, in which Gordon Jackson scooped the award with the loss of one solitary mark, saw Don gain the newcomer's award with the loss of 37 marks. He recalled at the time how easy it was, for he was winning open to centre trials with more than the 37 marks he lost on the Scottish. The event was not as testing for the rider and machine as it is now, for in that era it still retained the clubman's holiday image, which is precisely what the organizing Edinburgh club wanted to promote.

Don got close to winning the premier award on many occasions, but none so close as the 1964 event. If the organizers knew then what we now know, he would have won it, but sportsmanship prevailed and he was awarded third place. On the final run into Edinburgh, Mick Andrews, lying in second position, split the oil tank of his AJS. The marks lost for this type of fault, if noticed on the final inspection, would have been enough to relegate Mick to third place, and put Don up to second place. True sportsman, Don did not mind and, in fact, helped Mick to clean up the mess and disguise the fault.

Even Sammy Miller, the leader, was not devoid of trouble that year, for at one stage he suffered a cracked frame and had it secretly welded. If the organizers had been aware of these antics, Don would have gained the outright winner's award, an award which has eluded him to this day. To illustrate this sportsmanship between trials riders, later that year this situation was reversed. When competing in the National John Douglas Trial, held in October, Don flipped his Greeves over backwards. The bike, 685 HWC, landed heavily and snapped the handlebars on impact with the ground, effectively putting Don out of the event. Despite having put up a creditable performance, Dot rider, Richard Brian, went into voluntary retirement, releasing his handlebars to Don. The bars fitted, and Don went on to win the event.

Billy Wilkinson was not so lucky in the Ilkley Grand National of March 1961, for when leading Sammy Miller, his steering-head bolt sheared and the fork assembly came adrift. With no help at hand, Billy was forced into retirement.

The sort of sportsmanship shown by riders during the 1950s and 1960s, who considered that it was riding capabilities which counted, cannot happen today, as the event is contested by massively-supported works riders running to orders, whose bosses treat the event as a huge advertising campaign, rather than a sporting event. To this end, the sections have increased in severity, in an effort to weed out even the top men on their trick machines. Entry fees have also risen dramatically. At one time, these included the rider's accommodation, and even free petrol but, sadly, all these perks have ceased.

All is not quite as bad as the picture painted, however, for the Edinburgh and District Motor Club have recognized the upsurgence of the pre-'65 movement, and put on an event especially to cover that era. Not a full six-day trial, but a half-day bash, run as a prelude to the main event on some of the original sections, and catering exclusively for pre-'65 trials irons. This gives an airing to some of the classic machinery which used to frequent the Highlands two decades ago, and the riders, who are now a little older, a little greyer, and a little heavier. The old-timers see this now as their event, and attack the half-day with as much enthusiasm and dedication as do the young bloods in the full event. Ariel, AJS, BSA, Dot, Enfield and Greeves machinery can now be seen performing again in their natural habitat.

Once again, the blue and silver Thundersley

Brian Stonebridge taking his trials model, 220 ETW, through deep water during the Grasshopper Chingford MCC Dick Turpin Trial on 23 March 1958

bikes are in the Highlands performing in much the same way, on the same sections, as they did in their heyday—a job for which they were originally intended and eminently suitable. But let us not forget the early Greeves riders who campaigned this event with so much dedication, for it was Jack Simpson on his 197 who took the 200 cc award in the 1957 event, which was the first year Greeves entered a factory team. It comprised Simpson, Peter Hammond and Norman Storer.

To commemorate Jack's award, the newly-launched Greeves trials machine for 1958 was given the name Scottish. The name appeared on the fuel-tank badge below Bert's signature. It was a very suitable choice of name, for it summed up the endeavour and intentions of the factory—to produce a mount capable of tackling anything, including the world's premier trials event.

The first 20TA Scottish model to come off the production line was snapped up for Don Smith by his sponsor, Chelmsford dealer Derek Cornell, who employed Don prior to his military service. This machine led Don, an up-and-coming rider of the day, to many wins and eventual acceptance into the Greeves fold as a full works rider. With the tragic death of Brian Stonebridge in October 1959, it was Don who took over the development of the Scottish range.

Bert Greeves had designed the Scottish back in 1957, using the original 20T as a basis, but it was Brian, the superb development engineer, who finally got the formula right before it went into production. Refinement and further development of the Scottish was then put into Don's hands, and he looked after the model until it was phased out in 1965.

The sequence of events leading to the launch of any new Greeves model usually followed the same course: design, test in competition (this phase could sometimes be called 'test to destruction'), refine and relaunch. Normally, works mounts used by the factory stars, once proven, became the basis for machines available to the general public for the following season. The Scottish was no exception, as during its production life, no fewer

than five variants were made before it was phased out in favour of the Anglian.

This method of producing standard machines based on works bikes can best be illustrated if one studies Don's works mounts, 685 HWC and, latterly, JVW 88C. The former, used in the 1962 Scottish, bristled with new ideas, some of which were incorporated in production machines at a later date. Not all works-bike modifications were pressed into production; some ideas were axed because they were too radical, and others were shelved on the grounds of sheer expense. The engine mounting plates used on 685 HWC (or what was left of them) may have been satisfactory for a works rider in the pursuit of ultimate weight saving, but to a one-day-a-week clubman, who makes a few mistakes, they would not have been strong enough. Don always used alloy rims on his machines in the search for lightness, but it was not an idea passed on to the standard machines in the interests of both strength and expense.

The development of the Scottish pursued its own course, but was helped by lessons learned not only in trialing, but also on the scrambles track. Being a second runner to the scrambler, sometimes its improvements did take a little longer to filter through the system. When first introduced, the 20TA bore a close family resemblance to the 20SA scrambler, the frame being an exact copy, even down to the new T-shaped seat pillar/frame tie. To conform to the trials specification, and to meet the legal requirements of a machine destined to be ridden on the road, such items as trials tyres, speedometer, number plates and hooter were added. The riding position, being further towards the rear when compared to the scrambler, required the use of a new set of footrests, which were attached to a small subframe bolted to the rear frame lower mounting points. The frame also carried the rear-brake cross-over shaft. To complement the footrests, and in true trials tradition, the machine was fitted with a sprung rubber trials saddle, supplied by Dunlop.

The engine unit used in the 20TA was the Villiers 9E, which was fitted with a wide-ratio gearbox and heavy competition flywheel. The standard Villiers S25 carburettor was retained, but fitted to a longer competition inlet stub, lifting the instrument out of its recess in the crankcases—the recess was covered by a closing plate to retain the smooth crankcase lines. The new Scottish was treated to a revised exhaust system, developed by Brian Stonebridge, which featured a one-piece up-and-

Left **A meeting of enthusiasts, circa 1958. Left to right: Bert Greeves, John Griffiths (*Motor Cycling*), Jack Simpson, Derry Preston-Cobb and Peter Vine**

Right **Billy Wilkinson in action at the Scottish Six Day Trial, early May 1959**

over pipe connected to a long silencer unit bolted to the rear subframe's mudguard mounting loop. The silencer, a proprietary Villiers item, was modified by cutting and cranking it inboard under the seat, where it was connected to the pipe by a simple clip. This silencer pipe joint was never completely oil tight, and was criticized regularly by motorcycling press testers of the day, as there is nothing more unsightly than drips of oily, two-stroke exhaust residue on a nice clean machine.

In line with the standard trials models, Greeves produced trials specials, the designation bearing an 'S' suffix. The special models were built to a higher specification, which necessitated a correspondingly higher price. The 20TAS was the up-market model for 1958 and was fitted with an uprated version of the 9E motor, the only cosmetic difference being the use of a dull-chrome-plated fuel tank, instead of the standard light-blue, stove-enamelled version.

The following year saw the introduction of a full 250 cc Scottish, using the newly-introduced Villiers 31A unit, fitted with a heavy flywheel and a four-speed, wide-ratio gearbox. The extra 49 cc of the 24TAS delighted testers of the era who praised its 'plonkability', clean pick-up, pulling power and high-revving endurance. Some testers even wrote about the massive power increase over the 197 cc version—12 bhp at 4500 rpm, instead of 8.4 bhp at 4000 rpm, was a large step in those far-off days. The 250 weighed some 7 lb more than the 200, but this was of no consequence when set against the increased power output. Handling and instant power controllability were praised, even on the most slippery of sections, for snap throttle openings would enable the machine to draw away with the minimum of fuss, a feat not always possible with the 9E. One improvement introduced on the 24TAS was the provision of a rear chain oiler. The oil was contained within the tubes of the swinging arm, the filler being sited on the right-hand side, near the pivot, and metered to the chain via a needle valve. This system was destined to be used on all future trials models, and certainly helped prolong the life of the final-drive chain.

The next major step in the development of the Scottish was the introduction of the TC series for the 1960 season. By far the biggest advance was the use of the Villiers 32A trials motor instead of the 31A. The new 32A trials-specification unit was a purpose-built motor, which incorporated the heavy flywheel and wide gear ratios, together with a new cylinder designed specifically for trials work. The quoted power output was 12.4 bhp at

5000 rpm, a slight increase over the 31A.

The C-series Scottish was very similar to the earlier A-series, but the changes incorporated in this model were there for a purpose. Not readily noticeable was the change in the steering-head angle, the cast front beam having been redesigned to give a 2-degree steeper steering angle. This modification improved the low-speed handling and reduced the wheelbase to $51\frac{1}{4}$ in. The opportunity was also taken to modify the front-fork assembly to increase the steering lock, this was achieved by introducing cranked top and bottom fork crown plates. The new plates placed the fork tubes, which were now made of Reynold 531 tubing, some $\frac{1}{2}$ in. further forward, which increased the lock by 20 degrees. Another modification, not readily apparent, was the softening of the front and rear suspension systems, the front using softer-compound Metalastik bushes, and the rear Armstrong units being fitted with new springs of a lower poundage. The rear chain guard, which previously covered the rear sprocket, now terminated at the suspension unit. The tendency of owners to remove the rear portion of the guard to aid wheel removal swayed the factory into making the shortened version, thereby saving new owners the trouble of searching for a hacksaw.

In 1961 the TD-series trials machines were introduced, and were a continued and logical development of the earlier series. The new TD now used the scrambles frame, introduced on that model a year previously. As mentioned earlier, the trials machines sometimes had to wait for modifications to filter down from the scrambles side of the competitions shop, and this late change illustrates that fact quite well.

The new frame featured a larger-diameter top tube and a heavier, cast-alloy frame member to accommodate the change to Timken taper-roller steering-head bearings. These new bearings, proven in competition, were much stronger than the original ball variety, and were quite capable of standing up to the punishment received in the heat of battle. The rear subframe was changed to a one-piece, triangulated type and topped by a neat little wrap-around seat, which again first saw service on the previous year's scramblers. On this model, the factory took the opportunity to further improve machine handling on long hills by resiting the engine unit within the frame. New engine cradle plates were made to lower the engine by $\frac{1}{2}$ in. and to move it forward by $\frac{7}{8}$ in.

The next major step forward was the introduction of the 24TES for the 1962 season, for this machine was a complete redesign over the previous year's model, being based on the factory machines used in the 1961 Scottish. Prior to this, Greeves tended to employ the same frame which, with minor modifications, could be used in both branches of off-road competitions, but now the trials machine received a new, purpose-designed and competition-proven frame. The new assembly had a redesigned top tube ($1\frac{1}{2}$ in. $\times$ 16 gauge), which curved downwards behind the engine unit and attached to the rear of an all-welded, channel-section engine cradle, manufactured from 12-gauge plate. To this sturdy frame was bolted a triangulated rear subframe, constructed of $\frac{7}{8}$ in. $\times$ 16-gauge tubing, and a rectangular-section swinging arm running on a pivot bolt of increased diameter.

To complement the chassis came a new set of front forks, with a beefed-up loop featuring strengthened bush housings. The loop was constructed of 1 in. $\times$ 18-gauge, and not only attached to the rear of the bottom links, but now extended forward to a point below the damper mounting.

In the quest for greater power, the special trials model of the E-range was treated to a square alloy

Left **Sammy Miller seated on a 20TD Scottish, with Bert Greeves in the background, Earls Court 1960**

Right **P. Atkinson attempting his own version of the Highland Fling on Grey Mare's Ridge during the 1961 Scottish Six Days**

cylinder of the type previously used only on the scramblers. In order to retain the tractability of the trials model, the compression ratio was reduced. This, allied to the use of a Villiers S25 carburettor, produced a motor that was capable of plodding when called for, but could deliver instant power when the situation demanded it. Another step forward, using technology developed on the scrambles track, was the use of a long, tapering exhaust silencer of the low-level type, which neatly tucked in round the front of the engine cradle and emerged on the right-hand side, above the magneto housing and gearbox.

The E-series trials machines enjoyed a relatively long life, being in production for some four seasons, the ultimate machine being the 24TES Mk II, produced during 1963 for the 1964 season. The Mk II version featured fibreglass mudguards, a small seat, British Hub Company full-width alloy hubs, and a low-level exhaust system on the left-hand side. The front pipe was square in section and fabricated from four pieces of sheet welded together, terminating in a small, flat silencer mounted above the primary-drive case. During its production run, the TES scored many wins, not only with works riders aboard (Smith, Wilkinson, Adsett, Davis etc), but also in the hands of privateers. One notable win, when piloted by Sammy Miller, was the National Welsh Trophy Trial held in May 1963. Sam, not normally associated with two-strokes (his two-stroke days were to come later with the Spanish Bultaco marque), was not originally entered for the trial, but took over a 250 cc entry when offered a mount by Bill Brooker. Bill never let an opportunity slip, and even tried to sign up the Ulsterman for the works team. Miller, although grateful for the loan of a machine, passed up the chance, preferring to stick with his legendary Ariel 500.

Works 24TES, 313 WPU, at the 1961 Scottish. This Mk I machine has a Mk II front guard and lightweight fork legs

MY FIRST BIKE BOUGHT 1963

Above **Start of a typical trials event. Basingstoke club president, ex-police superintendent T. A. Willmott, about to start the eventual winner, Mike Jackson, in a March Hare Trial during the early 1960s**

Above right **Dave Bickers on a TES Mk II during the Inter Centre Trial in March 1964**

Left **January 1963, and Peter Stirland pilots his Scottish through deep snow to gain a first-class award**

The degree of success gained by the factory in 1964 can be gauged by the awards received by Greeves riders in that year's Scottish. No fewer than ten riders received special first-class awards, 19 first-class and 12 second-class awards. To this impressive total—more than any other manufacturer's—were added the 150 cc cup, the 250 cc cup and the third best performance.

The crowning glory of the season, however, was the European Trials Championship. Works rider Don Smith gained the premier award in the French, Belgian and German rounds, and amassed enough points to take the Championship outright. On the home front, Gordon Adsett took the runner-up prize in the British Experts Trial, riding a TES Mk II into second place behind Sammy Miller. For Gordon, who then worked for Comerfords and had been using a Greeves since his recognition by the factory in 1962, this was his second invitation to the Experts. His first effort had ended after he was excluded on time, caused by repair work being carried out after hitting a jaywalker in the middle of a section.

The following year Greeves' riders figured heavily again in the Scottish, taking ten special first-class awards, 26 first-class and 16 second-class awards, the 150 cc cup, and the best performance by a non Scot. It was at this event that Mary Driver notched up a unique record; out of six starts, she gained the best-woman award six times in a row. The works entrants, Davis, Smith and Wilkinson, chasing the manufacturers' team award, were leading that category for the first four days, but problems on the fifth day let the Triumph team through to win.

After a three-year lay-off, Gordon Jackson returned to competitive trials riding in the Dobrovini Cup Trial, held in mid-June 1965. Unfamiliar with the machine and faced with unexpected muddy conditions, nevertheless he managed to gain fourth place riding one of the factory's new TFS models, LHK 46C. After the trial, Gordon said that he had thoroughly enjoyed the event. He continued to ride for Greeves and, at the end of the year, took the premier award at the West of England Trial, but this time mounted on a TGS Anglian.

As development progressed, the TES was

Above **Top-end details of the TFS model**

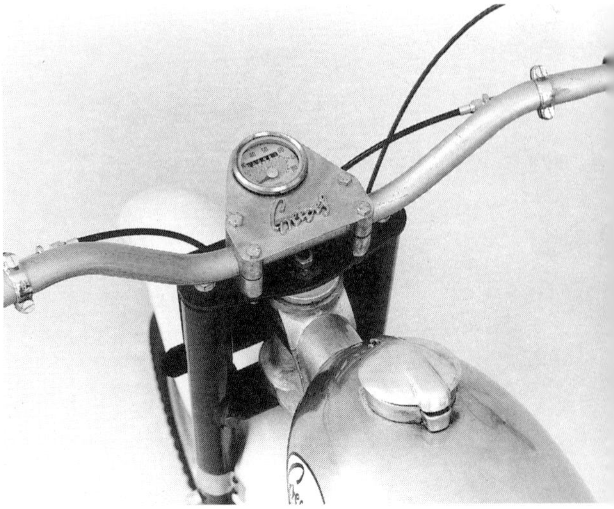

Above **Rider's eye view of the 24TFS—simple in the extreme**

Below **The legendary John Surtees with a 24TFS**

phased out in favour of the TFS trials model. The TFS was the last true Scottish, even though it did not bear this name, for with the advent of alloy fuel tanks (which first appeared on the TES Mk II), the cast-alloy Scottish badge was discontinued in favour of a Greeves transfer.

The TFS used the same frame and cycle parts as the model it superseded, but it was equipped with a pliable plastic front mudguard, as used by the Challenger motocross machine. The new plastic guard, being white, necessitated the rear fibreglass guard being finished in the same colour, instead of the blue finish found on the TES Mk II.

The success of the Challenger motocrosser led the factory to adopt its race-proven cylinder for use on the 24 TFS. The new Greeves engine had the same cylinder-stud spacing and cylinder height as the Villiers 250 cc motors, enabling the Challenger cylinder to fit the 32A crankcases of the TFS without resorting to expensive machining. The only modification required was the use of an 18-gauge compression plate, which lowered the compression ratio to a level more suited to trials. The new trials engine retained the use of a Villiers S25 carburettor, mounted on a specially-fabricated manifold which was bolted to the existing Monobloc mounting points.

To complement the cylinder, the factory designed a new, long, tapering expansion chamber, which was tucked well in on the right-hand side of the engine, but positioned higher than the TE type and attached to the rear spring unit's top mounting bolt. Many TFS models were fitted with alternative silencers, some utilizing a Palmer design, which was fitted in a similar position to that of the TE series and featured a barrel-type silencer. Other machines, mainly works development mounts, used a system similar to the later Anglian, a type developed and used by Don Smith as early as 1962.

At about this time, Greeves were making inroads on the US leisure market with a machine suited to the peculiar conditions found there. The Americans wanted a machine which was suitable for hunters, fishermen and recreational riders to get about on. A trials machine would have been the ideal choice, but these machines were tuned for 'plonking' and lacked the performance sought by fun-loving riders. The motocross machine would have been the ideal choice for the weekender who got his thrills from sheer speed, but would have been quite unsuitable for the rider who liked to take it easy once in a while. With these two opposite ends of the scale defined, a compromise was reached which favoured a 'trail' machine—so was born the TFS Trail for the American market only.

The Trail model was well suited to its market, for it fulfilled all the requirements of the widely differing American scene. Capable of over 70 mph, the Trail was no sluggard, for it was powered by a 33A unit, topped by a Challenger cylinder, with a compression ratio of 11:1. The quoted output was 23 bhp at 6500 rpm. This figure, slightly below that of the Challenger motocrosser, was achieved by the use of a Villiers S25 carburettor, which provided good low-speed characteristics and easy starting. The wide range of terrain, well within the capabilities of the machine, was looked after by wide-ratio, trials gearbox internals, allowing the machine to be ridden at a snail's pace or flat out on unmetalled roads. The construction of the machine followed closely that of the 24TFS, but utilized chromed steel guards and fuel tank, a large air filter and a 19 in. front wheel, a size favoured by the Americans for desert riding, as it was usually shod with a 3.5 in. tyre to prevent digging in on loose sand washes.

American journalists who tested the Trail liked its slow-speed capabilities and handling on nasty terrain, but criticized the high-speed handling of the trials-based frame. One tester went so far as to advocate the use of Challenger forks to cut out a high-speed wobble which marred flat-out testing. Generally, the machine was liked by all who tried it, some calling it an ideal poacher's bike, for it was no problem to outrun even the best equipped game warden. Although the machine was ideal, sales did not take off, for the same reason that British bike sales were beginning to fall on home ground; this was the mid-1960s and the effects of the Japanese invasion were beginning to be felt.

The average clubman is always impressed by results gained in national and international competition, and this is reflected by sales which rise at a proportional rate to successes. This was the factory's original intention and it paid off. The awards received by works riders and clubmen alike did wonders for the sales of the Scottish, as every budding rider wanted a machine that was seen to be capable of winning. This image was now becoming a little dented by the insurgence of a new contender for the trials crown. Just as the Japanese were making their presence felt in road-machine sales, the Spanish were making an appearance on the trials scene, with good results. Something had to be done; the Scottish had outlived its usefulness and a new design was needed. The Scottish was phased out at the end of the 1965 season, to be replaced by a new breed of trials machine which would carry the Greeves name on for another four years.

The Greeves trials machine of the Scottish era is remembered affectionately by many riders who rode it in competition, and it can best be summed up by quoting a phrase from a test report of the 24TAS in *Motor Cycling* of April 1959: 'In essentials, the 24TAS Scottish must go on record as a piece of functional machinery which cannot be faulted, designed with intelligence and care, and built with stoutness essential in a serious competition mount.'

Above **Don Smith's immaculate 1965 works mount had many detail changes from the standard production model**

Below **Billy Wilkinson, the 1969 Scottish winner, at Devil's Staircase on the third day—the end of an era for the Villiers-powered Greeves trials bike**

Below **Club rider A. L. King negotiates a rocky hazard on his TFS during the Clayton Trial in August 1967**

6 ISDT adventures

The International Six Day Trial, or International Six Day Enduro as it is now called, is an annual event to test the stamina, endurance and cunning of the world's best off-road riders. The event is best summed up by calling it the Olympics of motorcycling, because it covers all facets of off-road motorcycle racing. The ISDT is unique because it not only tests the rider's ability to pilot his machine over all types of terrain, but also tests his skill to monitor and manage his progress, repair and service his machine, and, above all, to actually *survive* the six days. When the daily schedule is seven to eight hours of battling over forest and mountain tracks, the occasional slide is an occupational hazard. Usually, it means another bruise and a few seconds' delay, but bigger spills may take a few minutes in straightening out the machine. Rarely are things more serious, but now and then riders do get hurt. National pride is always at stake, whether it be as a team member or as an individual, for every entrant goes for gold.

International Six Day trialing first began as a friendly match between the British and French, held near Carlisle in 1913, in conjunction with the then popular English Six Day Trial, each country submitting a three-man team. All three Frenchmen retired, giving the British their first recorded win, a result which was to be repeated many times during the events which followed. As that first British win was achieved on home ground, the French were invited to stage the next event, which was duly scheduled to be held at Grenoble in the following year, 1914. Due to the commencement of hostilities, the trial was postponed at the last minute. The large contingent of British riders who had left home to compete in the event, some taking several days to arrive at the venue, knew nothing of the worsening situation and were duly given 24 hours to leave the country. Riders scattered to the four winds, trying to make it home as best they could. Those who had not had their machines commandeered by the French Army faced the problem of roads cluttered by military convoys and a fuel shortage. Two entrants even tried to return over the Alps, but never did make the Channel crossing from Le Havre, having gone missing en route.

The 1939 event held in Salzburg was also overshadowed by the threat of war, but this time the event was staged. Teams began pulling out as hostilities escalated, but it was not until late on the fourth day that the decision was made to withdraw the British team, who left via the Swiss border the following morning. The British Army team who, in the absence of War Office instructions, thought they were fireproof, carried on. They, too, finally left by the Swiss border, but later in the day.

After the war, the event was reinstated, with Czechoslovakia playing host in 1947, and it has continued in much the same way, under virtually the same set of rules and regulations, ever since.

The objective of the ISDT during this period was to cover a set course of some 2000 km (1200 miles), at a laid-down average speed, according to machine capacity, with penalty points being awarded for lateness. In addition to the set course, there were a series of special tests which earned bonus points for the rider and were used to determine final placings. These special tests took the form of hill climbs, cross-country runs, acceleration/braking tests, and a final speed test. Bonus points were assessed by a formula, which took the average of the best three riders in class and used it as a standard test time. To earn an ISDT gold medal, the rider had to have zero penalty points and more than 500 bonus points. The silver medal required no more than 25 penalties and more than 300 bonus points. If a rider actually finished the event (not an entirely easy feat), and gained more than one bonus point, he was awarded the bronze.

The most prestigious division of the ISDT was the Trophy competition, which was entered on a nation-by-nation basis. The team consisted of six runners, using machines of varying sizes manufactured in the team's country of origin. The winner of the Trophy then exercised the right to stage the following year's event. If the Trophy was won on home ground, the privilege was extended to the runner-up. The Silver Vase was contested by national teams, too, each of four riders, the maximum being two teams per country. Trophy and Vase team riders had to stay together as a team, as any retirements automatically attracted a penalty of 100 points per day per rider missing. Other team events contested over the six days were for manufacturers and the various clubs and associations who could afford to field a team.

Greeves, as a manufacturer, did not enter ISDTs until a later date, but the first recorded Greeves rider was a private entrant in the 1954 Welsh event based at Llandrindod Wells. The rider, J. G. Mallalieu, gained a gold medal in the standard category. Riders who elected to ride the special schedule, the same schedule as the Trophy, Vase and manufacturers' teams, whose average was ten per cent higher, were on the hunt for special gold medals. Other medal winners that year were Monty Banks on a 197 Tandon, who gained a bronze, and James-mounted Peter Stirland who took a gold. Both riders were later to ride Greeves machines and add to their collection of medals.

As the Jawa-mounted Czech team took the Trophy in Wales, they staged the next round on their home ground, which effectively put an end to the participation of any Greeves-riding privateer for a while.

The 1958 West German event, centred on Garmisch in the Bavarian Alps, saw the first factory-backed Greeves machines in action. Brian Stonebridge, riding 6 LHK, and Jack Simpson, on 5 LHK, were teamed up with Peter Stirland on his Enfield 350 and Velocette 500-mounted Jim Sheehan to form the Vase B team. Other Greeves entrants were Bill Brooker, Peter Baldwin and Pat Brittain, with Albert Glassbrook representing the Birmingham club.

The first day was full of surprises. After standing all night in torrential rain, in the open—for the organizers had seen fit not to supply a covered *parc fermé*—many machines were reluctant to start. Was this purely for economic reasons, or was it an attempt to test the weatherproofing of the fragile electrics used in that era? Even Sammy Miller on his Ariel was a non-starter—not with water in the works but, above all things, food poisoning. By the end of the first day, the Trophy and both Vase teams were a man short, thus effectively putting paid to a Vase win by the Stonebridge Vase B team—with high bottom gearing, the fragile Velocette clutch of Jim Sheehan's machine had cried enough. Peter Stirland's run was not without trouble, either, for at one time he pulled out a suspension-unit mounting stud, which was replaced without incurring any penalty points.

Neither Peter Baldwin nor Pat Brittain was happy with his Greeves engine, both suspecting big-end wear, but it was not until the third day that Pat retired and confirmed a big-end failure. Peter's motor did last the event, but only with careful nursing. Further casualties ensued when Albert Glassbrook cried enough on the fourth day, suffering from a flesh wound and exhaust-pipe burns. The following day, Jack Simpson was rushed to hospital with a bruised and lacerated leg, following a spill.

All in all, not a very inspiring start for the Greeves factory, but they were spared a whitewash by the faultless run of Brian Stonebridge, who gained a well-deserved gold, backed up by Bill Brooker and Peter Baldwin, who both gained bronze medals.

The factory team travelled in style that year, in Bert's faithful Ford V8 Pilot, Brian and Jack's machines, together with a third bike, being carried on the trailer. The third machine was taken and ridden by Bert, but was not entered in the event.

The machines which Stonebridge and Simpson rode were from a series of six, from 2 LHK to 7 LHK, produced at the factory in early 1958 especially for the Bavarian event. These machines were first aired in public at the Welsh Three Day event in June, for that event included the selection tests for the ISDT squad.

The machines themselves were basically production 20TAS trials models, modified for the ISDT by the provision of a scrambles seat and footrests. Other ISDT requirements were the fitting of a tank-top bag for tools and spares, a centre stand for ease of hurried maintenance, and an air bottle for rapid tyre inflation. A QD lighting set and rock guards completed the specification, the latter items being on offer by the factory as optional extras anyway.

Gearbox ratios, normally wide on the trials machine, were changed for a set of standard road

Brian Stonebridge's ISDT gold-medal winner at Earls Court in November 1958

ratios, or even scrambles close ratios, depending on the terrain and the rider's choice. The engine, which started life as a competition 9E unit, was effectively increased in swept volume by the addition of a specially-cast, square, alloy cylinder of 66 mm bore. This new assembly, the forerunner of the MDS cylinder, featured detachable transfer ports, which could be changed as dictated by the type of engine response required—an idea first seen on the round iron barrels used in the Welsh selection tests. This arrangement was fed by a 389 Amal Monobloc carburettor and Garda air filter, as was common practice on the scramblers of that era.

Also seen for the first time on these works machines was the fitment of new, heavily-finned, cast-alloy brake drums. These aided cooling and also prevented the drum from distorting under heavy braking action—a problem known to occur in the pressed-steel versions, which had a tendency to swell when the brakes were applied hard.

Of the original six machines, three are known to survive today. 6 LHK is owned by Bert Greeves, and looked after by Chris Goodfellow, an ex-factory employee who displayed it at the Brands Hatch Festival of a Thousand Bikes in 1985. Number 6, as it is now known, was first exhibited to the public at the 1958 Motorcycle Show, where it took pride of place, still bearing the scars and caked mud from its recent ISDT gold-medal success. Jack Simpson's mount, number 5, has recently come to light and has been painstakingly restored to its original former glory by enthusiast Ian Booker. Number 2 was sold off by the factory in 1959 and is still in the

MY 2ND GREEVES 32A ENGINE BOUGHT 1974

hands of the original purchaser, Albert Glassbrook, who continued to use the machine in the manner to which it was intended.

When purchased, Albert Glassbrook's machine was not to his liking, for he had little faith in the single-cylinder engine, which was removed and replaced by a 250 2T unit. With the bike in this guise, he contested the 1959 Czech event as a member of the Birmingham MCC. British entrants for this event were organized by the ACU, but had no manufacturer's support, a daunting task indeed for any privateer rider, but his efforts were rewarded. Peter Rose, the only other Greeves entrant, went out on the second day with gearbox trouble, but Albert pressed on, only to run out of fuel and clocking up penalty points while searching for replenishment. Despite losing his clutch on the fifth day, and retiring after only 22 minutes of the final speed event, he gained a bronze medal.

Glassbrook was out again in the 1960 Austrian event, centred on Bad Aussee, this time in better company, as there were eight other Greeves riders competing. First-day Greeves casualties included Sammy Miller, from the Vase team, and 'Tiger' Timms, from the Army team, both going out with sheared head bolts. Later analysis proved that the material used to construct the special alloy sleeve bolts—necessary with the alloy cylinder—was of the wrong specification. The coefficient of expansion was lower than that of the cylinder, resulting in the bolts shearing at the lower end, leaving some $\frac{1}{2}$ in. of bolt remaining on the crankcase stud. Riders soon came up with a solution; a pair of special, thin-nosed pliers that could reach between the cylinder fins to unwind the remains of the sleeve bolt, and a pocket full of spare bolts.

The remaining Greeves riders put up good performances, with Triss Sharp gaining a gold and helping to put the British Trophy team into fourth position. This was achieved despite a brush with a private motorcyclist on the fourth day. Other golds were won by Bryan Sharp and SSM M. G. Edwards of the Army team. Silver medals were gained by privateers Peter Rose, Ian Hillier and Albert Glassbrook (on his 2T-twin-powered Greeves, 2 LHK), with Sgt 'Bill' D. Brooker of the Army team also in the running.

The organizers of the Austrian event were accused of inflexibility and lack of experience in the running of the trial, as it was fought out in the forests during the day and the jury room at night.

Above **Simpson leads Stonebridge at Abergivesyn during the Welsh Two Days in June 1958**

Above left **Preparing to leave for the 1958 ISDT in West Germany. Left to right: Brian Stonebridge, Bert Greeves and Jack Simpson**

Left **Pat Brittain's 1958 ISDT mount—prior to the event. He retired on the third day with big-end failure**

Above **A Russian competitor looks on as Sammy Miller (214) prepares to start on the first day of the 1960 ISDT from Bad Aussee, Austria. Miller retired on the same day when a cylinder-head retaining sleeve sheared**

Above right **A BMW rider watches as British teamster Triss Sharp takes his Greeves through an Austrian village during the 1960 event. Unlike Miller, Sharp won a gold**

Left **Sammy Miller checking his mount before the event. Looking on is the Castrol representative, Malcolm Edgar—Greeves were contracted to rivals Shell!**

Right **Triss Sharp during the speed tests on the final day of the 1960 ISDT**

BÄCKEREI
M
MW 108

201
201

The Italian judges raised an issue of 'outside assistance' in clearing a section on the fourth day and, on being out-voted, walked out of the jury room. The final day was marred by another jury-room battle, which postponed the results and prize-giving ceremony by 24 hours. This battle, brought about by a local farmer moving the course markers, initially gave the Austrians the trophy but, after due deliberation, it was awarded to the Czech team. After more protests, disputes and a secret vote, the trophy was finally awarded to the Austrian team. Needless to say, the Czechs were not happy with this result and took the matter to the FIM autumn congress.

After the problems of the Austrian event, it was finally decided that the 1961 event should be staged by the British. To this end, the 36th ISDT was centred on the Welsh town of Llandrindod Wells again, the seventh trial to be based there. This time, the event was sponsored by the Daily Herald newspaper.

The inhabitants of Llandrindod were due for a noisy awakening once the ISDT activities started—they had played host to a Church conference during the previous week, when the hotels had been filled with the clergy. Being on home ground, many Greeves machines were in evidence, but not all their riders were British. Both Dutch Vase teams included factory-prepared machines, ridden by Frits and Rob Selling. Other Dutch, Belgian and Irish riders competed, including B. R. Brunson, who represented the United States. Eric Adcock appeared on a new Dot machine, the frame being constructed of square-section tubing and featuring a Marcelle alloy cylinder. This machine aroused considerable interest in the Greeves camp, as the two factories were arch rivals in the off-road battle. How would the new Dot perform, the Greeves men asked? Not very well was the answer, because it seized solid on the second day.

The dubious honour of being the first Greeves rider, and also the first two-stroke rider, to lose points fell to A. N. Jones during the start-up on the first morning. The uncovered *parc fermé* and over-night rain had proved Murphy's law once again. If a Greeves carburettor can collect water, it will, and in this instance it did, and Jones' bike would not start.

Triss Sharp was going well on the second day when disaster struck on the fast home run; his gearbox locked up, shearing the main shaft. The unsupported clutch body wreaked havoc inside the primary-drive case. This incident put paid to the hopes of the Vase A team, costing them 100 points a day penalty on his retirement.

The dawning of the third day saw Jones in trouble again with water in the works; this time rectification took over an hour, as water had somehow entered his engine. Dutch Vase B entrant, Jan Van Der Hock, came a spectacular purler on his way down from the Rhiw Fawr summit, and he was rushed away to hospital with a broken collar bone, his retirement effectively putting the Vase B team out of the running. Another rider having trouble with water in the carburettor was Monty Banks, who incurred penalties for a 15-minute stop at the Llandrillo control on the fourth day to empty it out.

Drama on the fifth day saw Bill Brooker come into control with seconds to spare before incurring a penalty. Bill was lucky, as he actually believed he was over the time, but he kept his clean sheet after all. His next problem was to gain enough bonus points to get into the gold, and this he did with some style on the final speed test. Bill's performance, together with that of fellow Greeves rider, Bryan Sharp, ensured a third place in the Vase contest, the other members of the team being Sammy Miller and Gordon Blakeway.

All in all, Greeves riders gained seven gold medals in Wales, together with six silver and seven bronze—a truly excellent performance.

A distinguished visitor to the Welsh was American Bud Ekins. As three-times winner of the Big Bear Run, (America's toughest cross-country race), his comments, as reported, were of some interest. Commenting on the trial, he thought it was fine—even better than girls—but still reckoned it to be hard work. He considered it less damaging to man and machine than the Big Bear Run, and even better organized. Bud also claimed that the International was won or lost in the workshop prior to the event, this statement being borne out by the state of many British machines at the finish of the event.

With the continuing success of their ISDT teams on modified standard production machines, Greeves decided to develop a machine specifically for that event. During 1962, prior to the West German event, again centred on Garmisch, the factory had been testing a new International model. Three machines were built, ultimately for the ISDT, but they were also used during the German and Welsh Three Day events to evaluate their performance.

The 1961 ISDT was held in Wales. Pictured here is 313 WPU, one of the factory's official entries

The new machine, designated 24INT, was based on the new 24TES trials frame, which featured stronger forks, a stronger frame loop which curved downwards to join at the rear of the gearbox, and a square-section swinging arm. The wheels, which had high-tensile rims, were fitted with the new full-width, 6 in. diameter alloy hubs, providing superior performance over the old finned variety. The footrests (usage demanded a fitment further forward) were welded directly to the substantial rock guards, which protected the engine casings. A centre stand, lighting set, $2\frac{3}{4}$-gallon tank, air bottle and tool bag, completed the specification.

The engine chosen to power the new machine was the MDS scrambler unit, suitably modified for the job in hand. To make this potent motor more tractable, the compression ratio was lowered to 8.5:1. As the machine was a mixture of trials and scrambles components, so was the gearbox. Trials ratios were chosen for first and second gears, and were complemented by a scrambles third gear, making a nicely grouped cluster with a normal top gear acting as a semi-overdrive. This gave the machine a maximum velocity of some 70 mph. A Bond mini car primary-drive casing was fitted to this motor (normal practice on trials machines), achieving a two-fold advantage. Its construction allowed cooling air to reach the main-bearing housing, and its slimness cut down the machine's width. A new exhaust system was fabricated to stay within the silencing rules. It was similar to the TES version, but constructed from round-section tube and tucked in close behind the rider's left leg. Although quieter than the MDS, it still managed to emit a throaty rasp.

David Dixon test rode one of the new Internationals, KOO 928, for *Motor Cycle* in the summer of 1962. He commented that the machine was very forgiving, even when he had gone over the limit of his own abilities. He marvelled at the power output, and the controllability of the power, which enabled him to set up the machine for corners on the throttle. Adverse comments were levelled at the noisy exhaust and the starting technique, which he was unable to master during the short test. Having ridden both trials and scrambles Greeves, the tester, when going fast, preferred the scrambles riding position and trials-influenced forward engine position of the International, this configuration putting more weight on the front wheel.

The Sharp brothers—Triss riding KOO 927 and Bryan on KOO 928—put up another fine performance at Garmisch that September. Together with Vic Eastwood and Arthur Lampkin, they formed the British Vase B team, taking second

place only to the West Germans. The week was marred by only one incident when Bryan Sharp's rear wheel tightened up. On investigation, it was revealed that the speedo drive was at fault, and not the wheel bearings as initially suspected, for a fault of this nature would have spelt disaster for the team.

Bronze medals were gained by Dave Clegg, riding KOO 926, and R. A. Knott, who rode a 175 cc-engined Greeves. Five Greeves riders retired, including Monty Banks and Peter Rose, the latter riding a twin-cylinder 324 cc machine.

The summer of 1963 saw many distinguished Greeves riders gathered in the mountains of Northern Italy for the annual Valli Bergamasche three-day trial. The Bergamo, with its high average speed and varied tough going, made an ideal proving ground for the forthcoming six-day international event to be held that autumn in Czechoslovakia.

Originally intending it as a sporting holiday, some 18 British trials riders had made the trek southwards to compete in the sunshine. On assembly for the trial, Alec Wright, the Greeves charioteer, could not help noticing that the entry consisted of many works and national teams. Why not organize the British riders into teams, rather than compete against each other as individuals? His mind made up, he contacted the ACU secretary and the Greeves factory, gaining authority to enter an all-Greeves-mounted national team. For his enthusiasm, Alec was given three jobs to perform during the event; that of team selector, team manager and British representative on the International jury (the first sign of his abilities in this direction, as today he is Kawasaki's competitions manager).

The trial was a fantastic success for Alec and his riders. The international team of Monty Banks, Bill Brooker, Dave Clegg and Don Smith beat the Polish team to take top honours, while the works team of Bill Brooker, Don Smith and Dutchman Frits Selling beat the German Hercules team to gain the manufacturer's award.

Had it not been for the enthusiasm shown by Alec Wright and the other Greeves riders, the Bergamo would have been contested, as would any other trial, with each man going for individual honours. By teaming up together, the British contingent returned home with two unexpected major awards.

The following autumn, the Sharp brothers, this time with Peter Stirland, again represented the Greeves factory as a works team, the venue being the 38th ISDT held at Spindleruv Mlyn in the Krkonse Mountains of Czechoslovakia. Unlike many other events in the series, the going was over very rocky ground, which was unaffected by

Left **The 1963 ISDT model currently on display at the National Motorcycle Museum, Birmingham**

Right **Don Smith applying his front anchor fully during brake tests at the Welsh Three Day event in 1964**

the heavy rain, and there was no doubt that this terrain, with its absence of 'give', accounted for the many gearbox failures that year. Even the road sections of the course were bad and bumpy, which did not give the riders a well-deserved occasional breather. Sammy Miller also commented that some parts of the course were suitable for use as sections in a national one-day trial, as long, rock-filled slots and zig-zag climbs, of the Grey Mare's Ridge variety, were in abundance. Many Western European riders experienced carburettor problems during the initial stages of the trial, due to the poor quality of the Eastern Bloc fuel, but once carburettors had been tuned for the low-grade propellant, the problems eased.

Was it the fuel or an undetected lack of oil in the mix that caused the retirement of Triss Sharp within the first five miles on the first day? After dropping 20 points on the start-up, he went out abruptly with a seized big-end, thus ending the hopes of the Vase B team. Brother Bryan and Peter Stirland went on to gain golds, with Mary Driver (the only woman entrant) receiving a bronze. On the last day Mary had the misfortune to slide off a log bridge and end up in the river. Other British riders near the bridge at that time promptly forgot the outside-assistance rule and rescued Mary and the bike from the river, cleaned her down and sent her on her way. Greeves riders forced to retire that year were Carr, Hitchcock and the evergreen veteran Monty Banks. The trial overall was praised for being well planned and executed, the jury having had an easy time, as disputes were minimal.

The mount that Peter Stirland used in the 1963 Czech event, 458 JOO, having proved itself once, proved itself yet again in the hands of a private rider, Chris Brown, who used it to cover some 16,000 miles on a trek to India and back during the following year, without major mishap. It has since been restored to original specification by the staff of the National Motorcycle Museum, where it is on permanent show.

The Italian Valli Bergamasche three-day trial held in the summer of 1964 was a great success for the Greeves factory in showing how the newly-introduced Challenger motocrosser could perform in enduro-type competitions. The Sharp brothers, teamed with Dave Clegg and Peter Stirland, took second place to Moto Guzzi in the manufacturer's team contest and third place in the national team contest. Bryan Sharp took the overall runner-up prize but won the hotly-contested 250 cc class. Veteran Monty Banks, in due recognition of his age, received the oldest competitor award.

It came as some surprise that Bryan Sharp actually competed in this event. A couple of

DOO 93B
Greeves

Greeves
GREAT BRITAIN

weeks previously, he had withdrawn from the forthcoming ISDT Vase A team following a disagreement with the organizers over methods of team selection. At the time, it was suspected that he was persuaded to ride again without actually changing his point of view. Subsequently, it was revealed that he was *told* to ride and, in fact, was following orders. His performance in the Valli certainly assured him of an ISDT Vase place.

Preparations for the forthcoming East German ISDT were well under way, but changes had to be made to the Vase teams' line-ups, for Dave Clegg was tragically killed in a car accident and Peter Stirland was injured while scrambling. Triss Sharp was moved up to the Vase A team with brother Bryan, Ellis and Blakeway, the quartet finally taking ninth place in the Vase competition. It was noted during this event that the greatest overall improvement by British machines, in relation to class opposition, had undoubtedly been made by Greeves and the new Challenger. This observation was helped by the spirited riding of Triss and Bryan, who were never out of the top six in their class all week. The final speed test saw them dicing neck and neck, putting other class runners to shame.

This type of riding earned the factory another manufacturer's team prize, with four gold medals going to Triss, Bryan, Don Hitchcock and Frits Selling of the Dutch team. A fifth gold went to Monty Banks, who was delighted. After many years of trying, he had finally received his just reward, his first gold at the age of 52. Of the other Greeves entrants, R. P. Smith gained a silver, but the unfortunate Mary Driver was excluded on the first day after going over time due to a spate of punctures.

The East German event took on a carnival atmosphere at times when the evening's socialising centred on the British trade support vans, in particular that of Renold Chain, where competitors could relax and drink British tea, dispensed by Vic Doyle and his wife. The leisurely going of the week could best be summed up by the comments of three of the British Trophy team. Sammy Miller said, 'It was too easy,' Roy Peplow thought 'it was monotonous', and Ken Heanes could only call it 'boring'.

The Americans, who fielded two Vase teams for the first time, could be forgiven for calling it anything other than easy. Their troubles began in Britain prior to the event, when Ted Wassell, the team organizer, discovered that the transport he had booked for the East German transit was not forthcoming. Frantic searching resulted in the loan of a transporter from H. and L. Motors of Stroud. On reaching the venue, Ted then discovered that he was also in charge of a second US team drawn from European residents. His A team drew a lot of interest from all quarters, as it not only included Bud Ekins, the stunt rider and desert racer, but also Steve McQueen, the film star, neither of whom was destined to finish the event. Bud had a nasty brush with a bridge on the third day, resulting in a

Left **The 1964 ISDT variant of the Challenger MX1 motocrosser. The machine illustrated was used for selection tests only**

Below left **Close-up of the 1964 Challenger MX1-based ISDT model, showing the original Albion four-speed box, expansion chamber, Monobloc carb and Stefa magneto**

Below **Mary Driver with the machine she rode in the 1964 ISDT, staged in East Germany. Unhappily, she was forced to retire after being plagued with a series of punctures**

Frits Selling leads Triss Sharp at Valli Bergamasche, Italy, during July 1965

Peter Stirland at the Valli during late May of the following year

broken leg. Steve McQueen fell from his Triumph 650 on several occasions during the third day, at one time flattening an exhaust pipe, which he duly set about with a woodman's axe in the best Hollywood style. He finally retired after another fall rendered the machine beyond repair.

The Welsh Three Day Trial, normally used as a team selection event for the ISDT proper, was relieved of that chore in 1965. Team selection now took place during the Manx three-day event, not only to pick the teams, but also to give riders a chance of practice over the Manx countryside (intended to give the British entrants a bit of local knowledge). In contrast to previous years, there were no Greeves factory entrants, but Don Smith contested the Welsh as a lone hand. His appearance in a time trial was not disgraced. He was unpenalized and up front on the leader-board until a broken main shaft put him out on the very last afternoon. This retirement was vindicated in Italy during the summer Valli Bergamasche three-day trial, when Don, riding BTR 51B, teamed up with Triss Sharp and Frits Selling to win the manufacturer's team contest for the Greeves factory.

It was about this time that the British Army teams began receiving help from the factory in the shape of machines for use in national and international events. Was it because Bill Brooker was ex-Army and looking after his mates, or did Bert have his eye on an Army contract to replace the ageing B40? Whichever way it was, the Army teams had the benefit and certainly enjoyed themselves.

Being adventurous types, the Army team, led by Mick Noyce, riding the borrowed 6 LHK, contested both the 1964 and 1965 Valli three-day events, riding to and from the trials on their machines. Both trips were not without incident. On the return from the 1964 event, high up in the Alps, Gordon Norton punctured his front tyre. The whole team had enjoyed a substantial liquid lunch, and were quite incapable of changing the tube without nipping it. The job was finally entrusted to an Italian rider, who changed the tube and sent them on their way. For the 1965 Valli event, 6 LHK was fitted with a set of trials gearbox ratios—previously it had used road or even close ratios, which were quite unsuitable for this type of terrain. Mick got on better with the wide internals, but, unfortunately, lost a few pinion teeth during the event. Faced with the return journey of some

800 miles, he decided to rebuild the box prior to departure, using spares from Monty Banks' van, and the team returned to England without mishap.

The 1965 International event, held for the first time in the Isle of Man, should have been a home benefit match for the British riders taking part. This was not to be, as the event had been revised to grade the riders on the daily schedules rather than the special tests, as had been the norm in previous years. The daily schedules were hard enough, but were made worse by the atrocious weather, for the Isle of Man was being lashed by the tail of Hurricane Betsy.

Greeves fielded four works riders for this event: the Sharp brothers, now promoted to the Trophy team in recognition of their meteoric ride in the Czech, together with Peter Stirland in the Vase A team, and Bill Wilkinson in the Vase B team. The machines ridden by the works team were modified Challengers, which now featured the banana forks, hitherto seen only on the works motocross machines for the 1965 season. Bill Brooker looked after the interests of the works riders as best he could, but his primary duty was that of ACU-appointed deputy team manager, a real test of allegiance for what was to come.

During the pre-event servicing, while welding up his centre stand, Triss Sharp accidentally melted the nylon lining of his rear brake cable, but it was rapidly changed in time for the weigh-in. Casualties on the first day included the Dutch Greeves rider, Henk Wendelgelst, who forgot that the British drive on the left-hand side of the road. This lapse resulted in a collision with a car, which put him in hospital with a fractured pelvis. Lingelbach, of the Nick Nicholson, Greeves-mounted American team, went down with a dose of good old British flu and withdrew from the event altogether. Peter Stirland's first day was not without mishap, for as he footslogged his way out of a particularly boggy stretch, he kicked his air bottle, turning it on. The resulting icy blast, directed straight at the carburettor intake, stopped the engine. The primary chain of Bill Wilkinson's machine had become so slack by the third day that it began to jump the sprockets. The noise it made caused Bill to suspect big-end wear, but a replacement chain was fitted and he carried on, eventually retiring on the fifth day. A third-day casualty, on a particularly nasty stretch of sunken track just off Kate's Cottage, was Mary Driver, who became completely bogged down. With an international judge being nearby, all the spectators could do was shout encouragement to urge her on, but to no avail, and Mary retired completely exhausted and in tears.

Other Greeves riders to retire that week were Reg May of Comerfords and Mick Noyce of the Army team. Reg had to pull out with a broken gearbox mounting caused by the rough going. The bike, however, is still alive and well, and being ridden regularly by its present owner, Andrew King, the worthy editor of the Greeves Riders Association magazine, *Leading Link*.

Mick Noyce had the dubious privilege of being the last Greeves rider to retire. Riding 6 LHK, his battle ended on the Friday when he stripped the teeth from the final-drive sprocket. He had been having trouble with a fractured fibreglass front mudguard, which had collapsed under the weight of the clinging mud. Covered in mud and spray, he lay down in the road where he stopped. Colonel Daniels, the chairman of Army Motor Sports, who had been watching Mick's progress, produced a bottle of Scotch to revive the cold, wet and exhausted rider. Having consumed the Scotch, Mick and the bike were carried back to base in a truck.

On day four, the British team slogged on in worsening weather conditions, but by now the entire BSA team was out with ignition failures. The same problem beset Bryan Sharp, who also retired. Triss Sharp, the lone Greeves Trophy rider, carried on to finish the day, but was cold, wet and very dispirited with the whole affair.

It was noted that the continental teams enjoyed a very-well-organized back-up, being able to get food, drinks, dry gloves and spares at almost every control. British teamsters were not so lucky, as their comfort and wellbeing was looked after only by volunteers and retired riders. Spares back-up was just as poorly organized. Bill Brooker did his best in looking after his works riders, but could not be everywhere at once. Surviving British riders began to complain about the lack of support they were receiving for their efforts, and the complaints turned to revolt, with Triss Sharp deciding to quit. His refusal to turn out the next morning, and subsequent statements made to the press by himself and brother Bryan, slating the team management, resulted in swift reaction from the factory. All further support was withdrawn from both riders, and they were never to ride for Greeves again.

Sweden was chosen as host country for the 1966 event, and hopes were high following the previous year's fiasco in the Isle of Man. The Swedish Army looked after the marshalling, time keeping and communications for the event, which was held in good weather conditions. This, plus the organizational efficiency and easiness of the course, combined to produce a most enjoyable event. Sammy Miller was quoted as saying, 'It's too easy, when is the trial going to start?'—a point of view not shared by eight Greeves riders who subsequently retired. The factory, now out of the Trophy team since the departure of the Sharp brothers, fielded Jim Sandiford in the Vase A team, with Bill Wilkinson and Peter Stirland in the B team. The manufacturer's team comprised Stirland, Sandiford and Dutchman Frits Selling, who together put up a creditable performance to gain 13th place, with no points lost.

All the Vase and manufacturer's team riders gained gold medals that year, including Ken Sedgley and Army rider Peter Lasota, who was mounted on RHK 300D, a banana-forked works Challenger.

Brian Messenger, who was beset by plug troubles, only managed to complete 12 out of the 13 laps required on the final speed test. He failed by seconds to start his last lap before running out of time, this failure costing him two points and a gold medal. Still faithful to the Greeves marque was Monty Banks, who added another bronze medal to his collection. Colin Morgan of the Army team was indeed privileged in being lent 6 LHK to compete in the Swedish event, and gained a bronze medal, but not without difficulty. During the week, his frame down-tube broke under the seat, and all that kept the bike together was the rear chain. His Army team-mate, John Bull, recalls that Colin managed to carry on by riding smoothly and carefully, the rear chain being replaced at least twice a day. This endless supply of chain came from the ever-present Vic Doyle, the much-travelled Renold representative.

The highlight of the Swedish was the storming of an enormous, evil-smelling slag heap, which was used as the fifth-day special test. Riders attacked this 'hill' on a series of short straights and hairpin bends, which had been bulldozed all the way to the summit. Times were fast, probably due to the riders' inability to breath on the lower slopes, for the hill was wreathed in clouds of choking vapour issuing from an adjacent gas plant.

Attitudes towards British participation in international trials were beginning to change. The rising costs of preparation and competing, together with the poor results obtained, had led to factory withdrawal from the sport. In 1965, the last year of manufacturer support, before ACU help, Greeves spent £2200 on sending riders to international and ISDT-type training events. This figure was for entries and transportation, and did not include development, building and maintenance of the works machines. Bert was not happy with this expenditure and was quoted as saying, 'I would have been thousands of pounds better off, if I had pressed on with the development of the 360 cc scrambler instead.' In previous years, national pride had been at stake, in the hope of gaining a Trophy victory for the national team, but now, in a climate of shrinking sales, sound business sense had to be the order of the day.

To boost national prestige, the battle for an ISDT Trophy success was placed in the hands of the ACU. Helped by grants, donations and sympathetic motorcycle dealers, they managed to field a Trophy team annually, but without the success they hoped for.

Greeves machines were now being included in the British Trophy team line-up. They were built and serviced by the factory, but entered by Comerfords, the Thames Ditton sporting dealership.

The machines bore a striking resemblance to the factory Challengers, their specification including such items of equipment that were necessary to increase the reliability and maintainability of the machine.

Britain's fortunes were fading, the motorcycle industry was beginning to feel the effects of falling sales, but still the ACU pressed on in an effort to bring some glory back to the home country. There appeared to be only one ACU-sponsored, Greeves-mounted rider in the 1967 Trophy team, Jim Sandiford, who was to carry the flag for the Thundersley factory as a member of the team contesting the Trophy in Poland that year. Mounted on the Westbury-prepared MEV 9C, now owned by John Collard, Jim, unfortunately, was a non starter. After running out of road and experiencing a broken fuel pump on the team's Ford Transit van, as well as being arrested for non-payment of the team's bar bill, Jim had starting problems with his machine at the Saturday weigh-in. A new magneto, supplied by 360 Greeves rider Frits Selling, got the engine started, but the fault appeared to be with the carburation. Two time extensions were granted in order to correct the

The Vase A Team poses for the cameras prior to leaving Britain for the 1966 ISDT. Left to right: Gordon Farley, Alan Lampkin, Greeves-mounted Jim Sandiford, and John Lewis. The Greeves rider won a gold

fault, but when these expired, his place was taken by reserve Scott Ellis. The problem was finally diagnosed as porous crankcases, a fault which neither Jim nor the factory were very happy about.

All was not gloom on the home front, however, as Greeves scooped the best one-make team prize in the Welsh three-day event held the same year, using slightly-modified, one-day trials bikes, instead of the Challenger-based ISDT machines. Jim Sandiford was joined by John Pease (a factory competitions-department employee) and the veteran Monty Banks, who was called in to take the place of the missing Bill Wilkinson. They took the prize, even though John Pease had to remove his gearbox cover to extract a broken tooth which, if it had lodged between two pinions, could have caused a complete gearbox failure.

The adaptability and staying power of the Challenger was recognized by the ACU in 1968, when no less than four machines were fielded in the Trophy team that contested the six-day event held that year in San Pellegrino, Italy. John Pease and Jack Wilson rode the standard Comerfords 246 cc Challengers, backed up by Dennis Jones and Malcolm Rathmell mounted on the bored-out, 256 cc machines. The rest of the team, using 504 cc Triumphs, comprised John Lewis and Ken Heanes, the captain.

The advantages of using a small-capacity machine, with the corresponding lowering of overall speed averages, were becoming apparent, with some of the European entrants even using 50 cc mounts to great effect. The Eastern European dominance of this event must have been heart breaking for many of the seasoned British riders, for the regimented and disciplined riding of the Czech and East German teams was a model to be followed by all entrants. Politics aside, the reliability of the machines, and the doggedness and cunning of the riders, deserved the results obtained.

In the face of such adversity, the British still

carried on contesting the 1969 event, held again in the Bavarian Alps and centred on Garmisch. After an uneventful ride, Mick Wilkinson gained a gold medal, but many misfortunes overtook other Greeves riders. Silver medallist and Trophy teamster, John Pease, lost his rear brake on the second day, a problem not appreciated until he wanted to stop—the problem was overcome by the 'slide off' technique. Another problem encountered was a drowned engine on the fifth day. The other Greeves-mounted Trophy rider, Malcolm Rathmell, riding UPA 22F, did not fare so well, having snapped a drive chain on the fifth day and cooked a plug in the final speed test, but he still managed to gain a bronze.

Despite the problems, the British Trophy team gained an overall third place. Brian Messenger received a silver for his efforts, but Vase B rider, Don Buchan had to retire on the second day with broken ribs.

The Garmisch event saw many ex-Greeves riders mounted on other factories' machines. Frits Selling and Don Hitchcock used Jawas, while Peter Lasota, Peter Stirland and Jim Sandiford were Triumph mounted, and one-time teamster, Scott Ellis, even campaigned a 125 Puch! With the curtailment of active factory support for ISDT entrants, riders had to seek support from other quarters. If one was not good enough to warrant ACU sponsorship and a bike, then the only alternative was to approach someone who would supply the necessary back-up, hence the defections to the Eastern European, Spanish and even Japanese factories.

The writing was on the wall; the factory had to make cuts, and ISDTs were sacrificed in favour of motocross. Companies like Triumph and BSA, with huge competition budgets, could afford such a sport, but the small (by comparison) Greeves factory, which probably spent more on ISDTs, had to say no and put its limited funds into branches of motorcycling that would show a profit.

The final ISDT fling was the 380 QUB Griffon-mounted Army team's assault on the 1975 event held in the Isle of Man. The results obtained here ensured that the Greeves went out with a bang, in more ways than one, for no rider lasted longer than a couple of days. The machines, on loan from the Royal Artillery Display team and fitted with special generators to power the lighting set, were plagued with constant seizures necessitating frequent cylinder changes before the event even began. Needless to say, the assistant Army team manager, Jim Moore, was not very happy about the situation. Neither were his team riders.

Motor Cycle News added fuel to the fire by publishing the team's rude remarks about the mounts, which brought a swift reaction from the factory. A Greeves representative flew out to the island on the following day to try and calm things down, but it was too late; the team was out of the running, and the credibility of the Griffon blown. The factory never did overcome this setback, even though it was known at the time that the 380 in unmodified form was not suitable as a six-day mount. As far as the ISDT was concerned, the factory went into hiding to lick its wounds, never to contest the event again. A sad end to two decades of participation in the world's toughest off-road motorcycle event.

Gold-medal winner and Vase B teamster, Billy Wilkinson (30) leaving Villingsburg—the headquarters were in an army camp—at the start of the 1966 event, which was run in Sweden

7 Silverstone and Oulton

As the 1960s dawned, road racing in Britain was dominated at club and national level by the traditional big singles from AJS, Matchless and Norton in the 350 and 500 cc classes. Further down the scale, in the $\frac{1}{4}$-litre stakes, the situation was far less defined. For the select (and well off) few, an NSU Sportmax, or one of the brand-new Aermacchi Ala d'Oros was the thing. For the vast majority, however, it was either a case of a sleeved-down, bigger single, with all the weight penalties this incurred, or a home-built special, such as the REG and Jones ohc twins.

There was a third option; the two-stroke. In those days, although the humble 'stroker' had begun to make a serious impression on off-road competition, on the tarmac things were still very much the preserve of the four-stroke establishment. The first sign of a change had come with the German Adler twins of the mid-1950s. As far as Britain was concerned, however, it was not until 1960, when Mike O'Rouke finished seventh in the Lightweight TT, on an Ariel Arrow tuned by Hermann Meier, that road-race buffs viewed the two-stroke as anything other than a ride-to-work runabout.

O'Rouke's success spawned a number of Ariel-twin racing conversions, including those successfully campaigned by Robin Good and Peter Inchley. It also sparked an interest in other British 'strokers', notably Cotton, DMW, and Greeves, although it would be fairer to say that of all the British two-strokes raced during the 1960s, the top dog was certainly the Thundersley marque. The originator of what was later to be known as the Silverstone era was a young draughtsman, employed at the time by Marconi in his home town of Chelmsford, Essex.

Reg Everett had been born on 13 August 1940 at the height of the Battle of Britain. His first bike had been an ex-War Department Triumph, purchased on his 16th birthday. The Triumph was soon made to look like a racer, but at 19 he obtained his first *real* racer, an ex-Derek Minter BSA CB34 Gold Star. The young Everett and his Small Heath single had their first race together at Snetterton on Easter Monday 1960. But pitted against pukka racers, like the Manx Norton or Matchless G50, the Goldie usually came out second best.

The following year, 1961, still saw Everett mounted on the Gold Star, but on 28 May came his first association with a two-stroke—and Greeves. This was at the Silverstone 1000-kilometre race for production roadsters. In his own words, Reg had 'talked local dealer Derek Cornell into loaning me a brand-new 249 cc Villiers 2T-engined 25DC Sports Twin.'

Cornell, who traded as Derek Cornell Motorcycles in Broomfield Road, Chelmsford, held, among other agencies, the Greeves dealership for the area. His sporting interest however, lay firmly with the trials and motocross machines, not road racing. This makes the incident all the more surprising, and says much for Everett's enthusiasm at the time. The 25DC was run in by 'collecting some spares for the Gold Star from Eddie Dow's shop in Banbury.'

At Silverstone, Reg Everett was partnered by fellow Gold Star racer Martin Hayward. The guy who did the spannerwork that day was none other than Keith Wash, now the designer and owner of three-wheel manufacturers Hedingham Sidecars. Derek Cornell's lack of enthusiasm was demonstrated by his absence.

In the event, the Greeves twin went well until over half distance, when it refused to restart following a pit stop and change of rider. However, it was the machine's handling which had really impressed Everett. This was reinforced when the same bike was raced against pukka racing machines at Brands Hatch on 25 June. For this event, all the lighting equipment was removed and the machine was fitted with a pair of rudimentary

expansion chambers produced by Keith Wash—with no special measurements!

A fifth place in the heat and an eighth in the final—in which he lapped faster than on the Gold Star—convinced Everett that there might be a future for a Greeves-based racer. Unfortunately, after the Brands race, Derek Cornell took the bike back, so all thoughts of this were put aside while the remainder of the 1961 racing season was completed on the Goldie.

During the closed season, in the winter of 1961–2, Reg decided that his racing career needed different machinery. Initially, a Matchless G50 was favoured, but in the back of his mind was the memory of the way that Greeves had handled; 'If only I could have a Greeves with a faster engine,' he thought. Thus was born the idea of using a road-racing version of the motocross engine, at that time being campaigned so successfully by riders such as Dave Bickers.

Reg had met Greeves' competition engineer, Bob Mills, at Derek Cornell's showroom while preparing the twin for the 1000-kilometre race, and in late 1961 he decided to visit the Greeves factory to see him. 'I want to build a super Greeves racer,' Everett told the Greeves competition-department man, but all Bob Mills could reply at the time was, 'Sorry we haven't got anything suitable.' However, this was to change, as later Bob Mills was able to organize the necessary components from various roadster and motocross items, enabling a kit of parts to be provided for Everett. Even so, as Bob Mills puts it today, 'This was all highly unofficial.'

By now Reg Everett was living in Basildon, where he assembled his Greeves racer, which included an MDS motocross engine, in the front room at home. Among the parts were a roadster frame, forks and wheels. The full-width alloy hubs were built on to alloy rims, which were fitted with Avon racing tyres. The $1\frac{9}{32}$ in. carburettor came from the Gold Star, and the seat from a Manx Norton. The fuel tank was an alloy item from a Greeves motocrosser. The only modification to the engine was the GP carb, while the balance, including the exhaust system, was pure motocrosser.

In practice during March, before the 1962 season opened, the home-built Greeves single proved to have fantastic acceleration, but with performance dying at the top end of the scale. Its

first race was at Brands Hatch on the first day of the new season—Sunday 1 April. As *Motor Cycling* reported, 'In his heat, R. J. Everett notched an impressive victory on a motocross-engined Greeves with road-going forks. He also led for over half the final before being passed by E. R. Cooper (247 NSU), but still managed second although his engine began to tighten on the last lap.' Quite some debut!

There was also another Greeves racer in those early days. This was a competition-kitted roadster twin, which American actor Dick Wyler raced in 1961 at British short circuits, notably Crystal Palace and Brands Hatch, with help from the Greeves management and Comerfords, the large Thames Ditton dealership. It made its debut as a pukka

Left **Beginning of the Greeves road-racing story. Reg Everett (34) leads the field away at the Silverstone 1000-kilometre race for production roadsters on 20 May 1961. The machine was a Villiers 2T-powered 25DC twin**

Below **Everett on his 246 cc racer, which was constructed from a mix of roadster and motocross parts. It gained a considerable number of top placings during 1962, which led to factory interest in road racing**

racer at Crystal Palace on 7 August 1961, after being raced in standard trim by Wyler and Griff Jenkins at the Thruxton 500-miler in July. Following this successful outing, the bike received a face-lift by being converted into a short-circuit racer with a fibreglass tank, special Avon fairing and Amal Monobloc carburettor. Stripped of all non-essentials, this machine crossed the Atlantic during the winter of 1961–2 when, together with fellow racer Ron Grant, Wyler went back to his native America for a short period. Upon return to Britain in the following spring, the Greeves was sold by Comerfords.

Besides Wyler, another rider raced this particular machine at Brands Hatch. His name? Gerald Davidson, who later was to join Honda UK in Chiswick, London, eventually becoming a senior director of that company, before leaving to head a Jersey newspaper group in May 1985. However, as we shall see, it was the performance of Everett and his motocross-based single during the 1962 season which was to lead to road racers being built by the factory.

After his successful Brands Hatch debut, Everett's next race was at Snetterton on Easter Sunday, 22 April. Unlike the Brands affair, which was restricted to club riders, the Norfolk event was a national—open to all British licence holders, including the likes of Derek Minter, Dan Shorey, Tommy Robb, and even Mike Hailwood! Surprisingly, the humble Greeves managed to finish sixth, in front of many other far more specialized, and expensive, machines. The race was won by Dan Shorey on a works 196 Bultaco, with Derek Chatterton on a brand-new Aermacchi second, and veteran Arthur Wheeler on his famous Guzzi flat-single third—illustrious company!

On the following day, Easter Monday, it was down to South London's Crystal Palace circuit for more action. After a heat win, Everett recorded twelfth place in the hotly-contested final won by NSU rider Blake Osborne. Thereafter came a succession of wins and places throughout the summer of 1962 at Snetterton, Thruxton, Crystal Palace and Brands Hatch.

During a meeting at Snetterton in August, Reg let fellow competitor Brian Woolley look inside the engine—at least the barrel and head, as Woolley

thought it would be possible to extract more power from the motor or, more to the point, the type of power more suited to a road racer. However, although Brian Woolley was to play an important part in the Greeves road-racing saga, it was not at this stage. The only 'tuning' carried out on the machine in 1962 had come in July when Bob Mills made an expansion chamber and presented it to Everett on one of his unofficial visits to the factory development shop. As Reg puts it, 'Without Bob Mills' help, the bike simply wouldn't have existed. And he was my only contact with the company at that time.' However, at some stage that summer, unknown to Reg Everett, someone else at the factory *did* get involved. That was Bert Greeves himself.

Everett's last race meeting of the season had taken place under cloudless skies, in high temperatures and with little wind, which contributed to absolutely perfect conditions when the BMCRC staged their final event of the season, the Guinness Trophy Meeting, on Sunday 7 October at Snetterton. As *Motor Cycling* reported; 'As a contrast to Terry Grotefeld's rather processional win on his Aermacchi in the 250 cc event, R. J. Everett flogged his prototype Greeves throughout the race in an attempt to wrest back third place which he lost to R. A. Freeman (Honda) after the first lap. The final assault failed only because the Greeves didn't have enough steam!'

As will become apparent, while Reg Everett was scratching around the British short circuits, eyes other than the spectators' were on his every move. A mere couple of weeks after that final race of the 1962 season, *Motor Cycle* in the 18 October 1962 issue ran the headline 'Greeves on Greeves', going on to say, 'At Brands Hatch last week manufacturer Bert Greeves put in many very impressive laps on Reg Everett's privately owned prototype racing 246 cc Greeves. Bert's best lap of the 1.24 mile circuit was in 69 secs (64.7 mph). Not bad for a 56 year old!'

Following this revelation, in late October came the first news of a brand-new, all-alloy 247 cc (68 × 68 mm) racing engine from the Villiers concern. This was the Starmaker, to be used in a Cotton production racer which was scheduled to make its debut at the Earls Court show in the following month. Hard on the heels of this, the following week's *Motor Cycling* headline read, 'Greeves Production Racer', with Bert Greeves commenting, 'I want to see British machines establish supremacy and prestige—particularly in the 250 class. I've long thought about making a short circuit racer as a training machine to help this idea along.'

Thus, the Greeves boss summed up his reasons for introducing the new 246.3 cc (66 × 72 mm) Villiers-engined (but not Starmaker) Silverstone. He also hedged his bets by stating that the new machine 'was intended as a training machine for beginners in racing.' Designated the 24RAS, there was no mistaking its identity, since it employed all the usual Greeves features—plus others for its intended tarmac usage.

The centre section of the frame was standard motocrosser, with the cast-alloy down-member blended into a steel top tube and steel-plate engine mountings. The rear end had been reduced in width by 2 in. at the suspension pivot, and the

Far left **Richard Wyler raced a converted roadster twin in 1961, but did not achieve the level of success enjoyed by Reg Everett**

Left **Gerald Davidson—years later the boss of Honda UK—riding Wyler's bike at Brands Hatch in August 1961**

latest Villiers 36A engine specified for the production models, although the prototype shown used a 34A unit (which had identical bore and stroke measurements). Both the prototype and production models featured alloy cylinder barrels and heads of Greeves design and manufacture.

Technical details included a $1\frac{1}{4}$ in. Amal GP carburettor; 6 in. full-width, British Hub Company alloy hub units with $1\frac{1}{8}$ in. wide shoes; 19×2.75 front wheel, 18×3.25 rear, with Avon racing tyres; fibreglass $2\frac{3}{4}$-gallon fuel tank and seat base. The wheel base was stated as 52 in., with a height of $33\frac{1}{2}$ in. to the top of the forks, which were $1\frac{1}{2}$ in. shorter than those on the motocrosser. The exhaust system consisted of a short pipe leading to a high-level expansion chamber, which ran along the offside of the cylinder barrel, and a tail pipe which tucked under the seat. Output, with the 34A unit, was a claimed 25 bhp. Other features included a $\frac{1}{2} \times \frac{5}{16}$ in. rear drive chain, Girling rear units and Dunlop alloy rims. Strangely, this prototype carried only a Smiths chronometric speedometer and no tachometer. It was also stated that an initial batch of 30 machines was underway.

A mere seven days after this story appeared, another headline in *Motor Cycling* of 7 November 1962 read; 'Greeves—Beart Tie-up'. This referred

Above **Frame of the prototype Silverstone (called the Special), which was built by the factory in the autumn of 1962**

Right **The completed factory Silverstone prototype. Intended by Bert Greeves to be a trainer, it had a speedometer instead of a tacho**

to the fact that the Essex factory had reached an agreement with Francis Beart, whereby the famous Guildford tuner would prepare one of the new Silverstones on which he would enter Joe Dunphy in British short-circuit events during the following season.

The agreement had been reached after a test session at Brands Hatch on 1 November. With Beart there to watch, the 1962 Senior Manx Grand Prix winner had completed 15 laps on the 34A-engined prototype—still unstreamlined—and was reported as amazed by the performance. Interviewed afterwards, Dunphy said, 'I'm really surprised by the way the Greeves went. The handling was very good, and the brakes quite exceptional, while the power was there all the time. It was really difficult to find fault, in fact the machine was very much better than I'd dared hope.'

Francis Beart was also enthusiastic and impressed by what he had witnessed, prompted, no doubt, by Bert Greeves' statement; 'We are taking the introduction and development of this machine very seriously indeed'.

However, Mick Wollett, in his regular 'Sports Gossip' lead story in that week's *Motor Cycling* accurately predicted 'the start of something big.' This centred around the fact that although, 'the prototype machines from Cotton and Greeves might be modest and down to earth in specifications, who knows where a season's intensive development will lead?' Wollett also went on to say that this race-track development process could make the British newcomers very serious challengers indeed in the short-circuit events for which they were designed, and would lift them out of the 'beginners only' class for which they were primarily intended. He also saw that, whatever happened, the British race-going public would be seeing some red-hot, inter-factory rivalry on the short circuits for the first time in many years and that this could do the sport, and motorcycling in general, nothing but good.

Then came the London Earls Court show, staged on 10–17 November. Although the Greeves stand was in virtually the same location as their first appearance, nine years earlier, the 1962 effort was massive by comparison, the Essex company having the largest floor area of the entire show, some 2040 sq ft.

Among those to be photographed aboard the Silverstone (although the tank decal said Greeves Special) was none other than the legendary Geoff Duke. Another highlight was the *Greeves Times*, given away free from the stand. Written, edited and produced by Derry Preston-Cobb, it was an interesting news-sheet which, in addition to describing the full 1963 range, had gen on the new racer, and personal paragraphs about the Thundersley staff.

One of the thickest crowds at the show, certainly on the opening Saturday, surrounded the new road racer. Bert Greeves was on hand, telling potential customers that the price would be below £300 complete with fairing—provided that purchase-tax exemption was granted. He also told the press; 'We cannot fix a definite price before

12
2

21

we've finished the exact specification, which will include various modifications, including a lighter frame.' At the same time that this quote appeared, another snippet of race news was reported. This centred around a number of new production racing machines being offered for sale in Japan. At the 1962 Tokyo show, Honda, Tohatsu and Yamaha had displayed new, over-the-counter hardware, and it was to be Yamaha—with the twin-cylinder 250 TDI—that was to prove the real menace to the emerging British 'stroker' singles. Although for several years the Japanese bike was neither quick enough nor reliable enough, when Yamaha finally sorted it out, from 1967 onwards, it became such a threat that within a short period it annihilated all opposition in anything outside GP racing. However, all this was very much in the future as 1962 drew to a close.

Two weeks after the Earls Court show closed, rivals Cotton became the first of the British manufacturers (Greeves and Cotton had now been joined by DMW with a 250 production racer) to finalize their specification. The Gloucester firm had also seen their application to the Treasury for purchase-tax relief granted. This followed registration of the machine, the Villiers Starmaker-powered Telstar, with the ACU.

Motor Cycling, in their issue of 19 December 1962, carried the world's first track test of the new Greeves racer, under the headline, 'Ideal for New Racers'. Tested while development was still taking place, the prototype Silverstone now had some 500 miles on the clock (it still had the Smiths chronometric speedo fitted). The test session at Brands Hatch was held in miserably wet conditions. Perhaps because of this, and the wide power band of the 34A engine, deficiencies which showed up later with this particular machine went largely unnoticed. However, tester Bruce Main-Smith did comment about the riding position and lack of power from the 6 in. front brake.

Since the show, several modifications had been carried out; the rear of the expansion chamber had been relocated, the rear suspension units were now more upright, and the clip-on bars were separate halves, instead of the earlier complete unit type. Next items on the development agenda were a drive for a tacho, a fairing, a smaller tank, and experiments with springs of different poundage in both suspensions.

Bert Greeves, who was at the test session in leathers, was anxious to finalize all these details so that the specifications could be registered with the ACU. Once this was done, exemption from purchase tax could be obtained and the design could go into production. However, even as late as early February 1963, no definite price had been announced! At the same time it was revealed that, although the initial production bikes had been fitted with the 36A square-barrel engine with single Amal GP carburettor, it was on the cards that specially-tuned Starmaker engines would at least be tried as the season progressed, with a view to using this engine in later Silverstones. However, although the Starmaker unit was fitted to a few 24ME motocross models, in fact none was to find its way into the road racer. Instead Greeves opted to develop their own engine.

In March the final specification of the RAS Silverstone was announced. This included a new frame compared to the show prototype. There were also various other modifications; 18 in. wheels front and rear (although the 6 in. hubs remained unchanged) and a 2-gallon fuel tank.

However, the engine assembly displayed the biggest changes. Although Bert Greeves had seen the bike as a trainer, rather than a competitive racer, just about everyone else—including potential customers and the press—had soon shown him to be wrong; they all wanted a machine which stood a chance of winning. The result was what even Greeves themselves described as 'the most powerful standard production engine in the world for its size and weight.' This was a specially-prepared version of the basic Villiers 36A single developed for racing purposes only. A number of major components, including the Alpha crankshaft and Greeves barrel/head, were fitted by Greeves after purchasing the complete 36A unit from Villiers. This was a costly exercise and soon led to a wasteful stock of unused Villiers spares mounting up in the Greeves factory. It was also yet another reason why Greeves ultimately chose to develop their own engine.

The modified 36A had a capacity of 246 cc (66 × 72 mm). There was a completely redesigned,

Above left **Joe Dunphy in action on a specially-prepared lightweight RAS, with coil ignition, at Mallory Park during April 1963. The machine had been entered by Guildford tuner Francis Beart**

Left **Mike Philpott was loaned an RAS Silverstone for the Sunbeam Ramsgate Sprint on 5 May 1963. It recorded fastest time for its class**

low-level expansion chamber running down the nearside of the machine. The four-speed gearbox had internal ratios of 2.55:1, 1.55:1, 1.17:1 and 1:1. Primary drive was by $\frac{3}{8} \times \frac{7}{32}$ in. chain with a ratio of 2.15:1. As standard, the RAS came with an 18-tooth gearbox and 50-tooth rear wheel sprockets, plus additional 46- and 48-tooth items. It was also possible to purchase a 19-tooth gearbox component. Carburation was taken care of by an Amal $1\frac{3}{8}$ in. T5 GP 2S racing instrument, a selection of main jets being supplied with each bike. A small head fairing, made in fibreglass, was supplied as standard equipment, and the dry weight with this fitted was 188 lb.

The British motorcycling press finally announced the specification and price (£285) in late March, just as the road-racing season was about to get under way.

The first production RAS to roll off the Greeves production line, on 16 March 1963, was a works-supported Silverstone for Francis Beart's rider, Joe Dunphy. Beart modified the machine in several ways: narrower-section wheel rims, reduced compression ratio, and great attention paid to lightening the machine as much as possible—its weight was reduced to 179 lb. However, the most notable change was to the ignition system. The original set-up was replaced by a Bosch coil and a very small battery.

When the curtain lifted on the new racing season, observers saw that, besides the Beart machine ridden by Joe Dunphy, there were several of the new Silverstones at the start line, noticeably those of Tom Phillips (sponsored by Frank Higley), Horace Crowder (on a Brian Woolley-prepared machine) and Reg Everett, who had the actual show prototype. This had been redesigned with a 36A unit, but Everett was none too happy with it, although he had been told it was 'fantastic' by Bert Greeves. In his opinion, it 'didn't handle and wasn't a patch on my '62 bike.' This was probably due, in the main, to the additional power delivered by the 36A compared to the 34A, and its adverse effect on handling of the prototype chassis.

Soon the first results began to show that, generally, Greeves had come up with a bike that was capable of mixing it with the best—at least on the short circuits.

In early April Dunphy won at Crystal Palace (setting a new lap record), followed by a similar result at the end of the month by the man who was to emerge as the Silverstone rider of that particular season, Tom Phillips. Although Tom had scored the machine's first ever race success on 23 March in a club event at Oulton Park, his first major victory came on Saturday 21 April at a very wet Castle Combe meeting. Rain penetrated everywhere. It drowned ignition systems, trickled down backs and soaked through leathers, but it could not stop that man Phillips. At the start of the 250 race, Brian Richards (Bultaco) led the pack away with the Greeves rider close astern. Phillips slipped past to take the lead at Camp Corner. Then Adler-mounted Ron Willatts took the lead for a short time, but Phillips had no idea of giving up. The ding-dong, first-place tussle was resolved only as the pair went into the last lap, when Phillips snatched the lead back.

At the season's opener at Mallory Park on 7 April, Horace Crowder had had a far from happy first race on the British 'stroker', falling off and missing a whole month's racing through injury. Joe Dunphy on the Beart machine led for 13 of the 15 laps, only to be forced out with clutch trouble. Meanwhile, Reg Everett had made his debut as a works-supported rider at the international Hutchinson 100, staged at Silverstone, with an 11th place in the 250 race on Saturday 6 April. Then, at Brands Hatch on Good Friday 12 April, he gained a superb second place. A couple of days later, at a big international event at Snetterton on Easter Sunday, he was fastest in practice (it poured with rain!). At Crystal Palace on the following day, Everett was fourth in his heat, sixth in the final.

However, although things may have appeared satisfactory on the surface, Reg was still far from happy with the machine, its handling in particular. This came to a head on 27 April at Mallory Park. During the heat, he crashed coming out of Gerards Bend—because, he says, 'of the bad handling.' Ever since he had been given this bike, Reg found that it had had a marked tendency to get into 'a "tank slapper" unless the rider adopted a sitting-on-the-tank pose.' At Mallory Park even this precaution could not prevent the machine going out of control. The damage was so severe that it was totally written off. Luckily, its rider escaped serious injury, even though virtually everything on the bike was damaged—including both wheel hubs, the crankcases and even the gearbox casting!

Returning the wreck to the Greeves factory a few days later was not a particularly pleasant task—even though Everett maintains to this day that the machine deserved to be scrapped. Needless to say, Bert Greeves was none too pleased, which resulted in Everett going home bikeless, his own original scrambler-cum-racer having already been sold.

Brian Woolley then came back into the picture, entering Everett on his RAS, following yet more unlucky incidents with Horace Crowder during May.

Motor Cycle journalist David Dixon created a good deal of publicity when he turned up at a Brands Hatch clubman's meeting with a Silverstone provided by the factory for a real-live racer test. With Bob Mills and Ron Gill from Greeves in attendance, Dixon proceeded to astound spectators by finishing sixth in his heat, after being left on the line, followed by a superb battle in the final with Bob Cook on a 204 Ducati and John Mawby on a 250 Royal Enfield. At the end Dixon finished third, with all three very close together. As a spectator at that meeting during April 1963, I (*Mick Walker*) can testify to just what an impact this performance made!

Dixon made particular mention of the Silverstone's gearing, commenting; 'Even with my weight (13 stone) the Greeves was undergeared initially. On the standard 50-tooth rear sprocket, I was obtaining 8000 rpm (98 mph) in top half way along the Top Straight (the club circuit was used) in my heat. Fitting a 48-tooth sprocket improved top speed to 102 mph and lap times from 68s to 65s for the final and I am sure that with a 10 stone rider aboard, the model would pull a 48-tooth rear and 19-tooth gearbox sprocket to give 106 mph. He rounded off his racer test by saying, 'The Silverstone Greeves is more than a boy's racer. It is every inch a pukka racing iron—light, handleable, with an exceptionally useful powerband, and, ridden by better dicers than I am, capable of blasting off other machines costing twice as much.' And so it was to prove, with results coming in thick and fast for the Thundersley flier.

The Silverstone made its debut as a sprinter when a production RAS was loaned by the factory to Mike Philpott for the Ramsgate Sprint on 5 May. Philpott promptly set the fastest time for the 250 cc class quarter mile in 15.88 seconds.

The Blackpool show in mid-May saw the Greeves factory staff looking 'extraordinarily happy', as *Motor Cycle* put it, helped no doubt by six confirmed TT entries for the following month's Isle of Man classic—Greeves' first appearance in a World Championship road race. The latest version of the RAS on show now had its entire engine unit and exhaust system finished in matt black.

The six riders entered in the Lightweight TT were Joe Dunphy, Bob Richie, Barry Smith (Australia), Allan Harris (Southern Rhodesia), Tom Phillips and Reg Everett. In the event, only one Greeves finished the TT, Allan Harris taking eighth place at an average speed of 81.47 mph in a race won narrowly by Honda Four-mounted Jim Redman from Yamaha rider Fumio Ito.

There is quite a strange tale behind Allan Harris' TT ride—it nearly did not happen! Earlier, with the Silverstone catching everyone's attention, Reg Orpin of the London Velocette specialist, L. Stevens, was at a mid-week practice day at Brands Hatch in early May when Derry Preston-Cobb invited him to 'do a few laps' on a Silverstone. 'Better than that,' said Orpin, 'let my rider, Allan Harris, put in a few.' Harris rode the machine for a dozen or so laps, finishing in style with a fastest time that was a mere half-second outside the class lap record! After lunch the Rhodesian was eager to get back on board, but during the afternoon session he committed the sin of all sins by throwing the Greeves down the road in a big way.

Orpin approached Preston-Cobb, cheque book in hand, saying, 'As he's dropped it, I'd better buy the damned thing.' The confirmed four-stroke specialist was the proud owner—or not so proud owner—of his very first 'stroker' and, in his own words, 'the only thing I knew about two-strokes at this time was that I used to cut the front lawn with one on Sundays.'

The bike was quickly rebuilt, following its close inspection of the Brands Hatch tarmac, and promptly put into action, gaining a second place in the first race. A week later, at Mallory Park, Harris relegated the works Honda twins of Tommy Robb and Bruce Beale to third and fourth places. The scene had been set, the names Greeves Silverstone and Reg Orpin becoming synonymous. It was also performances such as this which convinced the mighty Honda concern *not* to market its production version of the racing 250 dohc twin the following season in Britain!

All summer long, riders such as Reg Everett, Chris Doble, Joe Dunphy, Allan Harris, Dave Simmonds and Tom Phillips were highlighting the Silverstone's capabilities. For example, Greeves riders put on an impressive display at the big international Cadwell Park meeting in September 1963, taking four of the top six places in the 250 cc race. This was won, as expected, by the West German rider Gunter Beer on an ex-works, four-cylinder Honda, for which he was reported to have

Above **The most successful Greeves racer in 1963, Tom Phillips, became holder of the ACU Star (British Champion) that year in the hotly-contested 250 cc class. He is pictured during practice for that season's IoM TT**

Above right **The man who started it all, Reg Everett (4), leading Honda-mounted Tommy Robb (50), Chris Doble (9) on a Greeves, and Joe Dunphy on the Beart Silverstone, at Brands Hatch in September 1963**

paid £5000 (nearly 20 times the cost of a Silverstone). For all that expenditure, Beer was hard pressed to win. Nearly 20,000 spectators, brilliant weather and the sort of racing that enthusiasts would willingly travel the length of the country to watch witnessed a superb Greeves performance.

Dunphy actually led for two laps on the Beart machine and set the class record at 71.96 mph, before his bike went off song and he was forced back into third place behind Beer and Tom Phillips. Then came Dave Degens and John Swannack, also both Greeves mounted, with Aermacchi-mounted John Ashworth completing the leader board in sixth spot.

The 17 October 1963 issue of *Motor Cycle* carried the news that Bert Greeves had said that the Silverstone would be 'substantially' revised. This was the first the public had heard of the new Greeves power unit, which was then underway and destined to replace the modified Villiers 36A in both road racing and motocross.

At the season's end, Tom Phillips and Greeves took the ACU Star (British Championship) for the 250 cc class with 54 points, two ahead of works Honda rider Tommy Robb. But perhaps the best news of all for the Greeves management was that the Silverstone project had been a commercial, as well as track, success. This is borne out by the fact that when production of the original RAS model ceased, on 24 May 1964, a total of 94 had been built (some sources suggest this figure was well over 100 units).

While the RAS models had been winning races throughout Britain during 1963, the factory had been busy designing an all-new motocrosser, the 24MX1 Challenger. This machine was to act as the

inspiration for the next generation of not only dirt racers, but tarmac racers too. The new scrambler was announced in February 1964, and was followed by the road racer some three months later—just in time for the first models to compete in the IoM TT.

Without doubt, the new engine, basically a product of the Greeves design shop with an Alpha crankshaft and Swedish Stefa flywheel magneto, was Bert Greeves' most important design—even though it shared the same 66 × 72 mm, 246.3 cc dimensions and capacity of the Villiers 36A unit.

Informed observers will agree that no one succeeds in obtaining competitive power *and* reliability without both knowledge and ability. In the case of the Greeves factory, the situation was even more difficult, if only because the Essex company was never more than a small-scale-production concern, even at its peak. The central problem was that quantities of parts were nowhere large enough to benefit from the economy of true mass-production techniques. On the other hand, special-production prices would have meant commercial suicide—this was the financial tightrope which Bert Greeves and his staff had to negotiate.

Ingenuity and careful planning had to be used to the full; every ounce of metal had to work for its place in the engine design. There could be no surplus, yet strength, stiffness and heat dissipation could not be sacrificed.

Much of the time spent on development of the road-racing engine was expended on the top end of the assembly—the cylinder head and, to even greater extent, the barrel. Experiments with various squish bands in the RAS head brought no real power boost, so it was decided to devote the major design work to the cylinder barrel. This was because the requirements of motocross and road racing differed considerably.

The original ISDT prototype of the Bert Greeves-conceived, 66 mm cylinder for the 197 cc Villiers engine, back in 1958, had a bore of hard chrome plate—applied by a German firm. Attractions were light weight, excellent cooling and the possibility of using very small piston clearances, since the expansion rates of the cylinder and piston were closely matched. Individually produced, the first half-dozen barrels were, in Bert Greeves' words, 'wonderful'. However, chrome flaking was experienced with some production cylinders and, at that time, there was no means of salvaging them. In addition, costs were higher—partly due to the cost of transport to and from Germany—while cast port shapes proved insufficiently accurate to provide the same level of performance on each engine.

With the 24MX1 engine, a corrugated, austenitic-iron liner was cast in the aluminium-alloy muff, and the entire assembly was heat treated for three hours before the bore was machined and the flange at the top faced off for the head joint.

At the time, when interviewed by Peter Frazer for *Motor Cycle*, Bert Greeves stated that 'iron is much better for lubrication since the surface retains oil without the etching required on chromium. The liner stiffens the cylinders too, and permits accurate machining of all the ports before casting.' A copying machine, designed and made at Greeves, reproduced any port profile consistently within the very satisfactory limits of ± 0.005 in.

Finning on both the barrel and head came in for particular attention. Compared to the RAS engine, the new Silverstone had a 50 per cent increase in cooling area for a weight penalty of only half that proportion.

Compared with the Villiers-based engine, the rear of the cylinder was quite different. In the RAS, the inlet port had been kept as short as possible to minimize the amount of heat applied to the ingoing charge. This called for a deeply-recessed carburettor joint face and, consequently a drastic interruption of the finning over a relatively large area. This resulted in a tendency to distort and produce uneven temperatures. Bert Greeves,

Right **Chris Doble (43) leads Dave Simmonds (40) at Mallory Park, July 1964. Both are on RBS models**

Below **Bert Greeves explaining his new Silverstone engine to** *Motor Cycle*'**s Peter Frazer, February 1964**

however, reasoned that although fuller finning meant a longer induction port, any slight raising of charge temperature was more than worthwhile as a means of achieving a more even cylinder temperature and, consequently, less distortion. On the later RBS engine the inlet-port length was shortened.

At the carburettor cylinder-joint face there was a pair of $\frac{3}{8}$ in. thick, Tufnol, heat-insulating gaskets. Between these was sandwiched a thin steel bracket for the remote float chamber of the Amal 5GP2 $1\frac{3}{8}$ in. carburettor (on the scrambler there was an 18-gauge, light-alloy shield to deflect warm air from the integral Monobloc bowl).

Obviously, there were other differences between the Silverstone RBS and Challenger cylinders; the $1\frac{3}{8}$ in. port on the racer (compared to the dirt bike's $1\frac{3}{16}$ in.) and the 22-degree downdraught angle of the bigger port, against only 8 degrees of the other machine. (Both carburettors, incidentally, were tilted a further 9 degrees by the forward inclination of the cylinder.) These differences, combined with equally differing variations in port timing, stemmed from the need for different power characteristics to match their respective uses.

A legacy of the earlier Villiers influence was the use of phosphor-bronze bushes in the piston. Internally, the assembly had strengthening ribs which, together with its Dykes top ring (the bottom one was conventional) hinted at its real purpose. In Bert Greeves' opinion, since the Dykes ring was pressure backed and formed an efficient seal, there was no point in fitting a similar ring in the lower groove. The piston and rings were of Hepolite manufacture.

In the crankcase, a high ratio of stiffness to weight was achieved by the use of several large webs to support the main bearings on both sides. These comprised a single row of 12 $\frac{9}{16} \times \frac{3}{16}$ in. caged rollers, with a ball bearing on the drive side, and a double row of $\frac{3}{8} \times \frac{3}{16}$ caged rollers on the other.

The Alpha crankshaft had the ring of the caged-roller big-end bearing pressed into an oval-section conrod with scallops and a slot in the eye for lubrication. A steel-backed bronze bush was fitted at the small-end. The nearside crankshaft end had a slot for the Smiths rev-counter drive, while at the offside-shaft end was the cam lobe and taper for the Stefa flywheel magneto.

Of prime importance affecting engine performance was the expansion-type exhaust system. This consisted of round pipe which led to a double-taper, round-section expansion chamber with a short tail pipe. Much of the porting and exhaust data had come from Brian Woolley.

The RBS Silverstone's power peaked between 7000 and 8000 rpm. Above this figure, it fell off steeply, while at the other end, real power was available from 6000 rpm, the motor pulling from as low as 3000 rpm. The factory quoted maximum power as 30 bhp at 7500 rpm.

On the track, the new engine produced no more maximum power than the RAS, but it was easier to ride, with additional mid-range torque. In theory, at least, the addition of a five-speed gearbox made things even easier for the pilot.

When the first of the new bikes appeared, early in May 1964, riders and sponsors were generally much in favour, considering the RBS a worthwhile improvement over the RAS. On the surface, its only weakness was the 6 in. front stopper left over from the earlier design. At 198 lb, it was some 9 lb heavier than the original. All seemed set for even more success. However, things were not to work out quite like that, or at least initially.

Riders soon found two major problems—a chronic top-end misfire and, quite simply, the Albion five-speed gearbox was a disaster. The former was relatively simple to cure, but gearbox and clutch disorders were not so easily solved.

Brian Woolley and Bob Mills had found the cure for the misfire while in the Isle of Man in June. Woolley described it as 'more like a volcanic eruption as soon as 7000 rpm was reached, banging and spluttering rent the air, and sheets of flame came out of the carburettor.' After going through the whole checking routine, including carburation, timing, softer plug and ignition points, they discovered that simply by removing the carburettor bellmouth, the motor would rev clean as a whistle straight up to 8000 rpm in each gear!

With the misfiring problem out of the way—Greeves had Mills, Woolley and Reg Orpin all in the island for the TT period—the situation could have been expected to be somewhat smoother for the remainder of the practice period and race week. But with almost twice the number of machines from the Thundersley factory being entered for the 1964 event, as Brian Woolley related recently, 'There now began a nightmare of early-practice broken motorcycles, rebuilding engines, transmissions and gearboxes, evening practice and a repetition of the work.'

In the race, Allan Harris on the Orpin Greeves went out after a mere 7 miles, a broken tachometer drive having snapped the primary chain. Dave Simmonds completed his first lap at 85.44 mph, and his second at 86.48 mph, only to suffer a puncture on the third while in ninth spot. The leading Greeves rider at the end of that lap was *Motor Cycle Mechanics*' staffman David Weightman on a 1963 RAS model, but he too retired on the next lap. This catalogue of failures continued until finally, at the end of the six-lap race, only one Silverstone was running—an old, factory-hack 1963 RAS ridden by Reg Everett, who came home eighth, and last, at an average speed of 77.42 mph. The race was won by Honda's Jim Redman at an average speed of 97.45 mph.

However, Everett's performance should not be scorned, as he reckons it was the slowest Greeves he had ever raced, and he was hard pressed to better a 90 mph maximum. In fact, he was so disappointed with the bike's lack of speed that this was his final race on one of the British machines, and he transferred his allegiance to a series of Yamaha twins sponsored by Ted Broad of Ilford. With these he became one of Britain's top short-circuit racers until his retirement at the end of the 1967 season.

August 1964 saw Orpin's runner, Rhodesian Allan Harris, crash heavily, breaking his arm, leg and shoulder. His place in the Orpin team was taken by close friend and fellow countryman Gordon Keith, while Harris himself, still plastered up, returned to Rhodesia in October.

For the newly-revived Manx Grand Prix, Reg Orpin and Bob Mills prepared the bike Keith was to ride for reliability above all else, following the dismal showing in June. Even more important, he was given strict instructions as to what revs to use and told never to use the clutch except when starting.

With factory man Mills to fettle the bike, the 26-year-old Rhodesian found himself the centre of a controversy, not helped by the Orpin-Greeves logo painted on the tank—no advertising was allowed then! On Manx Grand Prix entry forms, the organizing club plainly stated that works machines could not be accepted. However, even if the Greeves could have been accused of having a degree of factory backing, there were others in a similar position, most notably the brand-new Royal Enfield being ridden by Manxman Dennis Craine, with Geoff Duke and Hermann Meier also involved.

Interest was sky high in the return of the lightweights for the famous September races, helped in no small way by the incredible 19 different makes in the entry. This was in stark contrast to the Junior and Senior races, which were dominated by Manx Norton and the AMC AJS 7R and Matchless G50 singles.

Bob Mills, ostensibly taking the MGP period as part of his annual holiday, came to more than one rider's rescue during the fortnight of racing, helping any Greeves rider in trouble.

Performing very capably on his first visit to the Isle of Man, Gordon Keith put in 32 exploratory laps before practice even started, proving just how seriously he was taking the whole affair. Throughout practice week, he showed that he would be a formidable force in the race, and so it proved.

Motor Cycle, in their 10 September 1964 issue, ran the headline, 'Hail Keith and Greeves', going on to say of the winner; 'On a Greeves Silverstone Mark 2, he led throughout the four laps and steadily increased his advantage each time round without taking the slightest chance.'

Naturally, the Greeves rider's race speed of 86.19 mph, and fastest lap of 87.61 mph, made mincemeat of the previous records, for they had stood unchallenged since the last lightweight Manx GP had been run, back in 1948. That year,

Joe Dunphy at Brandish during the 1964 TT—he retired

Dickie Dale won on a Moto Guzzi at 73.36 mph, with a fastest lap of 74.36 mph.

Halfway round, at Sulby Bridge, on the first lap, George Collis had led on a Yamaha TDIA twin, with Keith five seconds astern on time, and Rex Butcher (Aermacchi) a further eight seconds behind. However, from then on, Keith reduced his deficit and, by the end of the lap, had grabbed a 7.4-second lead from the Yamaha rider. When he stopped for fuel, at the end of lap two, he led by some 20 seconds. At that stage, the Greeves was holding off five Aermacchis, a brace of Yamahas, two Cottons, a Bultaco, and an overbored Honda CR93 production racer.

Although he had started number 64, Keith had gobbled up most of the field by the third lap and lay third on the road. As the Greeves rider stretched his lead to almost a minute by the start of the last lap, reports from various parts of the course were unanimous in praising his fast, safe and stylish cornering. He was so confident in his machine, by this time, that he turned his last lap in 25 minutes 50.4 seconds, to set not only a new MGP class lap record, but also the fastest time ever around the island by a British production 250—putting many TT stars in the shade. At the finish, his average speed for the race, which was held in blustery winds and beautiful sunshine, was 86.19 mph, and he completed the course in 1 hour, 45 minutes, 4.8 seconds.

Other Greeves-mounted finishers were: 11th, Barry Scully; 19th, R. Waterer; 22nd, R. Kewley; 23rd, R. Eldridge; and 34th, J. Shacklady. There were 36 finishers from the 66 race starters and 86 original entries.

Motor Cycle's David Dixon had the chance to sample the MGP-winning machine, a couple of weeks after its return from the Isle of Man, on the Brands Hatch club circuit. Even though the bike still carried the much taller gearing used during the previous weekend at Snetterton, Dixon was able to draw a direct comparison to his ride on the RAS model 18 months previously.

With its motocross ancestry, the original Silverstone had power on tap from around 3000 rpm to 8000, an ideal mount for beginners. As Dixon observed, however, racing demanded ever more power, and this had been achieved higher up the scale of the the Mark 2 (still not referred to as the RBS by the press of the day). He also found that there was little power 'below 5000 rpm, then it started to flow in rapidly to 6000 rpm. At about 6400, a surge of revs and the needle swung without hesitation to eight on the revmeter—in first, second and third gears.' Because of the machine's high gearing, the top two gears couldn't peak on the twisty 1.24-mile Kent circuit.

In his report, David Dixon also commented on the handling, which he stated had considerably improved; 'Previously, the Silverstone was light at the front end, the resulting weaving has now been virtually eliminated. Over the ripples of Kidney, the sharp crest of Clearways and steep drop to Paddock—which showed up this fault on the old Silverstone—the Mark 2 was delightfully steady.'

What he did find strange at first was the 'riding-on-a-knife-edge' feeling given by the 2.75 × 18 triangular-section rear Dunlop. Not having raced on these tyres before, it took some laps before Dixon had become accustomed to the sharp transition from the vertical to full lean, and I (*Mick Walker*) can confirm this personally, having spent a considerable portion of my own racing career with these tyres.

Largely unnoticed on the Orpin-Greeves had been its larger, twin-leading-shoe front brake. Although commenting upon its power, even Dixon did not say anything about where it had come from—as it left the factory, the RBS came with the puny 6 in. British Hub assembly. When the RBS allocated to him arrived from the factory, the first thing Reg Orpin did was install the front brake assembly from a Velocette, with which he was familiar. Contrary to the few pressmen who had noticed, it was *not* 'a prototype assembly made by Greeves themselves.'

Another modification which Orpin had introduced (and, being hidden out of sight, went completely unnoticed) was a duplex primary-drive chain. During the season, this proved to be far more dependable than the single-row production item. Also, contrary to popular belief in certain quarters, at the time, the Orpin machine had not had its motor specially tuned—except for careful attention having been paid to the compression ratio, mixture and ignition.

Finally, that Stefa ignition! If you were able to keep the $3\frac{1}{2}$ in. diameter flywheel on the end of the crankshaft for any amount of time, you were doing well. Always a constant source of trouble, every flywheel had to be hand lapped on to its crankshaft. Without this, it would vibrate loose and ignition failure would follow.

In the same month as that morale-boosting MGP victory, the 1965 Greeves range was announced. Still referred to as the Mark 2, the RBS was listed at £325, and no changes were noted. As the last of the 27 RBS models had just been manufactured, this was hardly surprising. This small number is accounted for by both the problems encountered and the priority for production facilities given to the motocrossers.

Without a doubt, had Greeves been able to produce more road racers in 1964, its ultimate success would have been that much greater—with one proviso. Quite simply this would have been the need to find substitutes for the sub-standard Albion clutch and gearbox assemblies. Greeves' reputation took quite a knock from this, as the few customers able to buy an RBS model, while praising the balance of the machine, *hated* the Albion contribution. Moreover, it should be remembered that, while a satisfactory solution to these problems was some two years away, the Japanese, with their megabuck racing efforts, were solving their problems between races. However, in Greeves' defence, you could not buy a new Honda Four over the counter, and certainly not for £325!

Even if the situation was far from perfect, the Thundersley factory even made an impression on the four-wheel scene that autumn. This was at the first British Drag Festival where, among the cream of two- and four-wheel straight-line specialists, a humble Silverstone RBS-engined kart stole the thunder with its quarter-mile, standing-start runs of under 15 seconds. From the outside, at least, the engine appeared virtually standard, except that

Below left **The first lightweight Manx Grand Prix to be held since 1948 took place in 1964. The event was won by Rhodesian Gordon Keith on Reg Orpin's RBS Silverstone**

Below **The power unit of Keith's Orpin-Greeves**

the infamous flywheel magneto had been removed and battery/coil ignition fitted. To compensate for the lack of torsional damping of the flywheel rotor on the crankshaft, a strengthening band had been brazed around the clutch unit.

Even though relatively few Silverstones were built in 1964, the machine made an absolutely tremendous impact, as indicated by it being voted Machine of the Year in the annual *Motor Cycle News* poll. Perhaps this reflected a bit of British pride, but the underlying fact was that the Greeves had proved to be not only an effective motorcycle in the public's eye, but a glamorous one to boot.

With many of the marque's former leading exponents on different machinery, many spectators were initially confused as the 1965 season began, even though the latest model, the RCS, had been officially announced on 1 February, at a price of £345. Names like, Phillips, Everett and Simmonds were no longer Greeves mounted.

The most notable 'new boy' to the Greeves ranks was John 'Mooneyes' Cooper, the short-circuit star influenced by his great rival Derek Minter's success on a Cotton. However, in practice, Cooper's association with Greeves was never really a very successful—or happy—one. For the length of time that John Cooper was to campaign the Silverstone, it remained the property of the factory and was maintained by road-race mechanic Bob Mills, not by the rider. An instantly-recognizable feature was the use of an Italian Oldani front brake, but otherwise, externally at least, it was the same as any machine a customer could buy over the counter.

On the standard RCS, a new British Hub Company, 7 in. twin-leading-shoe front stopper was now standard fare, as was the fully-streamlined dolphin fairing with its clear perspex nose cone (the latter, until banned by the ACU, did an excellent job of improving penetration at higher speeds). To compensate for the increase in top speed, a 20-tooth gearbox sprocket was made available for faster circuits. The primary chain was of the duplex type, which reduced wear and race failures in that department. But the infamous clutch and gearbox continued to prove a source of embarrassment for the factory and a nightmare for owners. (As proof of this, many RCS models were converted to four speeds, using a Challenger-type gearbox.) There were small changes to the porting and exhaust which, although not making the engine noticeably quicker, did mean that power was available over a wider scale.

Above **The 1965 RCS featured a larger 7 in. front brake, full fairing with perspex nose cone, and several other minor changes**

Above right **Leading Greeves club rider Tony Plumridge (Mick Walker's brother-in-law) with his RCS in the paddock at Brands Hatch during early 1966**

Although blue remained the overall colour—except for the larger area of white taken up by the full fairing—there was a new tank logo contained in an oval sticker, with 'Greeves' in blue on a white background. The only extra listed by the factory for the RCS was a hydraulic steering damper at £7 10*s* 0*d*.

Compared to the tiny RBS production figure, the 66 RCS models manufactured seems quite large. All were produced during March and April 1965. Surprisingly, though, some remained unsold until much later that year. For example, my brother-in-law, Tony Plumridge, purchased his brand-new RCS from Ilford dealer Eddie Grimstead in October of that year.

Although the 1965 Lightweight TT was not quite the débâcle of the previous year, when only eight

of the 63 starters finished, it certainly was as far as Greeves were concerned. Of the eight machines entered, none reached the finishing line! Among their riders were Cooper, Syd Mizen, Barry Smith, Errol Cowan and Bob Richie. However, once again, the Manx Grand Prix made up for the disappointment of the June races, with 13 of the 53 finishers Greeves mounted, including the winner, Manxman Dennis Craine. He averaged 88.37 mph on Reg Orpin's machine, and set a new lap record of 89.48 mph for the class. As early as lap one Craine had showed his hand by lapping in 25 minutes, 38.8 seconds at a speed of 88.27 mph, bettering Gordon Keith's 1964 lap record by over 11 seconds. Third spot went to another Greeves rider, Peter Williams, later to become a TT hero and member of the John Player works Norton team in the early 1970s, who averaged 87.05 mph. However, with second and fifth places, Yamaha twins signalled their increasing challenge in the 250 amateur racing class.

Meanwhile, for his services to the factory, Brian Woolley had been given an RCS to replace his RBS. Initially, Barry Scully rode this machine, but he never really clicked with the bike and, in July 1965, Woolley offered his machine to a 20-year-old unknown called Trevor Burgess. They had got to know each other through their joint involvement in 50 cc racing—Brian as a tuner, Trevor as a rider. So began, as Brian said recently, 'a partnership which lasted for three rewarding seasons.' At the very first meeting with his new sponsor's bike, at Perton in August 1965, Burgess won both 250 cc races.

One of Woolley's first modifcations to the RCS had been to convert the bike to battery/coil ignition. He had seen several instances of the Stefa magneto flywheel shearing off the mainshaft. Coil ignition eliminated this possibility and gave the added advantage of making it far easier to time the ignition and set the contact-breaker points accurately.

Other modifications eventually included machining his own cylinder heads from blank castings, and using a central 'top hat' shape. Because the piston had a flat crown, he was able to experiment with squish clearances, finding that 0.030 in. was optimum (at 0.025 in. the piston touched the squish band at full revs). Compression ratio was limited by the big-end bearing, and the team found maximum reliability at 9:1. Above this, although quicker, reliability of the big-end suffered.

Slight alterations to the inlet timing gave another 500 rpm of the power at the top end. With these mods, the Woolley-tuned Greeves and Trevor Burgess were a difficult combination to beat on the British short circuits that year.

In Brian Woolley's opinion, the high spot of 1965 was at the Oulton Park Northern Championship meeting in October, when Burgess was headed only by Tommy Robb's Bultaco and beat the cream of the British scene, including the Yamahas of Reg Everett, Billy Nelson and John Ashworth—plus the redoubtable Peter Inchley on his works Villiers Starmaker.

When *Motor Cycling* published a racer test of the Woolley Greeves in their 1 November 1965 issue, Burgess' best speed through the electronic speed trap was 109.76 mph, and his fastest lap of the Silverstone club circuit was 79.9 mph. These figures compared with Gordon Keith's 1964 Manx Grand Prix winner at 102.27 mph and 75.2 mph, and Derek Minter's 1964 Cotton at 102.27 mph and 75.9 mph—the three tests being conducted under almost identical conditions, including the weather. It should be remembered that because of the short straight the machines were still accelerating as they passed the electronic eye.

Besides the specially-tuned Woolley Silverstone, the other machine which showed up well at any level was Reg Orpin's, which was virtually a factory bike. In 1965 it was equipped with a new Albion barrel-cam five-speeder, including a one-off, air-cooled clutch. This latter component was manufactured by Greeves and had been developed because of the standard Albion part's tendency to drag when cold and slip when hot. Not only this, but the Greeves assembly saved weight, as the standard item was machined from solid steel. Acting like a secondary flywheel, the Albion clutch absorbed power on acceleration; without this heavy assembly, the works motor responded far more quickly to the throttle.

However, as 1965 progressed, the Orpin camp experienced real rouble with the gearbox, so they set about curing transmission problems once and for all by converting a five-speed Manx Norton unit. Produced in the tool room at Thundersley, it was a massive failure, forcing the team back into using the dreaded Albion.

With Brian Woolley working on the porting and exhaust, power was upped to the 37–38 bhp figure.

Meanwhile, another set of problems had surfaced—this time political rather than mechanical. Back at the factory, the two factions—road race and motocross—were in competition for machining and testing facilities, but when it came to the crunch, the motocross team would pull rank, leaving Bob Mills and Reg Orpin to make do. Many a long night was spent in the Thundersley tool room, working quickly to finish before the motocross men started work the following morning. Even so, the Silverstone was still being developed at a rapid pace, but many of the changes which Reg Orpin would like to have seen made—such as rotary-disc induction and liquid cooling—were ruled out at that time simply because of the management's insistence that modifications made should, in theory, be adopted the following season into the production version.

In spite of all those hurdles, 1965 was—if one discounts the poor showing in the TT—another good season for the Silverstone, with riders such as Williams (now Orpin's top runner), Cooper and Burgess winning many races at national level on the short circuits. The climax, though, was that second Manx Grand Prix victory.

Now promoted to team manager, Reg Orpin had seen the humble Greeves 'stroker', which had started life as a clubman's short-circuit racer, challenge for not only national, but international, honours by the end of 1965.

So evolved the next stage of the production Silverstone, the RDS model, considered by most observers to have been the best of all the $\frac{1}{4}$-litre Greeves tarmac racers. Outwardly, its differences were confined to the removal of the perspex front number screen, a new-style fairing by Michenalls, and a few, but significant, alterations to the expansion-chamber shape. Mechanically, the RDS had its port timings altered, and was fitted with a suitably-modified piston.

The power output was looked after by a new Albion clutch, which featured more plates with both inner and outer splines (instead of the previous dog-tab design). However, the original six springs and 'star'-type pressure plate were retained. A Renold duplex chain took care of the primary drive but, unfortunately, the clutch was not the air-cooled version of the Orpin factory-development machine.

There was also a new gearbox—perhaps the most important feature of all. This assembly was not only much more reliable, but also more compact than the old HJ5 unit. Gone were the problems of seizing and indifferent gear selection. To cope with the forward positioning of the gear-change shaft, a special linkage was designed with a gear-change pedal which pivoted on the rider's footrest. It should be noted that machines such as Orpin's and Woolley's had the new box in 1965—for at least part of the season.

Motor Cycle Mechanics commented on the RDS in their July 1966 issue; 'The latest Silverstone racer. From boy's racer to respectable maturity among the kings of the track; that is the short and impressive story of the Greeves 250 cc Silverstone racer.' In just over the short space of two months, from 13 May to 15 July 1966, a total of 59 RDS models was produced.

When the 1966 road-racing season got under way, it was, of course, without the RDS—except for the factory-development model in the hands of Reg Orpin. On Saturday 5 March, it had been back to the hard stuff at Brands Hatch, the new season getting off to a fine start (in more ways than one) with the first of a series of clubman's meetings. Conditions were excellent and the standard of racing first class. As *Motor Cycle* put it; 'Some of the top liners may soon be viewing the exhaust pipes of a few of these boys.'

Two hotly-contested 250 cc races saw Paul Smart (Cotton) take victory in one, while the other went to Silverstone-mounted John E. Blanchard. *Motor Cycle* also commented, 'There appears to be a great future for teenager Charles Mortimer (Greeves), son of the famous ex-racer and organizer of the racing schools.' The young Charles notched a second and third, and was never far behind the leaders that day.

At the same time, I (*Mick Walker*) was just running in my own new Vic Camp Ducati Mach 1 racer at Cadwell Park and would do battle with these up-and-coming young stars throughout the 1966 season, together with other Silverstone riders, such as Bill Day and Derek Palmer, usually inspecting the tails of their expansion chambers at close quarters as we sped along the long Norwich Straight at Snetterton, or around the club circuit at Silverstone. The Greeves definitely had a speed advantage over even the best of the Ducatis in those days—although currently in the confines of classic racing events, the two machines are much more closely matched. I can only put this down to how the respective marques have fared with age, the number of machines on the track of each type, *and* spares availability.

Peter Williams, by now employed as a draughtsman at the Thundersley factory, was obviously keen to see Greeves come up with a really competitive short-circuit racer. To this end,

The 1965 Manx Grand Prix winner, Dennis Craine, with his Silverstone at Bradden Bridge

he and Reg Orpin conceived a tubular-framed RDS. Orpin had himself wanted to build a central-exhaust-port engine, and the tubular duplex frame gave him that opportunity.

As the power output of the factory-development bike was, by now, up to some 38 bhp, it soon became apparent that a water-cooled engine was necessary to overcome the increasing problems of piston seizures, but playing second fiddle to the motocross team meant development facilities were severely restricted. In practice, this was illustrated by the fact that instead of having a nice new barrel cast, Orpin and factory mechanic Bob Mills had to get by with a converted production item!

The central-port, air-cooled cylinder had most of its fins machined away and an alloy water-jacket muff welded on in their place. The cylinder head remained air-cooled, however. A Velocette LE $5\frac{1}{2}$-pint radiator (remember Reg Orpin was the boss of L. Stevens, the Velocette specialists) was mounted *behind* the engine, which had twin-plug ignition, with sparks supplied by two Swedish Stefa coils. It was in this form that the Orpin Silverstone appeared to do battle on the race circuits during 1966.

In addition to its tubular duplex frame, water-cooled cylinder, air-cooled clutch and extra engine tuning, the official factory-development machine differed in other ways. Reg Orpin had taken full advantage of his licence granted by the Greeves management, and later the machine even sported Italian components in the shape of Ceriani telescopic front forks and Oldani brakes. Certainly, it was the most stylish Silverstone around, looking every inch a winner. It could be picked out from the pack by the large alloy scoops on each side of the fairing.

Although the machine was a great improvement on what had gone before from the Essex marque and gained considerable success for the team at national and international level—the highlight possibly being Peter Williams' second place in Ireland's prestigious North West 200 in May 1966—it did not bring as much glory to the Orpin-Greeves camp as it had enjoyed in the two previous seasons. This was nothing to do with the bike or its rider, but simply an indication that the Japanese (notably Yamaha) were, at long last, getting their production racers to run really on song.

Whereas Orpin's official factory effort with Peter Williams was having a hard time against

Above **The Orpin water-cooled engine on display at the 1966 Earls Court show. A conversion was offered—with radiator—for £45, but it was not destined to prove a commercial success**

Right **Peter Williams (16), on the water-cooled Orpin machine, hounds Reg Everett (46), Yamaha TD1B, and Peter Inchley (78), on the rapid Villiers Special, at Brands Hatch on 1 May 1966**

ever-stiffer opposition on the southern circuits, Brian Woolley's northern campaign, with rider Trevor Burgess, was gaining a large number of wins and places. Typical of Burgess' performances that season was his success at Olivers Mount, Scarborough. At the national meeting staged at the end of May, with more than 10,000 spectators watching, Burgess won the 250 race from Derek Chatterton (Yamaha) and John Swannack (Aermacchi). He also recorded the fastest lap, at 64.55 mph, over the demanding North Yorkshire seaside course.

Then came the IoM TT—or, at least, it should have been, because at the last moment it had to be called off due to the infamous seamen's strike, finally being run in late August. The Lightweight took place on Sunday 28 August over six laps of the mountain circuit (226.4 miles). Among the half-dozen Greeves entries were Peter Williams and Carl Ward. Continuing Greeves' poor showing in the TT, not one of the 16 finishers was on their machinery, in a race won by maestro Mike Hailwood on his wailing six-cylinder works Honda.

The Manx Grand Prix was run in the fortnight following the TT. The 1966 Manx was my (*Mick Walker*) first IoM race (on a Ducati in the

Lightweight event), and I stayed in the room that Peter Williams had just vacated at 34 Murray's Road, Douglas, sitting with the Greeves rider as he had his last meal and I had my first during our respective stays that year!

With two consecutive wins under their belt, Greeves could rightly have expected to make it three in a row. Of the 108 entries, 22 were on Greeves including Paul Smart, John E. Blanchard, Chas Mortimer and Jimmy Guthrie—the son of the late, legendary Norton star of the 1930s, on the Orpin machine (but with production frame/forks and air-cooled engine).

Almost a quarter of the Greeves riders finished within replica time (awarded that year down to 21st position), but a Thundersley bike did not win, this honour going to a four-stroke. In fact, Italian bangers finished first and second, with Bob Farmer winning on an Aermacchi from Ducati-mounted Ken Watson—but by a slower speed than Craine's 1965 victory.

Blustery winds and scudding rain clouds accounted for the comparatively low speeds with, in addition, mist on the Mountain Section during the opening lap of the Lightweight event held on Tuesday 7 September. Yet at Ramsey, on lap one, the sun was shining as newcomer Paul Smart (who had started number 8) led the field into Parliament Square, although the fancied men were scattered throughout the field, it was hard to form a definite impression of progress. However, Smart was to retire and, at the end of the race, Guthrie (having his first ever ride on a two-stroke) was the leading Greeves rider down in fourth spot and averaging 84.52 mph for the four laps. Bill Day was seventh, Colin Fenton eighth, then a big gap with David Lindsay 18th and Chas Mortimer 19th.

Ten days after the Lightweight Manx Grand Prix, on Saturday 18 September, Trevor Burgess on the Woolley Silverstone once again underlined his northern supremacy by winning first his heat and then the final of the star-studded Croft Autodrome meeting. In the latter, he led the field home from Yamaha-mounted Reg Everett and flying Aussie Bultaco rider Kevin Cass. Many of the top stars were present at Croft that day, including Phil Read with a brace of Reg Dearden Nortons. The reason? A major international meeting on the following day at Cadwell Park, but against the likes of Hailwood, Simmonds, Robb, Shorey and Gould, even Burgess could not make much of an impression at the Lincolnshire circuit.

Left **Williams again, this time testing the lightweight tubular-framed (by Jim Lee) Orpin Special in August 1966**

Right **Brian Woolley's runner, Trevor Burgess, leads Dave Degens (8), Aermacchi, Martin Watson (37), Bultaco, and the almost obscured Rod Gould, Aermacchi, at Snetterton in October 1966**

During the 1966 season, the Woolley team had contested 34 short-circuit meetings, which usually entailed a heat and a final. Of these, seven ended in retirement. The reasons were a clutch problem on the start line at the Mallory Park season opener, a puncture, two big-end failures, one broken chain, a piston seizure and a loose sparking plug. Of the 34 meetings, 14 were of national status, and four international. Burgess had 14 wins, six seconds, three thirds, one fourth, two fifths and one sixth (with a broken exhaust).

The year also saw several races in the 350 cc class. At the time, this was becoming a fairly common practice because not only were 250 cc entries harder to get than in the bigger class, but machines such as the Greeves showed up well against the largest British four-stroke singles which, by then, were at least four years old. Burgess had created a 'sensation', as *Motor Cycle* put it, when at Silloth on 22 July, he had done the double on his Silverstone.

By the end of 1966 Silverstone riders were finding things considerably tougher than before. This was caused mainly by the Bultaco and Yamaha production racers, and Peter Inchley's Bultaco-framed Villiers Special, as I found myself when I raced my brother-in-law's Silverstone at the end of the season.

In an attempt to extract more power, a short-stroke (70.5 × 64 mm), water-cooled, rotary-valve engine was built during the winter of 1966–7 by a combination of factory personnel (including Bob Mills), Reg Orpin and Brian Woolley. However, this project was to prove a bitter disappointment to all concerned with, for example, the water-cooling cylinder (made by an outside supplier from patterns supplied by Brian Woolley) turning out to be porous, and other problems not helping matters. At this time, the Orpin camp also experimented with extra-lightweight frames built by Jim Lee.

On the production front, when the 1967 line-up was announced in October 1966, the Silverstone 24RES was launched at a price of £385. It had only very minor changes and virtually all of them were cosmetic.

A narrower front mudguard was claimed to improve air flow to the engine. Two locations for the footrests gave a choice of riding position, and a neater rear brake pedal was fitted. The most significant change was the colour scheme, with the frame now in silver, while the tank, seat and rear mudguard were finished in a striking contrast of Anglian red. The seat itself was completely new, with a rounded, instead of pointed, rear section and suede covering.

Although Ceriani telescopic forks were now available as extras on the motocross bikes, the Silverstone had no such option. Mechanical (and vastly more important) changes were minimal, to say the least, with minor porting modifications to the cylinder barrel being the only significant alteration within the engine.

RES production (although announced much earlier) did not get under way until 31 March 1967, and it finished three weeks later on 19 April, by which time 58 machines had rolled off the production line.

Although the Greeves (like its Cotton and DMW rivals) was cheap, even at its 1967 price, the more-expensive Bultaco TSS (£485) and Yamaha TDIC (£526) were considerably more advanced technically. Out on the track, their speed kept going up, so the earlier poor reliability of the foreign 250 two-strokes was no longer to be counted on. Quite simply, during 1967, at all but club level, the Silverstone was hopelessly outclassed, and instead of releasing a considerably-improved model to meet the foreign challenge, all the factory did was sit on its laurels and attempt to achieve results by a change of colour. They were to be punished for this serious error, with the RES destined to be the last of the Silverstone line—even though no one outside the factory realized it at the time.

The issue of *Motor Cycle*, dated 27 October 1966, which had announced the 1967 model line, had been dominated by the headline, 'Greeves Three-Sixty is here'. The magazine went on to say, 'Scooping the limelight in the Greeves line-up for 1967 is the 364 cc (actually 362 cc) Challenger Scrambler. With large capacity two-strokes really making their mark in the hands of factory riders, private owners have been waiting eagerly for this moment. The model designated the 36MX4 is far enough under way for the factory to put on their stand at the Show.' This illustrated just how the motocross faction within the factory held sway during that vital period. Instead of any substantial factory development of the tarmac racers, all the available resources were channelled into the dirt bikes.

The reason the management went along with this situation is easy to understand, given that a factory press release, dated 26 October 1966, revealed that over 60 per cent of production was exported, and an order for trials and motocross machines had recently been received from the factory's American distributor, worth around $1,000,000.

However, the 360 motocrosser did have some effect on the road-racing front. The first the public saw of this was on 28 May 1967 at Mallory Park, when Trevor Burgess rode a 350 Greeves, put together by Brian Woolley. Despite restricting the revs to 7200, he still managed to finish 14th in the 350 final.

Woolley claims the idea of converting the 350 motocross engine for road racing came from him—long before the Greeves management finally took the concept on board with the idea of building a production version. In theory, a larger single made sense, as Burgess had already shown in his dices against the likes of Manx Nortons and AJS 7Rs in the 350 category on his 250. Like the Orpin 250, the Woolley 350 did have official blessing, and quite a lot of assistance was given in the construction of the prototype.

With the motocrosser, the original 66 × 72 mm of the 250 grew to 80 × 72 mm, which gave 362 cc. With 36 bhp on tap for the production 360 dirt racer, it was reasoned that 40 bhp from a 350 road-racing version would be competitive. The conversion was carried out, not by reducing the bore size, but by shortening the stroke to 68.5 mm, giving 344 cc.

Writing in the July 1987 edition of *Classic Bike*, Brian Woolley revealed that, contrary to popular belief, the prototype 350 (only later named the Oulton) had been rapid and reliable. This is borne out by results gained by riders Burgess and Mike Scruby during 1967. In fact, Scruby had come in as a replacement for Burgess, after the latter suffered a broken collar bone at Aintree on Saturday 8 July, when he came to grief in a 350 heat at Village Corner and was later sidelined for the rest of the season with a second collar-bone injury.

So it was Scruby who notched up the 350's first victory at Darley Moor on Sunday 24 September. This came after taking a third place in his heat behind Charlie Wild (Aermacchi) and Stan Woods (BSA). However, Scruby got down to business in the final. Second to Woods at the end of the first lap, he relentlessly kept up the pressure until he took the lead on the fifth. The pair had built up an unchallenged lead, and when Woods went out with a dead sparking plug, Scruby was well ahead.

The debut of a very interesting 500 special, which used several Greeves components, also occurred in 1967. Constructed by Bob Stevenson (later to become boss of the Derby-based

Above **Last of the Silverstone line, the 1967 RES. The most significant change was to its colour scheme, which was now red and silver**

Left **Roger Cramp with the ex-Woolley RBS, into which he had fitted his own water-cooled rotary-valve engine, at Mallory Park in October 1966**

Below **Prototype of the 350 Oulton, created by Brian Woolley and raced by Trevor Burgess and Mike Scruby in 1967**

Spondon Engineering Company), this used a pair of 250 engines as a base but, unlike earlier attempts, Stevenson's creation had completely new crankcases. The 494 cc JRS Phantom, as it was known, utilized two Dot cylinder heads and two sets of Greeves Silverstone barrels, pistons, conrods and flywheels. However, the crankshaft was all his own work and featured a splined middle coupling. The assembly was then installed in a crankcase that had been specially cast to his own design.

Each crankshaft was supported by ball bearings on the outside, with two roller bearings in the middle. Crankcase chambers were sealed from each other by piston-ring-type seals (a method used by Brian Woolley on his Greeves engines). Primary drive was by three spur gears to a countershaft, which was supported on three needle-roller bearings. Chain drive was used between the sprocket on the countershaft and a BSA close-ratio gearbox. Coil ignition was used, with a twin-contact-breaker assembly adapted from an American Scintilla unit.

The engine unit was housed in a very neat, duplex cradle frame. This was equipped with leading-link front forks with external Girling hydraulic dampers together with an ex-works MZ front brake. The rear brake was an NSU item. The alloy fuel tank had a capacity of no less than 7 gallons.

Although very interesting from a technical standpoint, the JRS was never destined to be a race-track success. Its debut was marred when a gearbox bearing failed, forcing its retirement at Mallory Park on 20 August. A Mark 2 version, with a different frame, telescopic forks and new brakes, was built later.

Meanwhile, the L. Stevens semi-factory team, headed by Reg Orpin, had secured the services of Errol Cowan and Gordon Keith—the latter back for a second spell on Greeves. Even though their bikes had new frames, specially-cast cylinders with bridged exhaust and $1\frac{1}{2}$ in. Wal Phillips fuel injectors to clean up the bottom-end carburation, the writing was on the wall. Orpin wanted a rotary-disc induction, but the factory would not sanction it, insisting that the works machines kept in line with the production 24RES.

Paul Smart and Chas Mortimer had put together a series of good results throughout 1967 at national and international level on their Silverstones, and a host of clubmen had also continued to enjoy success. However, at the

65

Above **The production Oulton, which was largely a failure, both from a sales and racing viewpoint**

Above left **Bob Stevenson created this very interesting 500 twin, the RBS Phantom. Its engine owed much to contemporary Greeves thought**

Left **When the Phantom twin failed to live up to expectations, Stevenson conceived this 500 single with twin exhaust ports, receiving help from Brian Woolley**

major events, Bultaco and, more so, Yamaha were by now firmly in command.

At the TT, which saw 29 finishers in the Lightweight that year, the aptly-named T. T. Holdsworth brought his Silverstone home in eighth place, averaging 87.31 mph—a highly creditable performance.

The Manx Grand Prix, in September, saw the Lightweight event run in the worst weather conditions seen for many years. Torrential rain, gale-force winds and swirling mists caused a one-hour postponement, and even then, the organizing Manx MCC decided to cut the race from four to three laps.

Looking for further success, the L. Stevens camp was to be sorely disappointed. First, Reg Orpin was taken ill during the practice period with what was confirmed as a heart attack (although he eventually recovered to continue his Greeves racing involvement), and the two runners, Ken Watson and Jimmy Guthrie, hit problems. Watson did not even make the race, and Guthrie went out of the running at Sulby Bridge on the first lap with a seized engine. Even so, Bill Day, on his 'private' Silverstone, came home fourth, averaging 80.87 mph, and the former works scrambles star, John Griffiths, took the newcomer's award by finishing 13th.

The 1968 model range was announced in September, with *Motor Cycle* carrying the headline, 'Greeves Silverstone gets a big sister'. The magazine also commented; 'In view of the shortage of across-the-counter raceware the Oulton Special is particularly welcome.' Priced at £450 and officially dubbed the 35RFS, the newcomer sadly failed to repeat the performance of the prototype, and only 21 machines were produced. The reason was due, in part, to the Woolley prototype engine being stolen from the factory when the competition shop was burgled. Added to this, Brian Woolley recently stated, 'I had given the factory notes and drawings of the cylinder dimensions, but a disregard of my specifications, coupled with an uncorrected drawing-office error, meant that the production cylinder barrels bore no resemblance to the original design.' No attempt was made to rectify these and other problems which showed up in the production machines.

In retrospect, this is even more telling when one

considers that Bob Stevenson (the same man who had conceived the ill-fated JRS twin) was to gather a notable number of successes on a much-modified Oulton well into the 1970s, both at short circuits, like Darley Moor, and Irish road courses.

Yet another factor restricting sales was that, although announced in September 1967 and displayed at the annual Earls Court Motorcycle Show shortly afterwards, production did not begin until some *nine* months later, in mid-June 1968, when the racing season was half over!

As already mentioned, the Oulton power unit owed much to the 360 motocrosser. The bottom end was identical, save for the fact that the flywheel assembly had been machined differently to allow for the shorter stroke. Obviously, cylinder porting differed—understandably in view of the different power requirements. On the Oulton the twin exhaust ports fed into pipes with (unlike the off-road version) separate expansion chambers and long tail pipes. Carburation was taken care of by an Amal $1\frac{1}{2}$ in. 3GP2 instrument—the largest available and considered by many to be another factor limiting its potential. Again, a five-speed Albion gearbox was used, but the 350 was fitted with a new clutch assembly designed by Greeves themselves.

The Oulton's frame and cycle parts were those used on the RES Silverstone, and they were not really adequate for the additional power output. The machine was finished in black, with a contrasting cream-coloured fairing. Other differences, compared to the smaller Greeves racer, included a 220 lb dry weight, larger 5-gallon tank, and wider 3.00 × 18 Dunlop triangular tyres front and rear.

Alongside the 350, a larger 410 cc (85 × 72 mm) engine was built. However, this was the work of Reg Orpin and Bob Mills. The reasoning was that if 40 bhp was possible from a 350, the larger engine should have been good for 45–46 bhp. The idea was that with a superior power-to-weight ratio, the 410-engined bike would have been able to compete successfully against the larger Manx Nortons and Matchless G50—as an added advantage, it would benefit from not only the lighter weight but also the two-stroke's superior acceleration to gain a worthwhile advantage.

In reality, however, the 410 cc motor lacked one vital ingredient—reliability. Thus, as a factory-backed effort, it was quickly discarded, following a capacity increase to 498 cc (91 × 76 mm) and geared primary drive, passing on to Brian Woolley. It was then raced, as the Selva, by Bob Stevenson. The engine eventually went to East Anglian rider Frank Ball—a farmer and near neighbour of mine (*Mick Walker*) from Wisbech St Mary, Cambridgeshire—who did a considerable amount of work on the machine in the early 1970s, including fitting Ducati front forks and rear wheel, and a Spondon front brake, all supplied by my company, Mick Walker Motorcycles. Eventually, even Frank gave up the fight to develop the big single into not only a fast bike, but one which actually *finished* races. Long before this, however, Greeves road racers were effectively out of serious contention—with the leading figures, such as Woolley and Orpin also out of the picture—at least at factory level.

With declining sales in 1968, the factory desperately needed a replacement for the ageing 246 cc Villiers-based Silverstone motor. In what was to prove the final chapter of the Silverstone saga, Frank Cutler of Alpha—the suppliers of crankshafts to the Greeves concern for many years—was asked to supply two of his extremely powerful, although fragile, Centuri engines. These 247 cc (54 × 54 mm) disc-valve twins produced 45 bhp and (with extra development) could well have lifted Greeves back on to the winner's rostrum. Unfortunately, they were returned to Cutler with only one comment: 'unsuitable'.

Although Reg Orpin had retired from his association with the marque, Brian Woolley had not, even though his efforts were now strictly as a privateer. In 1968 he entered British 50 cc champion George Ashton, but largely was destined never to recapture the heady days of 1965–6 when Trevor Burgess (by now riding Ossas for importer Eric Houseley) had swept all before him. Woolley's last Greeves success was to come from the very special 350 raced by Bob Stevenson, who managed to achieve results that nobody else could emulate with the design.

In 1969 and 1970 riders such as Dave Street (first on an ex-Alastair Kirkcaldy Silverstone and then on a Geoff Monty-sponsored Oulton), Trevor Elliott on an Oulton (owned by Reg Orpin), and Ray Guy on the ex-Orpin Silverstone, all won races and continued to wave the Thundersley flag. But, except for Bob Stevenson's brilliant efforts, by the end of 1970 the Silverstones and Oultons—like all the other singles—found it impossible to compete with the now completely dominant Yamaha TD and TR twins.

Then, for some ten years, anything without

Above **Bob Stevenson on his Woolley-tuned 350 Greeves during the Skerries 100 on 3 July 1971**

Below **The final road-racing project from Greeves was this 498 cc (91 × 76 mm) unit. First used in experimental form in a factory motocrosser during 1971, it had a geared primary drive. It is shown here in the form raced by Cambridgeshire farmer Frank Ball during 1973–74**

'Yamaha' on the tank mouldered, forgotten in garden sheds and garages until the early 1980s when classic-racing fever struck. In an incredibly short space of time, the previously obsolete and largely forgotten racers of the 1960s were revived, rebuilt and reloved, to stage an action replay of events which had taken place two decades before. By 1983 there was even a Classic Manx Grand Prix. Although a Greeves did not win this inaugural event, a third of the finishers in the class were Silverstone mounted, with Manxman Brett Gaites the highest placed in fourth spot, averaging 81.72 mph for the three laps.

As this chapter was being written, the most successful Silverstone rider on the British classic-racing scene was young Martin Studder from Bourne End, Buckinghamshire, who, even against the most expensive and exotic 250s, is guaranteed to put up a real fight in races throughout the country organized by the CRMC (Classic Racing Motorcycle Club). Long may this state of affairs continue as a fitting tribute to a humble, single-cylinder, two-stroke racing motorcycle—conceived more by accident than design. The surviving examples of the Silverstone are a tribute to the men who designed, built, maintained and raced a truly British, two-wheeled, road-racing legend.

8 1960s roadsters

As the new decade dawned, many observers could have been forgiven for thinking that the day of the Greeves street bike was at an end. Those pundits, however, would have been wrong, as events in the 1960s were to prove.

When the 1961 line-up was announced, there were five competition models and four street bikes: the 197 cc 20DB Sports Single, the 246 cc 24DB Sports Single, the 25DC Sports Twin and the brand-new 324 cc 32DC Sports Twin. Actually, a handful of pre-production 32DC models (eight in total) had been built prior to the official launch. Powered by the Villiers 3T, which had been available from as early as 1957, the 325 once again gave Greeves a toe-hold in the larger-capacity enthusiasts' market.

Generally similar to the 2T, the 3T had, at first, been conceived for light car use. In 1958 it became available for two-wheel use without the fan cooling and reverse gear, which had originally been a feature for three- or four-wheel use. In fact, the 3T was simply a bored-out 2T, with the cylinder size increased from 50 to 57 mm. However, it remained a long-stroke engine at 63.5 mm. The carburettor size was increased from 22 to 25 mm, while the compression ratio dropped from 8.2 to 7.25:1. Power at 16.5 bhp was marginally better, but far superior was the level of engine torque. Maximum speed was a quoted 75 mph.

For 1961 both the twins benefited from improved gearboxes—a Villiers modification rather than anything undertaken by the Thundersley concern.

Actor Richard Wyler was partnered by Griff Jenkins in the annual 500-mile endurance race at Thruxton, in June 1961, on a Sports Twin and, although the pairing did not make the results, it did further the growing association between Greeves and the American star. Wyler's first connection with the Essex concern had come in November 1960, as little more than a crazy stunt. While practising at Brands Hatch with Joe Dunphy, Wyler had met the Essex company's directors, Derry Preston-Cobb and Bert Greeves. With the day's activities curtailed by heavy rain, the quartet sat having a cup of tea together. They got round to talking of warmer places and eventually centered upon the subject of how many European cities the actor had visited on location with the television series *Man From Interpol*. When the four parted on that cold November day, a seed of an idea had been sown in the fertile mind of Greeves' sales director, Derry Preston-Cobb.

Early in the following year, Richard Wyler was at home in his London flat when the telephone rang. Wyler picked it up, half thinking it was a film producer he was expecting to call, but it was Derry Preston-Cobb. 'How about taking two Greeves and showing Joe Dunphy those European cities you mentioned up at Brands,' he said. Wyler said, 'Okay', and with that the pair were given a 250 Sports Twin and one of the new 325s. Wyler settled down to the task, planning a trip to show fellow traveller Dunphy as many cities as possible in a whirlwind European tour of eight days, which would represent as tough a test for the machines as could be found.

At the last minute, the 250 was withdrawn for a press road test, but the Greeves management simply solved the problem by pulling a brand-new 325 right off the production line. To give it at least a fighting chance, they had a factory mechanic ride it all night to put 200 miles on the clock before departure time! At 6 o'clock the following morning, Wyler and Dunphy were ready to leave Britain via nearby Southend Airport, the riders pushing their heavily-laden mounts up the ramp to board a Bristol Freighter. An hour later, they were looking at a Dutch landscape, which included windmills and glasshouses, and the mass of shipping in the international port of Rotterdam.

After a quick cup of coffee, the Barbour-suited

Wyler and Dunphy were aboard their Greeves twins on the recently-opened motorway to Amsterdam. Within an hour, they were in the Dutch tourist centre, the first city on the list. Their visit had coincided with the annual RAI national motorcycle exhibition. At the Dutch *Motor* magazine stand, they met off-road rider and Greeves dealer Frits Selling. After the show came an excellent meal and then the night-club circuit.

With the previous night's revelling still fresh in their minds, the next day was a real challenge in more ways than one . . .

Planning on reaching Rome, via Cologne, soon proved harder to achieve than had been thought. Realizing that Cologne would have to be missed, they headed south in the freezing cold and, after hours of incessant rain, finally reached Frankfurt at nightfall. Next day, up at 5 o'clock in an attempt to make up time, all they succeeded in doing was 'feeling as cold as either one of us had ever felt in our lives'—and getting lost!

By now run in, or so the riders thought, both machines were behaving well and cruising at 70 mph plus. However, after a non-stop 180 miles on the *autobahn*, Wyler found that his much newer machine was *not* fully run in. The result—seized pistons!

With one new spare piston and four hours' work in a nearby NSU dealer's workshop, the engine was back together and running. Then came a slow 100-mile journey to Basle, Switzerland, where the night was spent. Wyler figured out a tentative plan. Cancel Rome. The following day he would check about putting the bikes on the train through Switzerland. He would call Bert Greeves and have him fly two piston assemblies to Milan, and they would be laughing—or so they hoped. That evening in the Basle hotel, Wyler reckoned that they had ridden 646 miles since leaving Britain in less than 24 actual riding hours.

On the following day, after going to the wrong railway station, the pair had to dash across the town to the correct one, arriving with only ten minutes to spare. Through the courtesy of an English-speaking German passenger, Wyler and Dunphy were able to find out where to purchase tickets and obtain the necessary documents for the bikes. In common with the other passengers, the German seemed very amused to see a couple of helmeted motorcyclists running all over the station booking hall with their machines!

Once aboard the train, the pair were able to relax, have dinner and enjoy the trip through breathtaking, snow-covered mountain scenery. At Chiasso, on the Italian border, they were horrified to see railway officials unloading the bikes. Although the passenger section of the train went through to Milan, the goods section did not! There followed another wait of several hours until a train arrived in which both riders and their machines could be carried together.

Actor Richard Wyler (left) and road racer Joe Dunphy in Milan during their European trip in early 1961

Eventually, they reached Milan, the package containing the valuable pistons was retrieved, the barrels bored and the offending machine running again as it had been designed to do. It even started with the first kick!

Back on the road, and taking things considerably steadier this time, the pair headed towards Genoa on the *autostrada*. It even began to get warmer for the first time on the trip. After

THE CHOICE OF THE EXPERT

Greeves

Genoa, the road ran westwards along the Italian Riviera, then through Monte Carlo and Nice, all very spectacular, with Wyler remarking that it was just like the Pacific coast of California.

On reaching the ultra-expensive Cannes, they were lucky to find a small, typically French hotel that was not only reasonable, but where they were even allowed to park the bikes in the tropical garden out front. Despite the thought of the following day's 500-mile ride, the day (Sunday) was spent soaking up the sun.

Monday morning and 6.30 am saw the pair stop for coffee at Frejus, having already travelled some 40 miles. About 250 miles from Cannes, they heard the blast of a loud and insistent motor horn. A van sped past, carrying two scramblers. They were Greeves! And who should be looking out but Dave Bickers! Unknown to them, he had won the Spanish 250 Moto Cross GP on the previous weekend—but Bickers did not stop, much to the chagrin of our two travellers.

In Lyon, traveller's cheques were cashed, and then came the long haul north. Later, at 11.30 pm, after being on the road for 18 hours and covering 500 miles, they were approaching their destination for the day—Saulieu. Next day, it was on to Paris, via Fontainebleau for a photo session outside the palace. More photographs—and a taste of the night life in the French capital. On the following day, Wednesday, the team completed the last 170 of the 2000 miles. The Channel Air Bridge was reached at 3 pm, and half an hour later they touched down at Southend Airport.

Except for the one bit of mechanical trouble—caused, as Wyler freely admitted, 'by my own impatience', it had been a memorable experience and a real test of endurance. They had travelled in freezing cold, in considerable heat, up mountains and through busy city streets, but both machines had coped admirably.

Soon after landing, the panniers were removed, the bars replaced by lower ones and the duo, together with Bert Greeves and Derry Preston-Cobb, were back at Brands Hatch again. There, both 325s were put through the final test over the Kent 'swervery'.

All four roadsters continued unchanged into 1962, but in April, a new model was added—the Sportsman, which one could have believed had been dreamed up by a stylist of the Italian school.

Left **Factory brochure showing Wyler with the 324 cc 32DC twin on which he undertook his European adventure**

Above right **Richard Wyler aboard the 25DC he shared with Griff Jenkins in the Thruxton 500-miler, June 1961**

Right **A 1962 197 cc 20DC**

'Trim, sporty, bang in the modern idiom', was how *Motor Cycle* summed it up. The public's first chance to see the new machine was at Silverstone that month during the Hutchinson 100, when an example was paraded around the circuit during the interval.

The Sportsman was powered by the well-known 249 cc Villiers 2T twin, but now with twin silencers. The machine came complete with a handlebar fairing, shapely fuel tank and front-fork spats, all in fibreglass.

First impression was of the striking, two-tone colour of banana yellow and light blue. Underneath this somewhat garish appearance was the frame and front fork used for so long on models like the DC Sports Twin, but a minor change was the repositioning of the footrests—$2\frac{1}{2}$ in. higher and 2 in. further back. This meant that they were better placed in relation to the low-level handlebars.

From the motocrosser model came the full-width, polished, alloy brake hubs. Brake diameter was 6 in., the front unit incorporating a slotted air scoop. The front brake torque arm was attached to the fork leg, parallelogram fashion, thus, it was claimed, eliminating judder under heavy braking. The four-bearing (including two in the cush drive) rear hub accommodated a rubber cush drive, but

Fibreglass wheel spats on Essex twins. Introduced for 1962, they proved unpopular

the roadster's sprocket carrier was modified to carry one thicker bearing. The front wheel carried a 2.75 × 19 tyre; the rear a 3.25 × 18 tyre.

Mudguards were of polished light alloy, and rear-wheel removal was simplified by a detachable tail-piece on the rear mudguard. This was held in place by three bolts. Each front-fork spat could be removed simply by undoing a cap on the pivot spindle and loosening the top locating bolt of the fork damper.

With a capacity of $2\frac{1}{2}$ gallons, the fuel tank had recesses for the rider's knees. A polished, light-alloy strip embellished the two-tone finish, and a final racy touch was added by the large-diameter, quick-action filler cap.

A semi-circular instrument console, housing a speedometer and lighting switch, was bonded to the handlebar fairing, and the complete assembly was attached to the machine at three points: the base of the steering head and the tops of both fork legs. The curved, sports-type screen was constructed from perspex. The fairing was recessed to take a 6 in. diameter headlamp, beam setting adjustment being provided by a screw at the lamp base. A horn was sited in the nearside wing of the fairing. The tool kit and battery were housed in the pressed-steel mid-section, which took the place of conventional battery/tool boxes.

The 25DCX, as the Sportsman was officially designated, cost £217 10*s* 0*d* or, with the 324 cc Villiers 3T engine and known as the 32DCX, £227. A point of interest is that a mere seven of the larger-engined Sportsman were actually made.

Later in 1962, at the Earls Court show in November, Greeves introduced yet another twin, the 25DD Essex. This used the 17 bhp specification 2T of the Sportsman. The Essex shared many features with the Sportsman, including the fibreglass fuel tank. However, not only did it have more deeply valanced mudguards—in the same material—but the more sober Moorland blue colour scheme. The brakes were the standard steel 6 in. units, although the full-width alloy ones fitted to the Sportsman were an option (at extra cost). Weight was 274 lb. It was available as the Model 32DD with the 324 cc Villiers 3T engine.

The 197 cc Sports Single 20DC, 250/325 Sports Twin 25DC/32DC, and 250/325 Sportsman 25DCX/32DCX continued, giving the marque its biggest ever range of roadsters. Without doubt, the end of 1962 marked the high point of the Greeves roadster story. From then on, the unexpected success of the Silverstone short-circuit road racer, followed by the ever-increasing competition on the dirt-bike front, meant that, although they survived for several years, the roadsters were to take more and more of a back-seat role.

In fact, from about this time, the storage and distribution of the roadsters was largely undertaken by Cornish dealer David Paull—by then roadster production was very much a limited-batch operation, taking up only a few weeks of the year—in conjunction with southern Greeves sales representative Mike Jackson. The situation was not helped when, at the end of 1963, Villiers chose to replace the popular 2T with the new 4T. This turned out to offer little more in terms of power, but was a harsher, high-revving unit, which had lost the smoothness of the earlier engine.

Originally making its debut in electric-start form in a Bond three-wheeler, the 4T was basically similar to the 2T, but had new features such as cylinder heads with angled finning to direct air on to the centrally-located spark plugs, and four transfer ports instead of two. The conrods were $\frac{1}{4}$ in. shorter than those of the 2T, although the bore and stroke remained the same, and the pistons were ported and had larger gudgeon pins. It also revved higher at 6000 rpm and developed 2.5 bhp more than the old unit. At the same time, Villiers made a great play of saying this had been achieved without the loss of any low-down pulling power (which was not true). Finally, the silencers

Above **A 1964 250 Essex twin under test by** *Motor Cycle*

Right **A 1962 2T-engined 25DC model**

Above **A 1964 25DD with new Villiers 4T engine**

Left **Although the 4T had an additional 2 bhp, it had none of the smoothness enjoyed by the earlier 2T engine**

Above **The final full year for the 25DC was 1964, when it had the 4T motor, full-width hubs and separate exhausts**

Right **1965 heralded the 25DC Mk 2, which was known as the East Coaster. It is seen here at Wivenhoe Harbour with Dave Bickers and model Beryl Moran**

had been redesigned with internal baffles, which had been conceived to take greater advantage of exhaust resonances.

Even though the new engine was available, not all Greeves twin-cylinder models were equipped with it immediately—whether this was a case of preference or to use up existing stocks is unclear. In fact, the 25DC Sports Twin did not begin to receive the 4T unit until the autumn of 1964. By then, only three roadsters remained; the Sports Twin, the 20DC Sports Single and the 25DD Essex Twin, now in Mk 2 form with 4T engine. All the other roadsters, including the gaudy Sportsman and all the 325 models, had been discontinued.

As standard, the Mk 2 Essex came complete with full-width alloy hubs which, for the two DC models, cost an additional £6 0*s* 0*d* in September 1964.

The Earls Court show in November that year saw a replica of the Essex Twin in the special trim supplied to the City of London Police. Otherwise, the roadsters continued unchanged.

Actually, the City of London Police had ordered and taken delivery of four 4T-engined Essex models, with special high-output generators. This was so that a two-way radio set could be carried. Because of this, a special fibreglass fuel tank was produced which held the set in its top. Other equipment included front crashbars and a black finish instead of Moorland blue.

Besides normal patrol duties, the police Essexes were used for the Lord Mayor's Show and other

Above **Villiers 37A-powered Essex singles, with high-output electrical equipment for use with radios, being handed over to the Staffordshire County Police, autumn 1968**

Left **City of London Police model, 4T-engined Essex twin with special high-output generator, shown during the winter of 1964**

important functions. Later, others were supplied to both the Staffordshire County and Stoke-on-Trent Constabularies. Police models were, in fact, delivered as late as autumn 1968, when a fleet of 15 were supplied by Stafford dealer Phil Bright. These, however, had the 4T motor replaced by a 37A unit with high-output electrical equipment.

May 1965 saw the final Greeves roadster appear, making its world debut at the Blackpool show. In essence, it was an all-black adaptation of the previous 25DC Sports Twin. Named the East Coaster, it was originally conceived at the request of the Greeves distributor for the eastern United States, although most British enthusiasts could have been forgiven for thinking it stemmed from the factory's location on the east coast of Britain. The East Coaster cost £222 10*s* 0*d*, compared with the Essex at £230.

Motorcyle Mechanics tested an East Coaster in their September 1965 issue, calling it the 'Getaway Greeves—with creamy power and perfect road-grip'. Maximum speed was found to be exactly 80 mph, with 0–60 mph acceleration in 13 seconds. Besides an awkward-to-reach choke situated under the tank, the tester's main gripe was the starting, which was 'quite frankly a real chore unless the engine is warm. The kickstart is mounted forward of the footrest and has to be pulled partially backwards by hand before you can get your foot on it. At the bottom of the arc, the foot comes too close for comfort underneath the footrest!' Although the lighting was 'surprisingly good, adjusting the height of the headlamp beam was complicated by the rigidly-mounted nacelle.'

When the 1966 model line was announced at the beginning of September 1965, only two roadsters remained: the 20DC Sports Single and 25DC East Coaster, now priced at £194 10*s* 0*d* and £230 respectively. Both were unchanged from the previous year's models. And when the 1967 Greeves line-up was announced, at the end of October 1966, there were *no* roadsters, only competition bikes. Although a few police bikes were built as late as 1968, the Greeves street bike died for three main reasons: the success of the competition bikes, the sophistication of competing Japanese machines and, perhaps most significant of all, the demise of the Villiers engine company. Eventually, this was taken over by Manganese Bronze, a company controlled by Dennis Poore, who then set up Norton Villiers. NV were not interested in supplying engines to customers such as Greeves and so sealed the fate of not only the Greeves roadsters, but also several other similar Villiers-powered models from the likes of Cotton and DMW.

9 Anglian and Wessex

Greeves
GREAT BRITAIN

The factory launched a new trials machine on to the market at the beginning of the 1966 season. The new machine, a logical advance on the Scottish series it replaced, was quite different and bore the name Anglian. Developed by the factory design staff and Don Smith, it carried many of the refinements used by works riders during the preceding season's events.

The Anglian was probably the most popular trials machine the factory ever produced, even more popular than the TES Scottish, which was in production for some three full seasons. During its production run of nearly four years, the Anglian appeared in three different guises, (TGS, THS and finally the TJS) and dominated trials events all over the country. The factory versions began to be seen in action towards the end of 1965, when Gordon Jackson used one to take top honours in the West of England Trial.

At the end of every year, the motorcycling press put on a light-hearted event entitled the Press Trial, or British Inexperts, as it is sometimes called, in which journalists, editors and trade barons have a bash. In the 1965 event many riders were Greeves mounted, probably due to the steadfast ways of the new machine in the extra muddy conditions which prevailed. After many mishaps, both Mick Woollett, of *Motor Cycling*, and Peter Frazer, of *Motor Cycle*, gained first-class awards in the sidecar class. Peter was piloting the Alec Wright outfit with a rather wet and worried Alec acting as ballast—when he was not paddling in the mud holes after being thrown from the chair on more than one occasion by the throttle-happy Frazer. Both Bert Greeves and Bill Brooker showed faith in their product by gaining first-class awards on a brace of the new trials irons.

Works rider Don Smith testing a standard production Anglian

In line with the launch of the Anglian, the factory decided that the production of a cheaper, utility trials machine was no longer needed. Thus, for the 1966 season, only one model was available: the 24TGS. The new bike's name was in recognition of the factory's East Anglian location.

The 24TGS had a new frame built on the lines of the TFS and still retaining the cast-alloy down-beam, but now bearing an integral subframe, with smaller muguard loop, welded to the main frame loop. The traditional Metalastik-sprung fork now ceased to be the standard wear of the trials mount, its place being taken by a set of banana forks, first seen in use on the previous season's scramblers.

The new fork utilized a pair of conventional Girling units to control the movement of the redesigned fork loop, and this featured a revised pivot position. The fork was said to have a better action and ability to cope with adverse conditions, mainly due to the increased range of movement effected by the new design. Originally attached by alloy clamps, the handlebars were now mounted on tubular-steel supports, held in place by U-shackles—a not entirely satisfactory move, as the shackles tended to bite deeply into the handlebars, which introduced a weak point.

The front wheel retained the WM1 × 21 rim and now used one of the original pressed-steel hubs in an effort to lighten the front end. Reversion to the pressed-steel hub required the use of the pressed-steel backplate, but this was modified to a fully-floating type, requiring the use of a torque arm anchored to the fork leg to prevent rotation under braking. The rear wheel was also modified, but still used the full-width alloy drum. It was fitted with a WM3 × 19 rim, giving the machine a better chance of climbing out of holes. Rear wheel adjustment now became easier with the use of snail-cam adjusters.

The use of well-valanced plastic and fibreglass mudguards now ceased, with a reversion to narrow-section, alloy mudguards, front and rear. The factory could not be accused of reverting entirely to old-technology materials, however, for a completely redesigned fibreglass fuel tank adorned the Anglian. The new tank and a complementary seat—with a base of the same material—helped to reduce the weight of the Anglian by some 4 lb over its predecessor.

In an effort to brighten up the trials scene, a new colour scheme was used on the Anglian—an idea initiated by many other factories—the frame and cycle parts being stoved light grey and the fuel tank pigmented bright red. A retrograde step? The Moorland blue traditionalist brigade thought so, but it had been long considered that the trials machine deserved a brighter finish.

'Smithy' in characteristic trials action, complete with cigarette, on his factory TGS

During the early production life of the Anglian, Greeves were dealt a blow that nearly spelt the end of the trials machine. This was the collapse of the Villiers empire, the repercussions of which were felt throughout the entire motorcycle industry. Had it not been for the foresight of the Metal Profile company in purchasing tooling, design and production rights of the Villiers 32 and 37A motors, the Anglian might never have continued. Metal Profile deemed the purchase desirable to protect the supply of engines to one of its own subsidiary companies, DMW, but also supplied other factories (Cotton, Dot and Greeves) with power units and spares to keep the Villiers-engined machines alive.

Initially, the Anglian used the 32A motor as standard, but soon changed over to the 37A once production had begun. Internally, the new motor was no different to the 32A, the main design

change being in the crankcases and gearbox shell. The new cases did not feature any cosmetic fairings to impede air flow to the main-bearing housings, and were of lighter construction. It had always been noted by the trials-riding fraternity that the first two ratios in the wide-ratio box were rather close together, as were the last two, with a large gap in the middle. Riders now wanted a box with three usable ratios and an overdrive top for road work. This was achieved by substituting a lower, roadster, third-gear pinion set in the new gearbox.

Greeves continued to use the Challenger cylinder and head on the new motor, but fitted a 1 in. Monobloc carburettor on a lengthened induction stub. A new exhaust system, designed especially for the Anglian, consisted of a pipe lying close to the cylinder fins above the primary-drive case. Initially, the silencer lay horizontally above the gearbox, but in later designs it was made to lay parallel to the rear subframe stay, the rider's left leg being protected by a square-shaped guard.

The trials-riding public received the Anglian well, being delighted with its excellent grip on a wide variety of surfaces and its ability to follow the chosen path. With its easy nature, it was hailed as a machine for both expert and novice alike. No one feature alone could be pinpointed and said to be the reason for the steadfastness of the machine. The new front fork with its $6\frac{1}{2}$ in., well-damped movement, the larger-diameter rear wheel, an all-up weight of 228 lb, and a powerful but controllable motor, all helped to enhance the reputation.

Considerable interest was shown in the Anglian, not only by trials riders, but also by off-road racers, for this was the era when the popularity of dual-purpose bikes was on the increase, a trend started by the DMW Mosquito, a go-to-work racer/roadster. By simply changing a few parts, it was found that the Anglian could be turned into a potent scrambler or endurance racer, each version being equally capable of holding its own against purpose-built machinery. This dual-purpose capability was noticed by Don Smith who, at the time, was running a sporting motorcycle business. To meet demand, he put together a kit of parts, which sold with the basic machine for an extra £10.00. The kit comprised a long, tapering expansion chamber, quick-action

Left **Engine details of the 1966 TGS Anglian**

Right **Stateside 24CS took you where most others could not follow. The original 1967 model is shown**

twist-grip, forward-mounted footrests and complementary brake lever. The biggest drawback to any scrambler converted from a trials machine is usually the gearbox, which has low-geared bottom and second ratios, with a considerable jump to third and top. As explained earlier, this problem had already been overcome by using a lower, roadster third ratio, which solved the problem nicely.

Another growth area being exploited by the factory was the ever-growing demand by the American market for a 'go anywhere, do anything' machine that was capable of tackling communication duties on construction sites and in forestry areas, as well as on cattle and sheep ranches. The major requirement was for an all-terrain machine requiring little maintenance—in other words, a substitute for the horse. To meet with this need, the factory introduced the 24CS Ranger, an American-market-only machine capable of performing the duties outlined.

Based on the Anglian, the Ranger featured knobbly tyres, dualseat, pillion footrests, lighting set, rock guards, rear carrier and a brush guard on the front mudguard. The engine was based on the 34A unit and featured normal, wide-ratio trials gearing. In line with the practice of the day, this unit used a Challenger cylinder and head, but reverted to the Villiers S25/6 carburettor to maintain tractability.

The Ranger suited the US market, as had the TFS trail bike before it, but the machine was now aimed at the commercial off-road rider, rather than the leisure rider, and was far more robust to cope with the tasks it would have to perform.

The high point of 1967 was the crowning of Don

Smith as the undisputed trials king. In winning the Swiss, Belgian, French and German rounds, he collected enough points to take the European Trials Championship for the second time.

Back on home ground, Billy Wilkinson showed everyone what an Anglian could do by winning the Allan Jefferies Trial—after many near misses, he finally took the premier place. This was a great triumph for the factory, for it was results that brought about sales, but this and other wins could not disguise the fact that it was a Bultaco, in the hands of Sammy Miller, that was getting the most publicity. In the previous two seasons, the Bultaco had come from nowhere to be the new trials front runner. Unfortunately, Greeves did not counter this meteoric rise to fame, preferring to carry on with the Anglian.

It was Don Smith, in 1967, who realized that something drastic needed to be done in order to get in front again. He confronted the Greeves management with the idea of a new model, the existing machine being based on a design that was already eight years old. Management liked the idea, for they, too, could see that all was not well on the trials scene, and Don was eventually given the go-ahead to build a new Greeves super trials machine. With his design and development skills (learnt from Brian Stonebridge), the factory engineering facilities, and a clean sheet of paper, the new machine should have been a world beater. Alas, it was not to be.

Above **The 1968 version of the 24CS. The most noticeable change was to the shape (and material) of the fuel tank**

Right Motor Cycle'**s Mike Bashford tries a 1967 THS with Ceriani forks and TGS front guard. Bill Brooker looks on**

Below right **The 1967 THS Anglian, an attractive mud-plugger**

At the last minute, the whole project was called off after a boardroom battle, one director not being confident that there was a market for the machine. Dispirited, Don had had enough and finally resigned his post. After riding a private Bultaco for a spell, he was finally offered a position with Montesa to develop their new trials machine, and thus began a new phase in his eventful career.

For the 1967 season, Greeves fielded a new Anglian, designated the 24THS. Being basically similar to its predecessor, the machine was treated to a new livery, the cycle parts being stoved silver. In line with Amal production, the factory fitted a new 26 mm Concentric carburettor, which was an improvement over the original Monobloc. That year saw yet another type of front fork fitted to the trials model, for the Italian Ceriani fork was becoming popular. It was not a standard fit to the THS, only an optional extra at this stage. However, in 1968, with the introduction of the final Anglian (the 24 TJS), banana forks were finally abandoned in favour of the Italian product. The TJS continued

SHK 66D

Above left **Drive side of the 1967 THS, showing the engine, Amal Concentric carburettor and exhaust details to advantage**

Left **Alec Cameron with the 1968 newcomer, the 24TJ Wessex, a cheaper version of the Anglian**

Above right **December 1967, and Mike Jackson competes in the St Peter's Trophy Trial, in Hampshire, on the actual Earl's Court Wessex, but it had been heavily modified**

Above far right **Works rider Gordon Farley aboard his TJS during the Manx Two Day Trial in September 1968**

in production for the 1968 season, with manufacture coming to an end the following year, when 24TJS 297 was the last machine off the line.

The Anglian had to come to an end sooner or later, since the supply of 37A units was drying up, and a suitable substitute was not forthcoming. In any case, the design was becoming obsolete.

In their wisdom, Greeves had deemed that a utility model of the Anglian was not required during its early production, but during the 1968 season they saw fit to produce a cheaper version, aimed at the less-experienced rider. Entitled the 24TJ Wessex (note the deletion of the 'S' suffix to denote the utility variant), the machine was a poor man's Anglian and fulfilled the need for a down-market, everyman's trials iron. The specification included banana forks, steel fuel tank and an absolutely standard 37A motor, complete with cast-iron cylinder and Villiers S25 carburettor—which, incidentally, was the same as the standard 32A set-up. A further financial saving was made in the engine cradle, which did not feature the numerous lightening holes of the Anglian.

The Wessex was used with great success by many lesser-known riders during its brief appearance, teaching many up-and-coming riders the art of trials riding. For those who could not afford an Anglian, the Wessex was the ideal choice, for it handled in much the same way. All it lacked was the extra punch and lighter weight of its big brother.

Long-time scrambler and trials ace, Mike Jackson, then employed as the south and southwest area sales representative, used a Wessex to great effect, contesting time and observation trials during the winter of 1967–8. His machine started life as the actual 1967 Earls Court show model. Now the managing director of the Andover Norton Company, Mike won such events as the Yeovil, Bishops Waltham, Wells and Newbury, with second places at Baydon Hardley and Sherborne. He first used the Wessex, bearing his own personalized number plate, WOW 67, to win the St Peter's Trophy trial.

Mike's Wessex, originally weighing in at 225 lb, had been pared down to 204 lb by the use of a Challenger cylinder, alloy tank, fibreglass front guard and an alloy silencer. The silencer did not come from the factory, either. It was obtained from a rival source, none other than Sammy Miller's after-market spares empire.

The Anglian, together with the Wessex, finally ceased production during 1969, having been toppled from its position as the best trials machine available by the emergence of the Spanish Bultaco, and beaten into submission by the lack of a suitable power unit. A final and fitting tribute to the Anglian was paid by Billy Wilkinson, when he took top honours that year in the world's premier event, the Scottish Six Day Trial. Billy's win signalled the end of British machine supremacy in the trials game, the leader-board being dominated, from that year onwards, first by Spanish and then by Japanese machinery.

10 The Austrian connection

As has been recounted in the previous chapters, Greeves owed much of their reputation to an amazing array of successes on the dirt, not just with the glamorous motocross racers, but also with the much more composed, but nonetheless able, trials irons. Names such as Scottish, Anglian and Wessex conjure up memories of some truly legendary performances over a decade between the late 1950s and early 1960s. However, from the mid-1960s onwards, the Thundersley factory was not making the sort of headway in the 'feet up' game as it had done previously. The Armada had arrived; top trials riders were now using Spanish machines, with many of the former Greeves stars mounted on Bultaco and Montesa machinery.

By early 1969, things were looking ominous on all fronts, with the roadsters gone, ever increasing competition off road and, to cap it all, a decision to throw in the towel and discontinue the Silverstone and Oulton road racers. As if all this was not enough, another hammer blow had fallen—this was the untimely demise of the long-running, Wolverhampton-based Villiers engine company and its sale to Manganese Bronze in 1966. This company pursued a policy of not supplying rival manufacturers. Fortunately, as related in the previous chapter, the Metal Profile concern had obtained production rights for the 32/37A Villiers engine designs, allowing Greeves at least a breathing space during 1967 and 1968.

Although Greeves had a suitable engine available for its motocross machinery, this was not the position for a trials mount, and so came into being the 'Austrian Connection'—the Puch-engined Pathfinder project, very much the result of a hastily-arranged shotgun marriage of British and Austrian design principles. Although the Pathfinder did have some initial success in the hands of one or two factory-backed riders, in production form, it failed to provide much in the way of sorely-needed revenue to assist the company's dwindling resources.

The first prototype of the much-vaunted, new-era machine made its debut at the Greybeards Trial in August 1969, ridden by none other than Bert Greeves. This bike, like the later production examples, featured a 169 cc (62 × 56 mm) short-stroke, conventionally piston-ported unit of all-alloy construction, with a six-speed gearbox. An aluminium cylinder head was fitted with a decompressor valve. The crankshaft had two main bearings, one roller and one ball race. Needle-roller bearings were fitted to the conrod at both the big- and small-end.

Lubrication was by petroil at a ratio of 25:1. A high (11:1) compression ratio, combined with the short-stroke engine dimensions and a pair of flywheels which needed to be heavily weighted to provide any semblance of the plodding power delivery so vital for an effective trials mount, did not bode well for its ultimate, much needed (and prayed for!) success in the life-or-death fight against the hordes of Spanish 'strokers' at that time taking the trials world by storm.

There were also other reasons why, at least as regards private ownership, the new Greeves was not entirely suitable. One was its flywheel clutch and the fact that its abundance of shims, circlips and distance pieces made the engine a nightmare to work on, even if one had the large range of special tools needed by the privateer, often working in primitive workshop conditions.

The first prototype Pathfinder differed quite considerably from the later versions. The most evident differences were the Puch roadster (from which the competition engine was derived) brake hubs, one-piece, high-level exhaust system, a front mudguard which was bolted directly on to the base of the bottom fork yoke, a fibreglass fuel tank and strange, funnel-type air filter.

Coded M59, the Pathfinder was originally

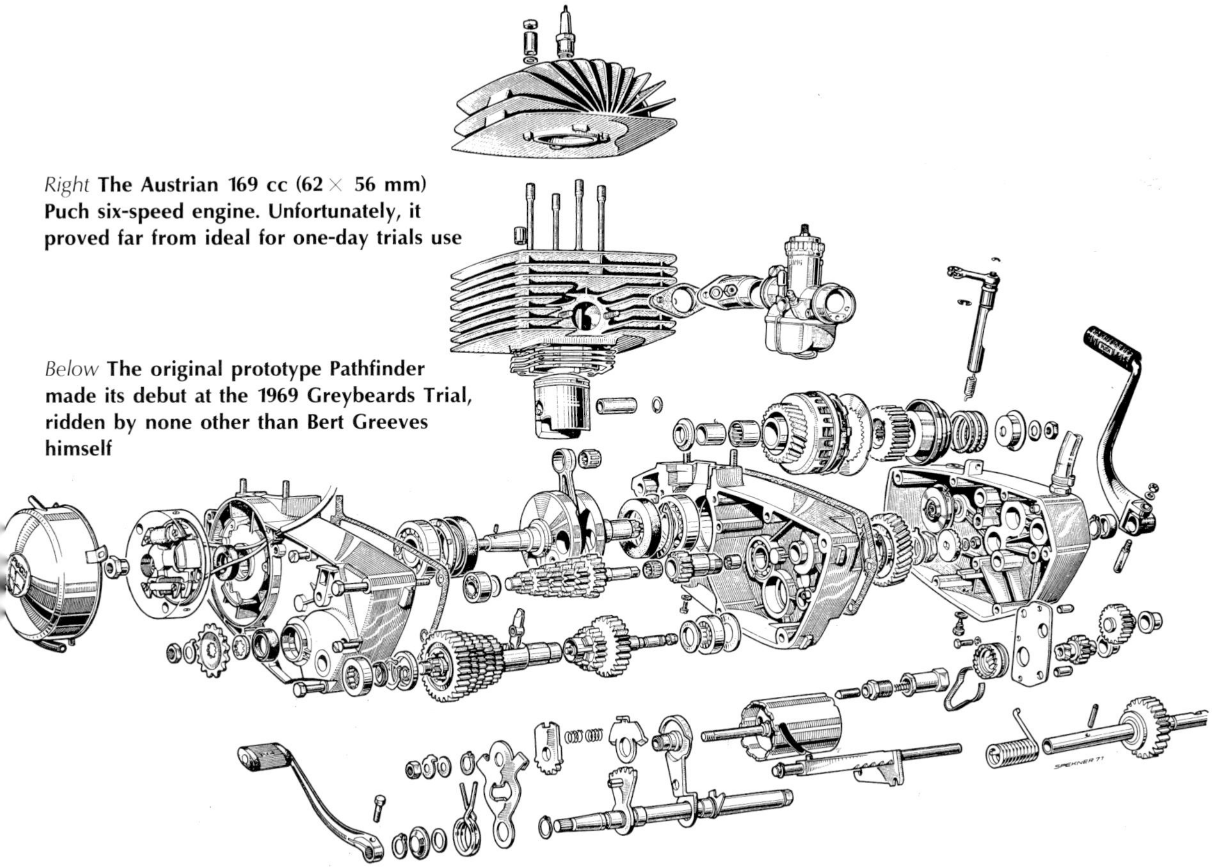

Right **The Austrian 169 cc (62 × 56 mm) Puch six-speed engine. Unfortunately, it proved far from ideal for one-day trials use**

Below **The original prototype Pathfinder made its debut at the 1969 Greybeards Trial, ridden by none other than Bert Greeves himself**

Above **Mick Wilkinson (not to be confused with Billy) also rode the Pathfinder. His best performance on the bike came when he won the Welsh Two Day Trial in June 1970**

Above left **Works rider Billy Wilkinson having his Pathfinder refuelled by Shell competition chief Len Ellis (centre), some time during early 1970**

Above right **The production M59 Pathfinder**

scheduled to enter production before the end of 1969, and to that effect, marketing director Derry Preston-Cobb wrote a letter, dated 11 December of that year, to Charles Deane, then the editor of *Motor Cycle Mechanics*. In this, Preston-Cobb included a list of amendments and alterations to the specification sent out a mere week previously. These included the engine details already mentioned.

When the detailed specification had been received, it had revealed that the frame was of all-welded, tubular construction, with duplex front down-tubes. The material used was Reynolds 531, suitably braced to produce a frame designed for the maximum strength and lightness. There were taper-roller bearings for both the steering head and swinging-arm pivot. The forks, like the prototype, were Italian Ceriani, with British Girling rear shock absorbers, but the brakes were now full-width, pressure-die-cast, alloy Grimeca assemblies—again, of Italian origin. These were laced to chrome-plated steel rims—21 in. front, and 18 in. rear, with 2.75 and 4.00 tyre sections respectively.

Both mudguards were still in alloy, but the front one was mounted much closer to the tyre. It had totally revamped brackets which were now attached to the fork legs. The unbraced handlebars were also in Reynolds 531 tubing and had the standard-issue, ball-ended alloy levers, as fitted to the earlier trials bikes. The fuel tank, with a capacity of $1\frac{1}{4}$ gallons, was in highly polished alloy. The seat was a small trials-pattern assembly with a fibreglass base.

Carburation was by a 27 mm German Bing with a central float, and the ignition by a 6-volt Bosch flywheel magneto. The exhaust system now sported a separate tail silencer—to quieten the prototype's noisy exhaust note. There was a folding kickstart lever on the offside, and the gear lever was mounted on the usual continental European nearside position. Transmission was taken care of by a set of helical primary-drive gears and a $\frac{1}{2} \times \frac{5}{16}$ in. Renold rear drive chain. Standard-gearing sprockets were 16-tooth at the gearbox

and 62-tooth at the rear wheel, but a selection of others was available.

In their publicity material, Greeves stated; '175 cc Pathfinder—The Trials Model to Challenge the World'. It is worth repeating in full what followed this heading which, in retrospect, can be said to have been more than a shade overstated: 'The combined engineering talents of Greeves—Great Britain and Steyr-Daimler-Puch—Austria bring you the Pathfinder, the trials model to challenge the world. The 175 cc (not quite correct!) Puch engine is a result of the pooling of knowledge from these two most enthusiastic factories intent on providing you, the trials rider, with a really potent unit with low maintenance costs. The six-speed gearbox allows selection of just the ratio for that 'nadgery' section or for a quick burst on the road—while frame-wise you benefit from all the Greeves know-how of quality, performance and reliability. We are therefore proud to present the new 175 cc Pathfinder. It is undoubtedly a new conception in trials models, offering the lightness and handling of an ultra lightweight with the power and performance of a two-fifty. It is certain that there will be a great future for the Pathfinder, both as a conventional trials bike, and for riding over all types of rough country!'

However, potential paying customers were not able to purchase the Pathfinder until the end of 1970, which certainly did not help the sales efforts. Well before this, at the beginning of that year, works-supported riders, Derek Adsett and Billy Wilkinson, had begun to make a limited impression on the trials scene, both at home and abroad, mounted on Pathfinders. The bike scored its first win in an international entry at Graz, near the Puch factory in Austria, when Yorkshireman Billy Wilkinson rode the prototype into equal first place with Scott Ellis on a 125 cc Puch Dalesman.

In mid-February the works pair competed in the international Lambrorell Trial in Belgium. Billy Wilkinson was the source of much attention, and the Belgians had their first opportunity of seeing the new Greeves in action. However, despite an early number, it was not Billy's day and the first half-dozen sections took 22 marks from him. Although he improved on the succeeding laps, he never overcame this deficit and finished in ninth position.

The other Pathfinder rider, Derek Adsett, had started the day needing to change defective suspension units, but following this, he made a sparkling start and was joint leader with Gordon Farley on a Montesa. On the second lap, however, Adsett slipped from form, but even so he eventually finished a creditable fifth place overall.

Sorry we've kept you waiting . . .

but it's all been worth while

Since its announcement considerable development has been carried out resulting in a really competitive model which will hold its own against its competitors. The 175cc 6-speed engine is the result of the amalgamation of GREEVES know-how and STEYR-DAIMLER-PUCH engineering ability—there is no lack of power. The jig-built frame has been specially produced for the PATHFINDER as have the new Greeves/Ceriani forks. GREEVES have combined all that is best in Europe and at only £259 in easy build form. Get in touch with your local Greeves dealer now.

Greeves GREAT BRITAIN

GREEVES MOTOR CYCLES, ARMSTRONG ROAD, BENFLEET, ESSEX, SS7 4PP.

Without doubt, it was later in June when the Pathfinder had its moment of glory, as the new ISDT British teamster, Mick Wilkinson, forced his Greeves to victory in the gruelling Welsh Two Day Trial. Despite a puncture and a prang with his Pathfinder, go-getter Wilkinson out-pointed first-day leader and AJS motocross star, Andy Robertson, on the second stage of the 290-mile marathon. Oddly enough, the British ISDT candidate had been deprived of a 500 Cheney-Triumph on the eve of the trial and only elected to ride the Greeves at the last moment!

When the production Pathfinder eventually went on sale, Greeves ran an advertisement saying, 'Sorry we've kept you waiting . . . but it's all been worthwhile.' Unfortunately, not enough paying customers thought so, and the £259 machine (in kit form to save tax) just did not sell in sufficient quantities. Many were put off because it was not a full 250—although, at 190 lb, it almost weighed as much—some did not like its peaky engine characteristics, and yet others did not like it having a 'foreign' engine. Greeves just could not win!

In 1971 an enduro version appeared. This was meant for the American market, with dualseat, modified mudguards, a chainguard and lighting equipment.

July 1971 saw a test comparison of the trials version by *Motor Cycle Mechanics*. It was pitted against a 250 Montesa Cota, Triumph 250 Trailblazer and a Suzuki TC120 Trail Cat, on a route which took the riders along the Ridgeway, starting near Reading and working their way down through Wiltshire to Salisbury Plain. The Pathfinder came out well—as perhaps it should have done when compared to machinery like the far-less-specialized Triumph and Suzuki machines. Even so, comments like, 'This gives a formidable combination, and the result is one of the best machines I've ever ridden', and, 'No one who rode it was willing to accept that the engine was only 175 cc', meant that the testers had been impressed.

The only faults which *MCM* could find were 'a notchy gear change between fourth and fifth and a decompressor which isn't necessary and gets clogged up with mud very easily, jamming the mechanism if it is used.'

For 1972 the specification was changed by fitting

Above left **Although widely advertised, the new-era Greeves trials mount failed to attract many buyers, even though the factory proclaimed that it could hold its own against any competition**

Above right **The enduro version of the Pathfinder appeared in 1971**

Right **The Pathfinder tested by** *Motorcycle Mechanics* **in their July 1971 issue**

a sump rock guard as standard, modifying the air filter system, replacing the Italian Cerianis with British Metal Profile 600 Series telescopic front forks, and providing lighting coils with a 17-watt output.

Although the Pathfinder was still listed as 1973 dawned, its future, together with that of Greeves as a serious motorcycle manufacturer, was in some doubt. This was because all motorcycle production at Thundersley—including the Pathfinder—had come to a halt during late 1972. The Austro-British marriage, which had begun with such high hopes four short years before, was over. The last chapter in the Greeves saga was about to begin.

11 The ultimate dirt racers

The misfortunes of the disastrous 1963 season were short lived, as the new front runner of the motocross stable, the 24MX1 Challenger, was unveiled during the closed season. This entirely new concept in motocross machinery was produced from Bert Greeves' drawing board, and can be attributed to a purely chance remark by Brian Woolley, who was employed as a freelance engine development engineer. Brian had realized the extent by which the original Villiers motor was stripped and parts discarded, in favour of the more robust or powerful items, which were required to ensure a competitive motor.

In order to be in the forefront of competition, the earlier MDS motor was stripped and then rebuilt using an Alpha crankshaft, Hepolite piston, Greeves cylinder and a Monobloc carburettor, which resulted in many unwanted and unsaleable parts being held by the factory, for Villiers would only supply complete motors. At one time, Greeves did offer the redundant iron cylinders to dealers at the knock-down price of £1.50 each, to ease the stock problem and also to recoup some revenue. It was rumoured that the Dot factory had actually managed to sell some of their redundant cylinders back to the Villiers factory, a magnificent coup indeed.

Greeves had the proven design ability and the manufacturing capability to produce the components required, completely removing the need for any further Villiers participation in the motocross programme. In view of the unwillingness of the Villiers concern to supply part-built motors and, indeed, the unsteadiness of the whole Villiers empire during these very uncertain times, the unprecedented step was taken for Greeves to go it alone.

The Challenger was billed as being fitted with the 'all new' Greeves engine, but this was not strictly true, for the crankshaft was made by Alpha, the gearbox and clutch supplied by Albion, and the magneto (a non-flywheel-effect type) by the Swedish firm Stefa. A more fitting description would have been, a new motor using no Villiers components, as the crankcase and primary-drive cases were now produced within the Greeves factory.

The heart of the new engine was a redesigned crankshaft, supplied by Alpha Bearings, which utilized a double-row, $\frac{3}{8} \times \frac{3}{16}$ in. caged bearing running directly on the hardened timing-side drive shaft. The drive side consisted of a $\frac{9}{16} \times \frac{3}{16}$ in. bearing, also running on the hardened drive shaft, backed up by a normal ball bearing outboard of it. Supported in this manner, the crankshaft assembly was stronger than the original Villiers system and, housed in a new, heavily-webbed crankcase of Greeves design and manufacture, ensured a bottom end that was nearly bulletproof.

The original square, alloy cylinder now gave way to another completely redesigned unit with 50 per cent greater fin area, but which only weighed some 25 per cent more. The cylinder fins ran uninterrupted from exhaust port to inlet port, taking on a trapezoidal shape instead of the more usual square profile. To complement the new cylinder, Greeves designed a new cylinder head, which looked lopsided, as the vertical finning was not symmetrical. Because the engine did not sit centrally behind the frame down-member, the fins were offset to draw cooling air in equal amounts from both sides of the frame and direct it on to the plug.

The carburettor looked as if the inlet tract had been shortened, there being no external stub, but the tract was of much the same length as the MDS—it just appeared that way because of the larger cylinder fins. To minimize heat transference to the carburettor, it was mounted on a $\frac{3}{4}$ in. insulating spacer and protected by an aluminium heat-deflector plate.

The primary-drive cases, of Greeves manufac-

Greeves
GREAT BRITAIN

Above **Factory brochure detailing the 24MX1 Challenger**

Right **A Challenger on the Dutch importer's stand at the Amsterdam show in 1964**

Left **Close-up of the MX1 motor, showing the original gearbox shape**

Right **Bickers, on his works Challenger, leads Joel Robert (CZ) during the 250 British Grand Prix on 4 July 1964**

ture and housing the single-row chain and Albion clutch, were held together by an aluminium band, in much the same way as the early Matchless type—and were just as oil tight! A compact magneto, of only $3\frac{5}{8}$ in. diameter, supplied the low-tension current to a high-tension coil, which was sited out of harm's way under the fuel tank.

The cycle parts of the new Challenger did not differ radically from those of the MDS, from which it was developed. The cosmetic appearance was altered with the use of a pliable plastic front mudguard and a new fibreglass fuel tank, both finished in white. Due to the incompatibility of plastic and dope fuel, the tank carried a specific warning to remind the unwary that alcohol fuels eat fibreglass resin.

As the new engine and Albion gearbox assembly was designed and built as a stressed member, the engine-cradle plates, needed for the Villiers unit, disappeared. Two tubular stays were fitted under the engine unit, not for strength, but to act as rock guards and provide a convenient point for attaching the footrests.

The Challenger did not suit everyone's style of riding; journalist Frank Melling confessed to not being able to manage more than a couple of laps without falling off, due to the machine's unpredictability. This alleged problem did not affect the likes of Dave Bickers, whose machine was prepared by the works mechanics. Frank did offer a valid explanation of the handling problems he remembered so vividly; his machine was never set up correctly and, for this reason, he did not ride hard enough to make the bike steer properly. The Challenger, being a pure racing machine, needed to be treated in the correct manner to obtain the desired results—it was not for the faint hearted.

Many journalists tried the Challenger, and none was more surprised by its handling qualities than Peter Frazer, off-road columnist with *Motor Cycle*, whose report appeared in the 29 October 1964 edition. Peter was given the dual task of testing the new Greeves and the Farnham club's new course, at Manor Farm, Dockenfield, at the same time. After testing the course, he decided that to gain a fair comparison of the Challenger, it would be entered in the inaugural meeting. Peter survived the heats and gained eleventh place in the final, an inspiring ride, considering his eight-year lay-off from competitive scrambling and the fact that he was mounted on a new machine for the first time.

Dave Bickers, supported by Alan Clough, John Griffiths and Freddie Mayes, set about putting the Greeves name back on the leader-board and contested as many events as humanly possible, including the BBC Grandstand series. Many wins were notched up during the hectic season, with Bickers winning the ACU Motocross Star for the sixth time.

Arguments had raged for some time as to which

Bickers leading a TV scrambles event

Above **By the end of 1964 Greeves were able to advertise that Challengers had won all the British, trade-supported, lightweight scrambles that year**

Above right **Road racer John Cooper tries an MX2 for size**

Right **An MX2 showing the kidney-shaped gearbox**

were the best front forks to use on a scrambles machine. The Greeves leading-link type, which had served the factory well, were still regarded by many as being the best available, but times were changing, with many top riders switching to telescopic forks. Even Dave Bickers tried a set of Bultaco origin to good advantage on his Challenger; they fitted and performed well. One surprising aspect was that nothing was said at the factory about the fitting of a foreign fork to a Greeves, for this was the period when riders could modify their machines if they wanted to (but only if they got the desired result!).

The first Challenger, bearing the frame number 24MX1–101 has reappeared. This machine was first raced by Dave Bickers on 26 April 1964, at Glastonbury in the National Wessex Scramble. It was not Bickers' usual mount, for he used numbers 103 and 105 on a regular basis that year. 101 was passed on to Alan Clough, who then passed it on to Bryan Goss, and he campaigned it for the rest of the season. This interesting and historic machine was purchased by GRA member, Charlie Pattison, in 1983, as an all-too-familiar basket case. Charlie has restored it to its former glory and now uses it vigorously in pre-'65 scrambles events.

The Challenger was not without some initial teething problems, and the biggest criticisms to be levelled against it concerned the gear-selection difficulties with the new Albion box, and the inability of the primary chain to transmit power without stretching. The gearbox had not been designed for scrambling, being more suited to road machines, and did not take kindly to being stamped into gear, resulting in a spate of gear-selector failures. This problem was overcome by the use of an improved selector mechanism, which was housed in a new gearbox featuring a kidney-shaped end cover.

At about the same time, the primary-drive chain was changed to the duplex type, and later the clutch was fitted with shock-absorbing rubbers, which increased the chain life dramatically. Primary-drive chain stretch was always a problem on the works machines prior to the

change to duplex and necessitated frequent adjustments. To adjust the chain tension, spacers were fitted to, or removed from, the gearbox mounting studs at the crankcase interface. This operation required engine removal and gearbox extraction, a practice not to be recommended in the pits during the heat of battle. To reduce the time taken for making adjustments, the factory mechanics made up horseshoe-shaped shims, which could be inserted with the aid of a tyre lever after the gearbox mountings were slackened.

For the 1965 season, Greeves introduced the 24MX2, which incorporated the gearbox and primary-drive modifications, together with a redesigned primary-chain case featuring a three-bolt fixing in place of the aluminium band. Other features of the MX2 included a slightly longer and lower fuel tank, and a mid-green finish for the cycle parts.

The hottest news of the 1965 season was the existence of a 360 Challenger, which Greeves intended to debut at the Cotswold Scramble in June, but could not make the deadline due to the shortage of the correct Hepolite piston. The new motor, based on the 250, had a cylinder with an

80 mm bore, but instead of using sleeve bolts, which would have protruded into the oversize bore, a new system of cylinder and head attachment was devised. The cylinder was bolted directly to a redesigned crankcase, with the head being held to the cylinder by a ring of six studs. Because of the enormous size of a single exhaust port and the distortion problems it would have produced, Greeves split the port into two and used two separate exhaust pipes linked to a common expansion chamber, with exit again low on the right-hand side of the machine.

The need to build a 360 cc engine was brought about by an edict from the FIM, who were attempting to outlaw overbored 250 machines from competing in the world 500 cc championship. This rule, not necessarily aimed at the Greeves factory, whose 252 cc Challengers were posing a threat, effectively barred machines of under 351 cc from entering 500 cc events.

Again on the international front, Nick Nicholson, the American west coast Greeves distributor, paid a visit to the factory while over for the Isle of Man ISDT, held in the autumn of 1965. His visit was a great boost to the factory, as during his stay he placed a $1,000,000 order for Greeves machines. Some three or four years before this massive order, John Taylor (later to become the US Bultaco and Ossa importer—and famous for the double Ossa-engined Yankee) enquired into the possibility of importing Greeves competition machines into the States. Frank Connor, who worked for John, reported that the request was treated with little sympathy, the excuse being that 'the factory could not tool up to meet the extra demand'! This refusal gave John the distinct impression that Bert Greeves was treating motorcycle production as a hobby rather than a commercial enterprise.

Hobby or not, by 1965 a high proportion of the factory's output was going to North America, the sales being sufficient for the Nicholson empire to specify what they wanted to suit the needs of the Stateside rider.

The Greeves scrambler was liked by the American enduro rider, since it offered a very stable ride over desert terrain. Equipped with a 3.50 × 19 in. front tyre to cope with the sandy conditions, and a lower all-up weight than the big four-strokes, the Greeves made long-distance desert races less of a strain on the rider. Events of this type—the Big Bear and the Baja being the most popular—were dominated by 500 and 650 cc four-strokes, until the rise in popularity of the Greeves scrambler. Suitably modified to suit the conditions, the Greeves certainly made its mark in the hands of riders like Gary Conrad and Preston Petty. So rapid was its rise to fame and dominance over the enduro scene that one American magazine paid the Greeves a supreme compliment by calling it 'the machine that revolutionized desert warfare.'

Back in Europe, Dave Bickers, backed up by John Griffiths, tackled the season's events. The going was not so easy this time, as other factories had used the Greeves absence from international competition to improve their products which, in some cases, turned out to be superior. Bickers, riding a works MX2, now fitted with banana forks, could only manage third place overall in the World Championship, behind CZ riders, Victor Arbekov and Joel Robert, but did manage to win the British round for the fifth time. Bickers' efforts at home, between the World Championship events, earned him the ACU Motocross Star for the seventh time.

After many months of testing, a new Challenger, the MX3, was introduced to the public. This new machine displayed a radical departure from the traditional engineering everyone accepted as being purely Greeves, for the MX3 was fitted with a set of banana forks, first used by Bickers during the previous season.

Traditionalists received a second body blow when it was announced that the MX3 could be supplied with a set of Italian Ceriani telescopic forks as an option. The Ceriani forks had the same length of travel as the banana forks (about 6 in.), were less robust and much more expensive, but they were becoming fashionable, a desirable factor in the eyes of certain riders. The MX3 retained the plastic mudguard, albeit slightly modified to fit the banana fork, but had an alloy blade mounted to a tubular stay when fitted with the telescopic forks.

Since the introduction of the Challenger as the number-one motocrosser, the factory had maintained production of the Villiers-engined MDS, in an effort to cater for the clubman on a limited budget. The MDS was still competitive at club level, but with the source of engine units at an end, and the emphasis being placed on national-level competition, the most beloved of all Greeves scramblers was finally phased out with the introduction of the MX3 Challenger.

Participation in international motocross once again ceased, for Dave Bickers had left the factory, in January 1966, to ride for CZ, which left Greeves with no riders of the necessary experience to challenge the top European contenders.

On the home front, the flag was kept flying by Freddie Mayes and Alan Clough, with Freddie taking the British Championship, relegating Dave Bickers to second place. This win gave Greeves its sixth consecutive championship, with the score standing at Bickers five, Mayes one.

The eagerly-awaited 360 cc Challenger, which Bickers had tested some two years previously, finally came into production for the 1967 season. The big Challenger used a proven version of the original 360 engine, mounted in a new frame that had been designed specifically for the job. The frame was lengthened by nearly 2 in., in an effort to improve high-speed handling, and now had a top rail which was split into two loops curving down to the rear-fork pivots and increasing the frame's stiffness. The front forks were Greeves banana type, but with the option of Ceriani telescopic forks if required.

To complement the 360, Greeves had designed and manufactured a completely new, conical wheel hub in cast alloy. The hub featured 6 in. brakes and was lighter than the full-width hub which it replaced. The rear hub now had a brake drum with a cast-in sprocket flange on the left, which simplified the brake operating linkage. The brake operating cable and cross-over shaft system of the MX3, being both complicated and heavy, was at last dropped in favour of a single rod.

In line with the new 360 came a redesigned 250—the 24MX5. As a logical follow-on from the MX3, the new 250 used the same cycle parts, but its main frame was 2 in. longer, again to improve handling. The biggest surprise was the change made to the bore and stroke of the new motor, the bore going up to 70 mm and the stroke reducing to 64 mm, making it truly oversquare. With the increase in bore size, no room was available for the usual sleeve nuts, which sandwiched the cylinder between the head and crankcases. Now the cylinder was bolted directly to the cases, and the head to the cylinder, as per the 360 system.

Yet another gearbox was used on the MX5, the third since Challenger production began, and was the best so far. However, even this one came in for its fair share of modifications, there being two versions of the end cover and selector return springs. To fit the lengthened frames of the two newly-introduced machines, Greeves manufactured another fuel tank in fibreglass, which was

American-specification 1967 24MXE smooth-track model—more commonly known as the TT Challenger

finished in dark green to contrast with the silver frame of the 360, and in a bluish-green to complement the dark green finish of the 250.

The 360 received a favourable write up in *Motor Cycle Illustrated*, of February 1967, when tested by self-confessed four-stroke man, Jeff Smith. In his blunt way, Smith stated that he was no two-stroke lover, considering them noisy and smelly. His biggest hate was having to sit behind a bunch of 'strokers' in the paddock, his ear drums being rattled, and his lungs filled with exhaust smoke. The four-stroke bias of the tester disappeared as the session continued, and Smith found that he could come to grips with the different power

Left **First 360 motor, with twin-port exhaust and Amal Concentric carburettor**

Right **Brian Wade leaping his works Ceriani-forked MX5**

Below **Wade goes ploughing with his 360**

characteristics of the Greeves. He praised the flexibility of the engine, and the superb handling qualities, but did not like the stiff clutch action and dispensed with it after starting. His dislike of the two-stroke was not quite so strong when the 360 was finally, and reluctantly, handed back to the waiting factory staff.

Another avid four-stroke fan to change his tune was Eric Cheney, the well-known frame maker. Having previously used four-stroke power units, Cheney turned to a 250 Challenger engine to power one of his new creations. Being somewhat out of the ordinary, the fuel tank of the device was placed under the seat, while the expansion chamber occupied the space under the dummy fuel tank. The fragile build of the Albion gearbox, the Achilles' heel of the Greeves design, had always received its fair share of abuse but, unfortunately, Challenger riders were stuck with it. Not so with the Cheney design, for a complete BSA Victor gearbox was grafted on to the rear of the Greeves unit.

The Cheney/Greeves design, commissioned by the Thundersley factory, was first tried by Bryan Goss at the Tweseldown meeting in December 1966, but from then on faded from view. The design was not scrapped, however, for it reappeared in a more conventional guise, early in 1969, as a frame kit to house a 250, 360 or 380 Greeves engine and gearbox unit.

The Challenger motor not only received fame on the motocross and road-race circuits, but also found its way into other branches of motorcycle sport, namely grass track and speedway. Both specialist followings were traditionally strongholds of the four-stroke single thumper, but with modification to the power-delivery characteristics, a two-stroke could be competitive. To prove this point, Alf Hagon constructed and offered for sale a 250 grasser, using the well-proven Hagon frame fitted with a short-stroke 250 Greeves engine.

On the speedway side, a 360 Challenger motor was hitched to a single-speed countershaft and installed in a Don Smith speedway frame. The 165 lb machine was tested by World Championship runner-up, Bengt Jansson, at the Hackney Wick Stadium in 1968. He considered it to be underpowered by speedway standards. Undaunted, Smith changed the cylinder for an overbored 83 mm (390 cc) item and tuned the engine for methanol fuel in an effort to extract more power—even the use of a Wal Phillips fuel injector was tried. The machine was a fearsome beast to ride once it was on song, but lacked the instant getaway punch from the gate. It was for this reason that the project was shelved, but the motor still lives today, languishing in the Smith garden shed, waiting for another opportunity to put it into use.

The factory policy of staying at home was again vindicated when the major emphasis was placed on the BBC Television Grandstand scrambling series, using Brian Wade and Arthur Browning as front runners. The man everyone was after that season, CZ-mounted Dave Bickers, still commanded a huge following, but now he was being harried by the Greeves duo, who managed a few decisive wins during the season. One such win occurred when Browning took the January 1967 round of the BBC Grandstand 750 series, the 360 Greeves rider beating the 360 CZ-mounted Bickers to the line. In the following month, Brian Wade won the 250 final at Ashover, Derbyshire, despite his clutch lever having fallen off.

The 360 Challenger continued in production for the 1968 season, backed up by another version of the 250, this time designated the 24MX4, which now used the frame and cycle parts of its big brother, the 36MX4. The new 250 never received much acclaim, for during its brief, one-season appearance, it was overshadowed by the news of a new generation of Greeves motocrosser—the era of the Griffon was about to commence.

Hectic action at the BBC Grandstand Trophy Scramble, Leighton, Somerset, on 5 March 1966. Bickers (1), now with CZ, and Chris Horsfield (6) lead Greeves riders Bryan Goss (2), Brian Wade (27) and Alan Clough (20)

The new machines were given their first airings at Newbury in mid-May 1968, piloted by Arthur Browning and Vic Allan. First called the 'tubular' Greeves by the motorcycling press, for a name had yet to be chosen, the machine did indeed have an all-tube frame, with a large-diameter, single down-tube replacing the traditional alloy beam. The down-tube swept under the motor to join two smaller rails, which continued upwards to join the top tube under the fuel tank. The swinging arm was attached to the frame rails at two pivot points, instead of the more usual, long pivot bolt.

The new design owed a lot to market research and pure design wizardry, for the sales teams had detected a reluctance to depend on 'traditional'

methods—the public wanted to see a technological advance—and the frame showed that the factory was not standing still. Being a continuous loop, the Griffon frame provided a secure mounting for the engine unit and overcame a problem which was beginning to be noticed on the Challengers. When the Challenger frame was stretched, the correspondingly lengthened front engine plates increased the loading on the alloy frame beam's mounting points, causing some fretting and elongation of the bolt holes. The expertise put into the tubular frame design was instantly accepted by the sporting fraternity of the day, for the factory had to march with the times to remain competitive. But the traditionalists shook their heads in disbelief, not wishing to be assured of the advantages that such a frame would offer; 'It doesn't look like the real thing,' they cried.

Real thing or not, the Griffon frame was *stronger* than the alloy-beam type. The cast-alloy section of the frame had outlived its usefulness, the original reason for its use being the inferior quality of the steel tube that had been available some 14 years previously. With the availability of the much superior—and lighter—Reynolds 531 tubing, used by Greeves for some time, and the advances in frame-building technology, the reversion to an all-steel frame now became a feasible proposition. To illustrate the thought which went into the frame's manufacture, the rear frame rails did not meet the top tube at the same point, being out of step by nearly 2 in. to spread the loading and prevent any localized brittling due to the heat of welding.

The engine, basically the same design as the MX4 range, now featured an overbored cylinder (82 mm) to bring the open-class Griffon up to 380 cc, the 250 remaining as before. By far the best feature of the new range was the use of an all-Greeves gearbox and clutch assembly. The factory had suffered enough jibes at the Albion gearbox, and decided to manufacture their own in an effort to increase reliability and to reduce their reliance on outside suppliers. Capable of handling the 39 bhp pumped out by the 380, the new gearbox was treated to a Greeves-designed and manufactured, all-metal clutch, which incorporated half-round driving keys, instead of the more-usual square keys. This method of power transmission was chosen to prevent the steel plates from scoring the alloy clutch drum. Together, the new clutch and gearbox saved nearly 9 lb over the Albion set-up.

Although not due for launch until the 1969 season, works Griffons were in evidence as early as May of the previous year, with Bryan Wade and Arthur Browning putting in 150 non-stop laps of Hawkstone Park to prove the new models. With an eye on export sales, Bert Greeves took one of the machines to the United States for his distributor, Nick Nicholson, to evaluate its suitability for the American market.

Once the formula had been perfected, the Griffon was put into production and, as a publicity

Above **The MX4**

Left **Dutchman Frits Selling giving the MX4 its first victory in the Netherlands during early 1968**

Above right **The 246 cc Griffon model 56**

Right **The 380 cc engine and gearbox of the Griffon**

Left **Bryan Wade at Westlake Village, California, in December 1968, during his American tour. The bike is a 380 Griffon**

Below **Dave Palmer, manufacturer of Palmer exhaust systems, with a Griffon-powered 250 grass-track racer in a Hagon chassis**

exercise to demonstrate endurance and reliability, two 380 Griffons were given a 100-mile track test at the local Wakes Colne circuit in February 1969. Each machine covered 133 trouble-free laps under snowy and icy conditions, piloted by six works riders: Arthur Browning, Vic Allen, Dick Clayton, Bryan Wade, Malcolm Rathmell and Richard Hughes. They took it in turn to gallop the Griffons around the $\frac{3}{4}$-mile circuit, in an effort to prove just how good the machines were under the atrocious conditions. The factory also took along a spare machine, not as a back-up to the marathon pair, but as a test vehicle to be tried by the eager journalists who had been invited to the launch.

Mike Bashford, of *Motor Cycle*, was very impressed by the machine's handling and its ability to traverse the ice-bound course thanks to its very wide spread of torque. Tractability was so good that he found it possible to pull third gear all round the circuit, accelerating strongly from tick-over with no hesitation in pick-up. He was so pleased that his report, of 25 February 1969, read: 'I'm convinced that the open class (380) Griffon is the most powerful, most handleable scrambler ever launched by the Thundersley factory.' However, one criticism raised by Bashford was the length of the gear lever, but an assurance by the factory that a shorter version would be fitted smoothed things over.

Richard Hughes was later the subject of much controversy, which attracted national press and television coverage. This centred around a dispute which involved Hughes, the Greeves factory and his parents. The latter would not sign his ACU licence over an issue concerning a girlfriend. Hughes, being under 18 years old, was therefore unable to race. The entire affair succeeded in creating more publicity for the Thundersley company than the new model!

The Griffon went into full production for the 1969 season, with nearly 80 per cent destined for the USA. Machines on sale in Britain were offered in kit form to exploit a loophole in the tax regulations prevailing at the time. These stated that a motorcycle, or motor car, supplied uncompleted, would be exempt from purchase tax, providing a saving of 10 per cent. Greeves, and many other manufacturers within the motor industry, turned this ruling to their advantage by supplying complete rolling chassis and engine units separately. The thought of saving £40 for a couple of hours' spanner work persuaded many enthusiasts to buy their new Griffon in this manner. Needless to say, this loophole has since been closed.

Vic Allen and Bryan Wade continued to show the opposition just what a well-set-up Griffon could achieve, by contesting the TV Grandstand series during the 1969 season. In the following year, Vic, who had little experience of continental motocross meetings, took top honours at the St Anthonis event, held in Holland in early March 1970. This event, the traditional start to the international year, was one of the most important of the season's openers and, indeed, an eye opener for the crowd. Having raced without success on the circuit once before, Vic became the first British rider on a British machine to win the event in six years. Fresh from his Dutch victory, Vic was in action again on the following day, this time at the TV Grandstand fifth-round meeting, held at Frome in Somerset. Backed up by Arthur Browning and Bryan Wade, he took the 250 and 750 Grandstand races, as well as the 750 invitation.

Sales of the Griffon continued in 1970, but results achieved by the non-factory riders began to dwindle, since the Greeves was becoming out-classed and over-priced when compared to the new oriental machines that were emerging. To stop any further decline, the factory announced a cut-back in competition support early in 1971 but, later in the year, introduced a new and even more powerful Griffon with which to fight back.

The work of Dr Gordon Blair of Queen's University, Belfast, the new 380QUB Griffon was quoted as giving 44 bhp at 6500 rpm. Dr Blair and his research team had developed the existing 380 motor, with the aid of the university's computer, to give a flatter power curve with a higher peak. The motor now sported revised internal porting and a single, external exhaust port. A Motoplat transistorized ignition system, mounted on a stiffer crankshaft, supplied the sparks.

Iberian influence on the new machine was high, not only in the ignition system, but also in the Amal carburettor and the Telesco forks, both of which were of Spanish manufacture. The forks were the strongest and most functional versions available at the time, and were 2 lb lighter than the previously-used Cerianis. The appearance of the machine was striking, the silver and red of the old Griffon having given way to a black frame with Golden Glow tank and side panels.

The impact made by the QUB Griffon was short lived, as the factory went into a period of withdrawal. By the end of 1972 all motorcycle manufacture had ceased. Motocross support was seriously curtailed, with only Dick Clayton turning out to keep the flag flying.

Vic Allan was given an opportunity to test ride the machine before production of the QUB ceased. By then an ex-factory rider and columnist with *Motor Cycle*, Vic had never been astride the QUB before, ending his factory days on the standard 380 Griffon. The first thing he noticed about the QUB was the extra power on tap, controllable power, pulling from well down the rev range, with a good power band for its size. Cornering was considered to be excellent, the rear wheel being able to be controlled in a slide, without the back-end bounce which marred the earlier Griffons. The change to Telesco forks was not liked, however, for not only was their action hard, but the fork had a tendency to flop from side to side when airborne—a retrograde step, in view of the extra expense, thought Vic.

Although bike production had ceased, the factory was not standing still, and development work continued. Some 13 years before, the factory had used 197 cc mounts to contest 250 events, giving away nearly 50 cc to their competitors. This situation had been rectified by the development of an in-house 250 conversion, thus taking full advantage of the 250 rules. Ideas were now afoot to do the same with the 500 class. Why use a 380 in the senior class, when a full 500 would develop more power and exploit the rules to the full? In order to achieve this, the factory built and used an experimental 498 cc machine, giving it a public debut at the Gloucester Grand National, held at the end of August 1971.

The 498 engine was a radical departure from the normal Griffon layout, being 91 × 76 mm. As the motor churned out more power than the 380, it was deemed advisable to use a gear-driven primary drive, instead of a duplex chain. Therefore, the motor rotated *backwards*. Using a transistorized ignition system and housed in a Griffon frame, the engine performed well, but development did not continue, as other ideas took priority.

Experiments had taken place on reed-valve induction, at first using a conversion made by Bernard Hargreaves, a reed-valve specialist from Lancashire. As results were promising, the factory went ahead and produced a reed-valve 250, which Dick Clayton first used in the British Championship round at Southend in June 1972. With spring-steel reeds in the manifold of a 32 mm Amal Concentric carburettor, and a four-transfer-port cylinder, the machine showed potential, but Dick just missed out on the points. Further development was carried out on the engine, together with frame alterations, which transformed the machine into a real flyer.

Delighted at the way the 250 was showing promise, the factory then began working flat out to provide Dick with a 380 reed-valve version. Alas, the debut could not be met, as Dick was admitted to hospital with an eye injury. Development continued once his eye had healed, but the reed-valve Greeves did not make the expected splash.

During 1974, the Ministry of Defence invited a number of motorcycle manufacturers to tender for the supply of a dual-purpose motorcycle to replace their ageing BSA B40. Greeves was one of those companies. They had long-standing connections with, and many friends among, the Army competition riders, and it was from this quarter that the suggestion came for a modified Griffon.

The modifications for the military Griffon were fairly extensive, especially to the bottom half of the motor, which was of unit-construction design with a geared primary drive. The cylinder and porting were left as standard, but although this provided shattering performance, it also made the machine totally unsuitable for the Army's needs. Attempts to civilize the machine by reducing the compression ratio failed completely to persuade the MoD to place a contract, and eventually the Canadian Can Am concern won the business.

Although tooling for production had been set up, only two or three machines were made, together with a quantity of spares. Only one machine is known to survive today, being in the capable hands of a respected GRA member.

The factory did manage to establish one contract with the Army, not to replace the entire B40 fleet, as they would have liked, but to supply the Royal Artillery display team with machines. The Greeves were ideal mounts for the type of work the RA had in mind, but when entered in the 1975 International Six Day Trial by a team of Army riders, they displayed many shortcomings (see Chapter 6), all the machines failing dismally.

Greeves took the opportunity to enter the market yet again with a civilian version of the RA Griffon. Aimed at the club rider who was not going to set the world alight, it represented an inexpensive and reliable mount with excellent low-cost spares service, compared to the high-powered, high-cost foreign machines ruling the motocross scene in 1975. After more than a two-year absence from the showroom, Greeves now offered a 250 and a QUB380, which were virtually the same as the last motocrossers on sale in 1972. Production was slow, as were sales, for the public did not want a 1972 machine at 1975 prices, only to be blown away by one of the new breed of European or oriental 'buzz bombs'!

The decline of this once highly-respected motocross machine manufacturer was swift. In withdrawing from European events and slowing development in order to cater for home events only, they lost valuable experience on the continental fields. This experience, obtained by fighting it out with some of the top factories, was never to be regained, and Greeves slipped further and further down the league table. Other countries, notably Japan, were pouring vast fortunes into the development of world-beating motocross machines and gaining results.

The financial side of international competition dictated the factory's withdrawal from it, they could not justify the expense of fielding a full international team to tackle the World Championship series. Once into the downward financial spiral, it was very hard to reverse the trend, the funds available to this comparatively small factory being strictly limited.

As related in Chapter 12, the end of motorcycle production came quickly, the last machine to emerge being the 380QUB Mk II, in 1977. Originally intended for a run of 250 machines, production came to a halt the following year after only 40 had been made. The Mk II QUB was merely an update of the original QUB, but it featured 'laid down' rear suspension units, as used by other fashionable manufacturers of the day. This idea was first tried by Dave Bickers during the mid-1960s, when he used a series of damper-unit top mounting holes, much in the same way as Velocette used a slot, to load up the rear suspension. The general public did not take to the Mk II QUB, and production ceased in 1978 (could this have been due, in part, to the use of a Japanese Mikuni carburettor?).

It is indeed sad to recall that the situation had been reversed two decades previously. Then, Greeves had seen the beginning of the build-up to near total competitions success, now the wheel of fortune had turned full circle.

Greeves motocross machines were beginning to be pensioned off at an alarming rate, as the orientals swept all before them. Many machines were destined to end their days down on the farm, or to be decimated at the hands of the inexperienced. Some were saved and restored, and these can now be seen performing at the many pre-'65 events (and events which cater for bikes from the pre-'70 era), lovingly restored and used in the correct manner.

A quartet of Barbour-suited Greeves gentlemen. Left to right: John Gazeby, Alec Wright, Don Smith and Dave Bickers. The outfit is Alec's 380 motocross chariot, and the location, Linford Park

12 Final days

GREEVES

In many ways, the decline of the Greeves marque had begun at the end of 1968. Not only had the roadsters and road racers been discontinued but, perhaps even more serious, with no more Villiers engines available, the classic Anglian trials bike was axed, too. This left only the Griffon motocrosser—introduced that year in two engine sizes—and, as described in Chapter 10, the ill-fated tie-up with the Austrian Puch concern, involving the use of its 169 cc, six-speed engine in a brand-new trials model, the Pathfinder.

Although the Griffon could be adjudged reasonably successful (although never gaining the aura of the earlier dirt racers), the Pathfinder never achieved any lasting acceptance in a market that was steadily being swamped, first by the Spanish and then the Japanese.

By 1973, motorcycle production had slowed to a trickle, but the real hammer blow to the factory was the end of the Invacar. This centred around a highly publicized, and expertly orchestrated, campaign—'ostensibly on behalf of disabled people, but really the greedy car industry,' as Brian Woolley put it, writing in the July 1987 issue of *Classic Bike*. This had come after Bert Greeves had sold his entire shareholding in Greeves to a private company, Tieplas Ltd, headed by Brian Gilroy, in May 1973. However, Derry Preston-Cobb had remained as a member of the new board of directors. Prior to this, Bert Greeves had been awarded the MBE on 1 January 1972. In addition, since the end of 1968, he had left the day-to-day running of the factory to others, including John Rallings. Always someone to take full advantage of a situation, the originator of the Greeves motorcycle had removed himself from the scene just at the right time. In retrospect, it is obvious that things could only go downhill—as they most certainly did.

The end of the Invacar came in 1974. The campaign against it, alleging it was unsafe, had come from a lobby that was strongly supported by the car industry, British Leyland in particular, and fronted by the late Graham Hill, the racing driver. Without doubt, it was Hill's reputation which was instrumental in the anti-Invacar faction gaining the upper hand.

However, the whole affair blew up in the faces of both the automobile industry and those disabled people who had supported the campaign. Instead of simply handing out new Minis and the like, free of charge—to quote Brian Woolley again—the government said, in effect, 'You claim that the Invacar is unsafe, then no more Invacars. Instead, here is a £5-per-week mobility allowance—now make your own arrangements.' Thus, many people lost their sole means of cheap independence, and the Invacar business disappeared overnight. It also meant that several key figures in the Greeves story were made redundant, including engineer Bob Mills, who by now had been 'promoted' to development superintendent.

Without Bert Greeves or the Invacar, the new board of directors at Greeves found the going ever tougher. At first, the situation was eased, to some extent, by acting as wholesalers for various motorcycle accessories, most notably DAG heat-dispersant paint. However, as time went by, even this part of the company suffered through mismanagement. This was highlighted by certain poor-quality lines being distributed under the G Range brand name, which did nothing for the good name previously enjoyed by Greeves. For example, a large quantity of inferior-quality boots from an East European country were marketed as trials boots—not only were they totally unsuitable for the task at hand, but they leaked as well!

Limited production of the Griffon motocrosser continued, as described elsewhere, after co-operation with Dr Gordon Blair of Queen's University, Belfast.

Above **Bert Greeves used this 360-powered sidecar outfit for fun and serious testing of the company's products**

Right **Bert and Mrs Greeves after he received the MBE from HM The Queen Mother, 22 February 1972**

In 1977 Derry Preston-Cobb retired. At the same time, the company was re-formed, with Brian Gilroy being joined by Spencer May and the controlling company changing its name to Speybrig Ltd. This was soon followed by a fire, which not only destroyed much of the office block and part of the stores, but was instrumental in restricting a planned batch of some 250 Griffon Mk II machines to a mere 40.

There was also frenzied activity, in the summer of 1978 and throughout the following winter, to obtain contracts from not only the British government, but also foreign powers, for military

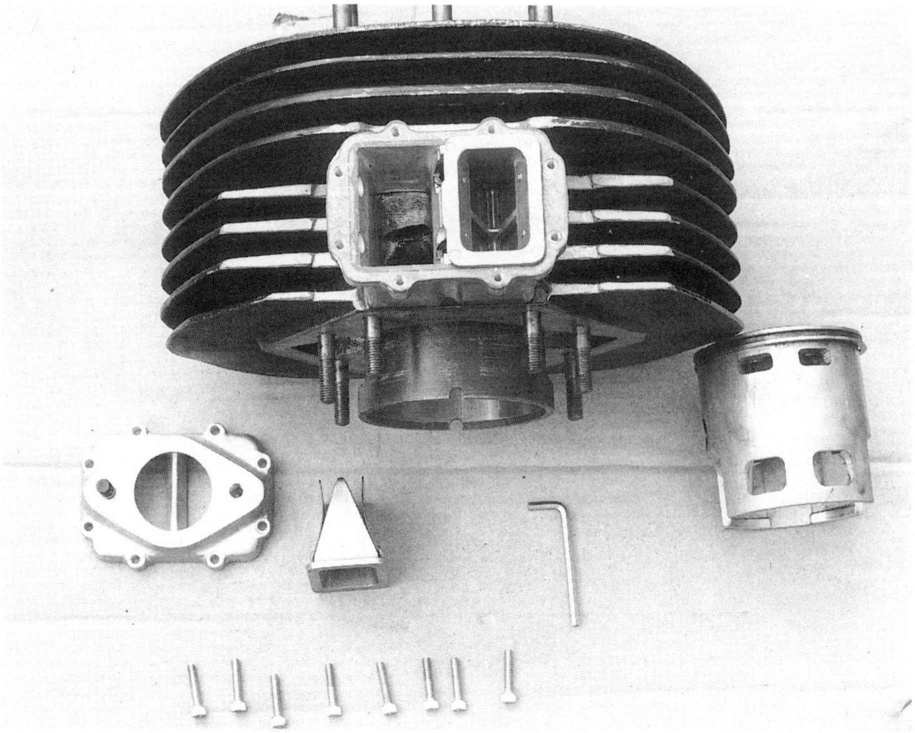

Above **A 380 Griffon at a motocross event in the early 1970s. By this time machines such as Husqvarna, CZ and Bultaco had already largely taken over, with the Japanese waiting in the wings**

Above right **Last gasp. The Gauntlet military motorcycle. Its failure to win orders signalled the end for the Greeves marque**

Left **A Greeves reed-valve cylinder, which was tested in 1975, but never entered production**

motorcycles. In the main, this involved a modified version of the 380 Griffon, initially called the Saxon and later the Gauntlet. The change of name was an attempt to make it sound better—Greeves Gauntlet. However, the only significant sale of a military nature during this time was to the Royal Artillery display team and comprised a dozen 380 Griffon Mk II motocrossers (included in the total production of 40 machines), plus two reserve bikes, which the team specified had to be kept at the factory at all times, in case they were needed suddenly.

In May 1978 the very last Greeves was produced (a Griffon Mk II). There were hopes of a co-operative venture with the Jordanian government to construct an assembly plant in that country to build motorcycles from parts supplied by Greeves, but this never came to fruition. If this plan sounds far-fetched, remember that the ruler of Jordan, King Hussein, has been a life-long motorcyclist.

Already struggling, Brian Gilroy and his team of employees—now around 50—were tottering after the failure to clinch the Jordanian export order. This was confirmed by the fact that, two months prior to the last machine being built, Greeves parts director, David Screttet, had let it be known to one of their few remaining dealers—Terry Silvester Motorcycles of Holmfirth, near Huddersfield—that the factory was interested in selling its entire parts operation. Keith Pursglove, of Terry Silvester's, remembers being surprised, but by May 1978 a deal had been arranged and the spares were being shipped north to their new home. The deal also included the two remaining, unsold machines—the spare Royal Artillery display bikes. One of these was soon sold, while the other was retained by the Silvester organization and today is on display in their showroom.

Relying entirely on the marketing of accessories, Greeves survived until 17 January 1979, when the accountants, Touche-Ross, were appointed receivers. The majority of the staff were made redundant within a few days by the receiver, A. R. Houghton, but a handful of employees remained for a few weeks (until 31 March) while the usual attempts were made to find a buyer (sadly, none

was found) and to administer the last rites to a company which, although never one of the 'big boys', still managed to achieve some truly amazing results. Not only this, but the East Anglian marque was known all around the world.

American Richard C. Renstrom, in his book *Great Motorcycle Legends*, perhaps illustrated best just how highly the Greeves name was held, even on the other side of the Atlantic, by including the Essex factory alongside such names as AJS, BMW, BSA, Ducati, Honda, Matchless, Moto Guzzi, Norton, NSU, Triumph and Velocette—all far bigger and longer established.

From humble beginnings, the Greeves factory had become known worldwide. Its giant-killing

Left **In the early 1980s the Greeves name was kept alive by machines such as this state-of-the-art hillclimber**

Below **The birth of classic racing has brought Silverstones back into action. One of the leading exponents is Martin Studer, pictured here on his 1967 RFS at Mallory Park on 5 May 1985**

1987, and a proud Charlie Pattison stands with the very first Challenger (1964), which he has lovingly restored to its original condition for pre-'65 scrambles events

activities of the late 1950s and early 1960s will never be forgotten. The man himself, the riders, the team of engineers and the machines—all played significant parts in producing a force to be recognized, feared even, by much larger and richer manufacturers.

At its height, Greeves was the most prestigious and respected sporting firm in Britain, perhaps Europe, and was viewed by many as a model of British motorcycle expertise. So why the rapid fall from grace and extinction suffered only a few short years after its greatest achievements? In my (*Mick Walker*) opinion, the underlying reason for failure, as with the majority of other British motorcycle makers, was their inability to adapt quickly enough to counter first the European, and then the Japanese invasions of their markets.

Up-to-the-minute technology, advanced production techniques and lower production costs employed by the Japanese ensured that they could beat the opposition and, therefore, swamp the market. The smaller, leaner Greeves organization—at least while Bert Greeves was at the helm—with its down-to-earth approach, managed to hold off the invaders for longer than most. However, once its founder had left the scene, it took only five years or so to die.

The Greeves name lives on today, thanks, in no small part, to the upsurge of interest in the collection and restoration of motorcycles from the classic period. Of all the British lightweights from this era, the Greeves motorcycles, in their various forms, stand head and shoulders above the rest—just as they did in trials, scrambling and road racing two decades, and more, ago. Because of this, representatives of the marque can be seen competing in the array of sporting events for classic machinery, which take place on almost every weekend throughout the summer months in Britain, and even overseas.

Enthusiasts are now catered for by the GRA (Greeves Riders Association). Established in 1984, the GRA now has about 500 members dotted around the world and was, when formed, the fastest-growing one-make club in Britain. What originally began as a few lonely Greeves owners, helping each other out with parts and information, has now taken on the shape of a successful and well-run organization.

The GRA membership is served by an enthusiastic and knowledgeable team of unpaid volunteers. To keep all members in touch, an excellent bi-monthly newsletter, *Leading Link*, is produced. This contains much useful technical and general information about the marque. The current membership secretary (August 1988) is Peter Smith, 8 St Georges Road, Winsford, Cheshire.

Bert Greeves, now over 80, is the GRA's president and is still as enthusiastic as ever, almost 70 years on from his first motorcycle.

Two companies currently specialize in offering Greeves spares, one in Britain, the other in North America. These are: Terry Silvester Motorcycles, Spring Lane Mills, Woodhead Road, Holmfirth, Huddersfield, West Yorkshire, HO7 1PR, England; and Frank Conley, 13 El Cuenco, Carmel Valley, California 93924, USA. Both carry comprehensive stocks of engine and cycle parts, and operate a full postal service to customers.

All this goes to prove that, although, at first glance, any Greeves could have been dismissed as just another lightweight 'stroker', in reality they were very different to the competition. They had *real* character and that is the reason why today they are held in such high regard by those who appreciate the difference.

Early Scottish being put through its paces in a modern arena event

Appendices

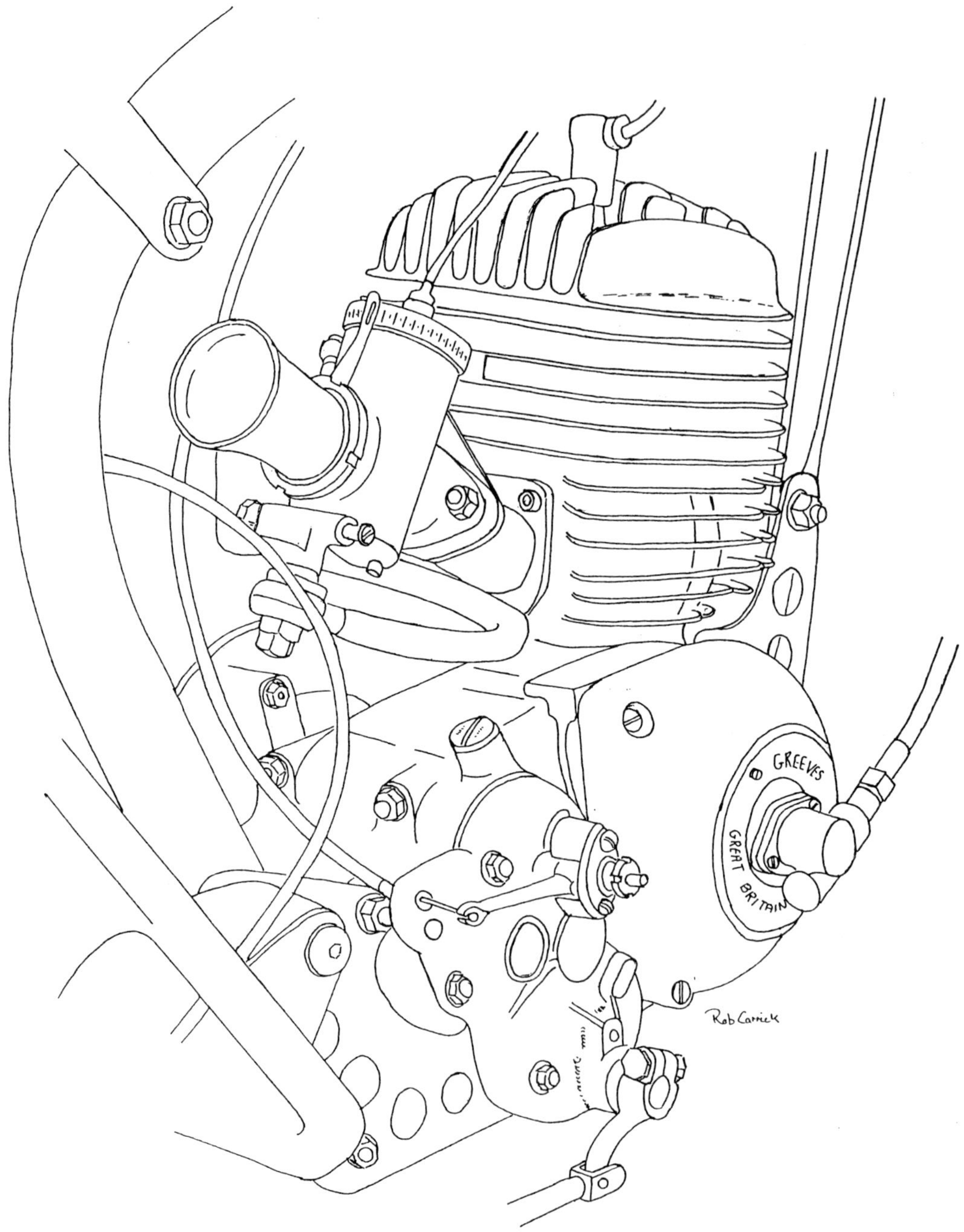
GREEVES
GREAT BRITAIN
Rob Carrick

Specifications

The stated year of manufacture is not necessarily the year in which manufacture began, some models being produced as early as the preceding autumn in order to have machines available for the start of the sporting season. Therefore, the year stated is the first full year of manufacture, or the season for which it was intended.

Models may have been produced during the year following that stated, but these are not included if the model was being run down or was an overspill.

Engine specifications given should not be taken as gospel, as they indicate the standard or lowest state of tune available. Engine specification and, indeed, machine specification could be altered in one, or all, of the following ways:

a) Factory options.
b) Rider options.
c) Parts availability.
d) On-going modifications programme.

Model	**20R**	**20R3**	**20R4**	**20D**	**20D**	**20DB**
Year	**1954**	**1955–6**	**1955–7**	**1954–5**	**1956–8**	**1961**
Engine	8E	8E	8E	8E	9E	9E
Number of cylinders	1	1	1	1	1	1
Bore (mm)	59	59	59	59	59	59
Stroke (mm)	72	72	72	72	72	72
Capacity (cc)	197	197	197	197	197	197
Compression ratio (:1)	7.25	7.25	7.25	7.25	7.25	7.25
Power (bhp)	8.4	8.4	8.4	8.4	8.4	8.4
at (rpm)	4000	4000	4000	4000	4000	4000
Ignition timing (btdc)	.156 in.	.156 in.	.156 in.	.156 in.	.172 in.	.172 in.
Number of gears	3	3	4	4	4	4
Suspension–front	LL	LL	LL	LL	LL	LL
–rear	SA	SA	SA	SA	SA	SA
Brake diameter–front	5	5	5	6	6	6
–rear	5	5	5	6	6	6
Tyre size–front	275/300 × 19	275 × 19	275 × 19	275 × 19	275 × 19	275 × 19
–rear	325 × 19	325 × 19	325 × 19	325 × 19	325 × 19	325 × 19
Dry weight (lb)	240	240	240	240	248	248
Price new (£)	141.00	134.00	141.00	150.00	163.00	170.00

Model	20DC	24DB	24DC	25D	25D	25R
Year	**1961–5**	**1959–61**	**1961–2**	**1954–6**	**1957–8**	**1955–7**
Engine	9E	31A	32A	Anzani	2T	Anzani
Number of cylinders	1	1	1	2	2	2
Bore	59	66	66	52	50	52
Stroke (mm)	72	72	72	57	63.5	57
Capacity (cc)	197	246	246	242	249	242
Compression ratio (:1)	7.25	7.4	7.9	6.5 7.5 (1956)	8.2	6.5 7.5 (1956)
Power (bhp)	8.4	11.6	12.4	10	15	10
at (rpm)	4500	4800	5000	4800	5500	4800
Ignition timing (btdc)	.172 in.	.172 in.	.172 in.	28 deg.	.187 in.	28 deg.
Number of gears	4	4	4	4	4	4
Suspension–front	LL	LL	LL	LL	LL	LL
–rear	SA	SA	SA	SA	SA	SA
Brake diameter–front	6	6	6	6 Twin 6 (1957)	6	6
–rear	6	6	6	6	6	6
Tyre size–front	275 × 19	275 × 19	275 × 19	300 × 19	300 × 20	300 × 19
–rear	325 × 18	325 × 18	325 × 18	325 × 19	325 × 19	325 × 19
Dry weight (lb)	238	245	245	252	294	260
Price new (£)	172.00	179.00	182.00	180.00	217.00	171.00

Model	25DB	25DC	25DCX	25DD	25DC	32D
Year	**1959–60**	**1961–4**	**1962–4**	**1963–5**	**1965**	**1955–7**
Engine	2T	2T	4T	4T	4T	Anzani
Number of cylinders	2	2	2	2	2	2
Bore (mm)	50	50	50	50	50	60
Stroke (mm)	63.5	63.5	63.5	63.5	63.5	57
Capacity (cc)	249	249	249	249	249	322
Compression ratio (:1)	8.2	8.2	8.75	8.75	8.75	6.5 7.5 (1955)
Power (bhp)	15	15	17	17	17	15
at (rpm)	5500	5500	6000	6000	6000	4800
Ignition timing (btdc)	.187 in.	.187 in.	.155 in.	.155 in.	.155 in.	28 deg
Number of gears	4	4	4	4	4	4
Suspension–front	LL	LL	LL	LL	LL	LL
–rear	SA	SA	SA	SA	SA	SA
Brake diameter–front	6	6	6	6	6	Twin 6
–rear	6	6	6	6	6	6
Tyre size–front	275 × 19	275 × 19	275 × 19	275 × 19	275 × 19	300 × 19 300 × 20
–rear	325 × 18	325 × 18	325 × 18	325 × 18	325 × 18	325 × 20
Dry weight (lb)	270	270	277	274	274	292
Price new (£)	199.00	199.00	217.00	219.00	230.00	198.00

Model	32DB	32DC	32DCX	32DD
Year	1960	1961–3	1962–3	1963
Engine	3T	3T	3T	3T
Number of cylinders	2	2	2	2
Bore (mm)	57	57	57	57
Stroke (mm)	63.5	63.5	63.5	63.5
Capacity (cc)	324	324	324	324
Compression ratio (:1)	7.25	8.86	8.86	8.86
Power (bhp)	16.5	18.5	18.5	18.5
at (rpm)	5000	5500	5500	5500
Ignition timing (btdc)	.187 in.	.187 in.	.187 in.	.187 in.
Number of gears	4	4	4	4
Suspension–front	LL	LL	LL	LL
–rear	SA	SA	SA	SA
Brake diameter–front	6	6	6	6
–rear	6	6	6	6
Tyre size–front	275 × 19	275 × 19	275 × 19	275 × 19
–rear	325 × 18	325 × 18	325 × 18	325 × 18
Dry weight (lb)	270	270	277	274
Price new (£)	205.00	209.00	227.00	230.00

Model	20T	20T	20TA	20TC	20TD	20TE
Year	1954–55	1956–57	1958–59	1960	1961–62	1962–64
Engine	8E	9E (Comp) 9E	9E	9E	9E	9E
Number of cylinders	1	1	1	1	1	1
Bore (mm)	59	59	59	59	59	59
Stroke (mm)	72	72	72	72	72	72
Capacity (cc)	197	197	197	197	197	197
Compression ratio (:1)	7.25	8.25 (Comp) 7.25	7.25	7.25	7.25	7.25
Power (bhp)	8.4	9.3 (Comp) 8.4	8.4	8.4	8.4	8.4
at (rpm)	4000	4300 (Comp) 4000	4000	4000	4000	4000
Ignition timing (btdc)	.156 in.	.172 in.	.172 in.	.172 in.	.172 in.	.172 in.
Number of gears	4	4	4	4	4	4
Suspension–front	LL	LL	LL	LL	LL	LL
–rear	SA	SA	SA	SA	SA	SA
Brake diameter–front	6	6	6	6	6	6
–rear	6	6	6	6	6	6
Tyre size–front	275 × 21	275 × 21	275 × 21	275 × 21	275 × 21	275 × 21
–rear	400 × 18	400 × 18	400 × 18	400 × 18	400 × 18	400 × 18
Dry weight (lb)	225	228	233	233	233	240
Price new (£)	147.00	161.00	175.00	166.00	172.00	205.00

Model	20TAS	20TCS	24TE	24TAS	24TCS	24TDS
Year	**1959**	**1960**	**1962–5**	**1959**	**1960**	**1961**
Engine	9E	9E	32A	31A	32A	32A
Number of cylinders	1	1	1	1	1	1
Bore (mm)	59	59	66	66	66	66
Stroke (mm)	72	72	72	72	72	72
Capacity (cc)	197	197	246	246	246	246
Compression ratio (:1)	7.25	7.25	7.9	7.25	7.9	7.9
Power (bhp)	8.4	8.4	12.4	12.0	12.4	12.4
at (rpm)	4000	4000	5000	4400	5000	5000
Ignition timing (btdc)	.172 in.	.172 in.	.172 in.	.172 in.	.172 in.	.172 in.
Number of gears	4	4	4	4	4	4
Suspension–front	LL	LL	LL	LL	LL	LL
–rear	SA	SA	SA	SA	SA	SA
Brake diameter–front	6	6	6	6	6	6
–rear	6	6	6	6	6	6
Tyre size–front	275 × 21	275 × 21	275 × 21	275 × 21	275 × 21	275 × 21
–rear	400 × 18	400 × 18	400 × 18	400 × 18	400 × 18	400 × 18
Dry weight (lb)	233	233	240	240	240	240
Price new (£)	184.00	174.00	205.00	185.00	185. 0	190.00

Model	24TES	24TFS	24TGS	24THS	24TJS	24TJ
Year	**1962–4**	**1965**	**1966**	**1967**	**1968**	**1968**
Engine	32A GR	32A GR	37A GR	37A GR	37A GR	37A
Number of cylinders	1	1	1	1	1	1
Bore (mm)	66	66	66	66	66	66
Stroke (mm)	72	72	72	72	72	72
CapaciTy (cc)	246	246	246	246	246	246
Compression ratio (:1)	9.5	8.86	8.86	8.86	8.86	7.9
Power (bhp)	15	16	17	17	17.5	12.4
at (rpm)	5500	5500	5500	5500	5500	5000
Ignition timing (btdc)	.172 in.	.172 in.	.172 in.	.172 in.	.172 in.	.172 in.
Number of gears	4	4	4	4	4	4
Suspension–front	LL	LL	LL	LL (Tele option)	Tele	LL
–rear	SA	SA	SA	SA	SA	SA
Brake diameter–front	6	6	6	6	6	6
–rear	6	6	6	6	6	6
Tyre size–front	275 × 21	275 × 21	275 × 21	275 × 21	275 × 21	275 × 21
–rear	400 × 18	400 × 18	400 × 19	400 × 19	400 × 19	400 × 19
Dry weight (lb)	235	232	228	215	215	225
Price new (£)	245.00	260.00	265.00	269.00 (Telefork £20.00 extra)	285.00	219.00

Model	25TA	Pathfinder	20S	20S	20SA	20SAS
Year	1958	1970–1	1954–5	1956–7	1958–9	1958–9
Engine	2T	Puch	8E	9E	9E	9E
Number of cylinders	2	1	1	1	1	1
Bore (mm)	50	62	59	59	59	59
Stroke (mm)	63.5	56	72	72	72	72
Capacity (cc)	249	169	197	197	197	197
Compression ratio (:1)	8.2	11.5	7.25	8.25	8.25	9.5
Power (bhp)	15	20	8.4	9.3	9.3	13.5
at (rpm)	5500	8000	4000	4300	4300	5500
Ignition timing (btdc)	.187 in.	.0866 in.	.156 in.	.172 in.	.172 in.	.172 in.
Number of gears	4	6	4	4	4	4
Suspension–front	LL	Tele	LL	LL	LL	LL
–rear	SA	SA	SA	SA	SA	SA
Brake diameter–front	6	5	6	6	6	6
–rear	6	5	6	6	6	6
Tyre size–front	275 × 21	275 × 21	300 × 19	300 × 21	275 × 21	275 × 21
–rear	400 × 18	400 × 18	325 × 19	325 × 19	325 × 19	325 × 19
Dry weight (lb)	260	190	213	218	223	223
Price new (£)	224.00	259.00	152.00	163.00	170.00	189.00

Model	20SCS	24SAS	24SCS	24MCS	24MDS	24ME
Year	1960–61	1959	1960–61	1961	1962–65	1963
Engine	9E	31A	33A	34A GR	34A 36A GR	Starmaker
Number of cylinders	1	1	1	1	1	1
Bore (mm)	59	66	66	66	66	68
Stroke (mm)	72	72	72	72	72	68
Capacity (cc)	197	246	246	246	246	247
Compression ratio (:1)	10.5		12.00	11.00	11.00	12.00
Power (bhp)	13.5		19	21	23	25
at (rpm)	6000		6000	6750	6750	6500
Ignition timing (btdc)	.172 in.	.172 in.	.172 in.	.172 in.	.172 in.	.095 in.
Number of gears	4	4	4	4	4	4
Suspension–front	LL	LL	LL	LL	LL	LL
–rear	SA	SA	SA	SA	SA	SA
Brake diameter–front	6	6	6	6	6	6
–rear	6	6	6	6	6	6
Tyre size–front	275 × 21	275 × 21	275 × 21	275 × 21	275 × 21	275 × 21
–rear	325 × 19	350 × 19	350 × 19	400 × 18	400 × 18	400 × 18
Dry weight (lb)	230	230	230	218	218	227
Price new (£)	185.00	193.00	199.00	250.00	260.00	275.00

Model	24MX1	24MX2	24MX3	24MX4	24MX5	25SA
Year	**1964**	**1965**	**1966**	**1968**	**1967**	**1958–9**
Engine	Greeves	Greeves	Greeves	Greeves	Greeves	2T
Number of cylinders	1	1	1	1	1	2
Bore (mm)	66	66	66	70	66	50
Stroke (mm)	72	72	72	64	72	63.5
Capacity (cc)	246	246	246	246	246	249
Compression ratio (:1)	10	10	10	10	10	8.2
Power (bhp)	25	25	25	27	25	15
at (rpm)	6000	6000	6000	5600	6000	5500
Ignition timing (btdc)	.137–.157 in.	.137–.157 in.	.137–.157 in.	.137–.157 in.	.137–.157 in.	.187 in.
Number of gears	4	4	4	4	4	4
Suspension–front	LL	LL	LL or Tele	Tele or LL	Tele	LL
–rear	SA	SA	SA	SA	SA	SA
Brake diameter–front	6	6	6	6	6	6
–rear	6	6	6	6	6	6
Tyre size–front	275 × 21	275 × 21	275 × 21	275 × 21	275 × 21	275 × 21
–rear	400 × 18	400 × 18	400 × 18	400 × 18	400 × 18	325 × 19
Dry weight (lb)	215	215	217	225	217	260
Price new (£)	285.00	300.00	320.00 (Telefork £20.00 extra)	340.00	330.00	212.00

Model	36MX4	250 Griffon	380 Griffon	380 QUB	380 QUB Mk II
Year	**1967–8**	**1969–77**	**1969–71**	**1971–5**	**1976–7**
Engine	Greeves	Greeves	Greeves	Greeves	Greeves
Number of cylinders	1	1	1	1	1
Bore (mm)	80	70	82	82	82
Stroke (mm)	72	64	72	72	72
Capacity (cc)	362	246	380	380	380
Compression ratio (:1)	10.0	11.0	10.7	13.0	13.0
Power (bhp)	36.0	28.5	39.0	44	44
at (rpm)	7000	7500	7000	6750	6750
Ignition timing (btdc)	.157 in.	.157 in.	.157 in.	.157 in.	.157 in.
Number of gears	4	4	4	4	4
Suspension–front	Tele	Tele	Tele	Tele	Tele
–rear	SA	SA	SA	SA	SA
Brake diameter–front	6	6	6	6	6
–rear	6	6	6	6	6
Tyre size–front	275 × 21	300 × 21	300 × 21	300 × 21	300 × 21
–rear	400 × 18	400 × 18	400 × 18	400 × 18	400 × 18
Dry weight (lb)	226	216	227	225	225
Price new (£)	385.00 (Telefork £20.00 extra)	365.00 (Kit form)	395.00 (Kit form)	475.00 (Kit form)	729.00 (inc. VAT)

Australian motocross star Tim Gibbes campaigned this 500 Matchless-powered Greeves in Europe during 1963

Model	24RAS	24RBS	24RCS	24RDS	24RES	35RFS
Year	**1963**	**1964**	**1965**	**1966**	**1967**	**1968**
Engine	36A GRA	Greeves	Greeves	Greeves	Greeves	Greeves
Number of cylinders	1	1	1	1	1	1
Bore (mm)	66	66	66	66	66	80
Stroke (mm)	72	72	72	72	72	68.5
Capacity (cc)	246	246	246	246	246	344
Compression ratio (:1)	12.7	9.15–9.35	9.25	9.25	9.5	10.0
Power (bhp)	31	31	31	31	32	40
at (rpm)	7400	7500	7500	7500	7500	7500
Ignition timing (btdc)	26 deg.	23 deg.	.137 in.	.137 in.	.137 in.	.137 in.
Number of gears	4	5	5	5	5	5
Suspension–front	LL	LL	LL	LL	LL	LL
–rear	SA	SA	SA	SA	SA	SA
Brake diameter–front	6	6	7	7	7	7
–rear	6	6	6	6	6	6
Tyre size–front	275 × 18	275 × 18	275 × 18	275 × 18	275 × 18	300 × 18
–rear	300 × 18	275 × 18	275 × 18	275 × 18	275 × 18	300 × 18
Dry weight (lb)	189	198	210	210	210	220
Price new (£)	285.00	325.00	345.00	385.00	385.00	450.00

Triumph T100A-engined Greeves at New Brighton road races, organized by the Wirral 100 Club in 1966

Frame numbers

1954	20D	402R
	25D	406/25D
	20R	404R
	20S	401S
	20T	405T
1955	20D	5051
	25D	5301
	32D	5401
	20R3	5151
	20R4	5201
	25R	5351
	20S	5251S
	20T	5001T
1956	20D	6051
	25D	5317
	32D	6401
	20R3	6151
	20R4	5222
	25R	6351
	20S	6251
	20T	6001
1957	20D	7051/20D
	25D	7202
	32D	7401
	20R4	7160/R4
	25R	7351/25R
	20S	7251/S
	20T	7001/T
1958	20D	8398/20D
	25D	8451/D
	20SA	8201/SA
	20SAS	8551/SAS
	25SA	8751/SA
	20TA	8001/TA
	25TA	8651/TA
1959	24DB	59/2401
	25DB	59/2701
	20SAS	59/1901
	24SAS	59/1701
	25SA	59/2201
	20TA	59/1001
	20TAS	59/1001
	24 TAS	59/1501
1960	24DB	60/2500
	25DB	60/2800
	32DB	60/2825
	20SCS	60/1805
	24SCS	60/2006
	20TC	60/1000
	20TCS	60/1000
	24TCS	60/1400
1961	20DB	61/2610
	20DC	61/2804
	24DB	61/2600
	24DC	61/2700
	25DC	61/2900
	32DC	61/3500
	24MCS	61/3650
	20SCS	61/2500
	24SCS	61/1900
	20TD	61/1000
	24TDS	61/1300
1962	20DC	20DC101
	24DC	24DC101
	25DC	25DC101
	32DC	32DC101
	25DCX	25DCX102
	32DCX	32DCX101
	24MCS	24MCS101
	24MDS	24MDS102
	20SC	20SC101
	20SCS	20SCS101
	24SC	24SC101
	20TD	20TD101
	24TD	24TD101
	20TE	20TE101
	24TE	24TE101
	24TES	24TES101
1963	25DC	25DC continued
	32DC	32DC continued
	25DCX	25DCX continued
	32DCX	32DCX continued
	25DD	25DD101
	32DD	32DD101
	24MD	24MD101
	24ME	24ME102
	24RAS	24RAS102
	20SC	20SC106
	20TE	20TE continued
	24TE	24TE322
	24TES	24TES159
1964	20DC	20DC301
	25DC	25DC287
	25DCX	25DCX216
	25DD	25DD194
	24MDS	24MDS1129
	24MX1	24MX101
	24RBS	24RBS101
	20TE	20TE118
	24TE	24TE433
	24TES	24TES331
1965	20DC	20DC398
	25DC	25DC330
	25DC Mk II	25DC350B
	24MDS	24MDS1402
	24MX2	24MX501
	24RCS	24RCS101
	20TE	20TE continued
	24TE	24TE501
	24TFS	24TFS102
1966	24MX3	24MX3-900
	24RDS	24RDS101
	24TGS	24TGS-102
1967	24MX5	25MX5A 101
	36MX4	36MX4 101
	24RES	24RES 101
	24THS	24THSA103
1968	35RFS	35RFS101
	24MX4	24MX4 101
	24TJ	24TJ 101
	24TJS	24TJS 101
1969	250 Griffon	56
	380 Griffon	58
1970	250 Griffon	56
	380	

A 250 Maico-engined Greeves, circa early 1960s

	Griffon	58
	Pathfinder	59
1971	250	
	Griffon	60
	380	
	Griffon	61
	380QUB	63
	Pathfinder	62
1975	250	
	Griffon	60
	380QUB	63
1976	250	
	Griffon	60
	380 QUB	
	Mk II	65
1977	250	
	Griffon	60
	380 QUB	
	Mk II	65

Carburettor settings

Model	cc	Motor type	Carb.	Main jet	Pilot jet	Jet taper	Set out	Groove	Throttle
20R	197	8E	S24/S25	120	35	3½	1.95		3
20R3	197	8E	S24/S25	120	35	3½	1.95		3
20R4	197	8E	S24/S25	120	35	3½	1.95		3
20D	197	8E	S24/S25	120	35	3½	1.95		3
20D	197	9E	S25/1	120	35	3½	1.95		3
20DB	197	9E	S25/1	120	35	3½	1.95		3
20DC	197	9E	S25/1	120	35	3½	1.95		3
20T	197	8E	S24/S25	120	35	3½	1.95		3
20T	197	9E	S25/1	120	35	3½	1.95		3
20TA	197	9E	S25/1	120	35	3½	1.95		3
20TC	197	9E	S25/1	120	35	3½	1.95		3
20TD	197	9E	S25/1	120	35	3½	1.95		3
20TE	197	9E	S25/1	120	35	3½	1.95		3
20TAS	197	9E	S25/1	120	35	3½	1.95		3
20TCS	197	9E	S25/1	120	35	3½	1.95		3
20S	197	8E	S25	120	35	3½	1.95		3
20S	197	9E	S25/1	120	35	3½	1.95		3
20SA	197	9E	376 1$\frac{1}{16}$	290	30	.106		4	3
20SAS	197	9E	376 1$\frac{1}{16}$	250	25	.109		3	3
20SCS	197	9E	389 1$\frac{3}{16}$	460	25	.109		3	3
24DB	246	31A	S25/1	130	35	3½	1.95		3 or 4
24DC	246	32A	S25/2	140	35	3½	1.85		4
24TE	246	32A	S25/2	140	35	3½	1.85		4
24TJ	246	37A	S25/2	140	35	3½	1.85		4
24TAS	246	31A	S25/1	130	35	3½	1.95		3 or 4
24TCS	246	32A	S25/2	140	35	3½	1.85		4
24TDS	246	32A	S25/2	140	35	3½	1.85		4
24TES	246	32A/GR	S25/5	140	35	3½	1.85		4
24TFS	246	32A/GR	S25/6	140	35	3½	1.85		4
24TGS	246	37A/GR	376 1$\frac{1}{16}$	190	25	.105		3	3
24THS	246	37A/GR	626	140	25	.106		2	2½
24TJS	246	37A/GR	626	140	25	.106		2	2½
24SAS	246	31A	389 1$\frac{3}{16}$	480/560	25	.109		3	3
24SCS	246	34A	389 1$\frac{3}{16}$	370	25	.109		3	3½
24MCS	246	34A/GR	389 1$\frac{3}{16}$	380	25	.109		4	3½
24MDS	246	34A/GR	389 1$\frac{3}{16}$	380	25	.109		4	3½
24ME	247	Starmaker	389 1⅛*	290/210	30	.106		5/3	3
24MX1	246	GR	389 1$\frac{3}{16}$	350	25	.106		2	3½
24MX2	246	GR	389 1$\frac{3}{16}$	350	25	.106		2	3½
24MX3	246	GR	389 1$\frac{3}{16}$	350	25	.106		2	3½
24MX4	246	GR	932	300	30	.106		2	3
24MX5	246	GR	930	280	20	.106		2	3

Model	cc	Motor type	Carb.	Main jet	Pilot jet	Jet taper	Set out	Groove	Throttle
Pathfinder	169	Puch	Bing 27	125	40	2.73		3	22.5.75
25D	242	Anzani	375 $\frac{25}{32}$	130	25	.106		2	3
25D	249	2T	S22/2	180	35	$3\frac{1}{2}$		3	3
25R	242	Anzani	375 $\frac{25}{32}$	130	25	.106		2	3
25DB	249	2T	S22/2	180	35	$3\frac{1}{2}$		3	3
25DC	249	2T	S22/2	180	35	$3\frac{1}{2}$		3	3
25DCX	249	4T	S25/6	180	35	$3\frac{1}{2}$	1.95		3
25DD	249	4T	S25/6	180	35	$3\frac{1}{2}$	1.95		3
25DC Mk II	249	4T	S25/6	180	35	$3\frac{1}{2}$	1.95		3
25TA	249	2T	S22/2	180	35	$3\frac{1}{2}$		3	3
25SA	249	2T	S22/2	180	35	$3\frac{1}{2}$		3	3
32D	322	Anzani	376 1.0	260	25	.106		2	$3\frac{1}{2}$
32DB	324	3T	S25/3	180	35	$3\frac{1}{2}$		3	3
32DC	324	3T	S25/3	180	35	$3\frac{1}{2}$		3	3
32DCX	324	3T	S25/3	180	35	$3\frac{1}{2}$		3	3
32DD	324	3T	S25/3	180	35	$3\frac{1}{2}$		3	3
36MX4	362	GR	932	300	30	.106		2	3
250 Griffon	246	GR	930	280	20	.106		3	3
250 Griffon	246	GR	932	310	25	.106		2	3
380 Griffon	380	GR	932	300	25	.106		2	3
380QUB Griffon	380	GR	1034	320	30	.107		2	3
24RAS	246	36A GR	5GP2 $1\frac{3}{8}$	390/420	25	.109		2	3
24RBS	246	GR	5GP2 $1\frac{3}{8}$	400/420	25	.109		Top	4
24RCS	246	GR	5GP2 $1\frac{3}{8}$	400/420	25	.109		2	3
24RDS	246	GR	5GP2 $1\frac{3}{8}$	400/420	25	.109		2	3
24RES	246	GR	5GP2 $1\frac{3}{8}$	400/420	25	.109		2	3
35RFS	344	GR	3GP2 $1\frac{1}{2}$	530		.109		2	3/4

* Twin carburettors.

NOTE. Villiers carburettors prefixed with 'S'; Amal instruments used otherwise except 169 cc Puch-engined Pathfinder, which used a German Bing.

Internal gearbox ratios

Manufacturer	Engine type	Ratio	1	2	3	4	5	6
Villiers	8E/3	Std	2.55	1.34	1.0			
	8E/3	Wide	3.25	1.7	1.0			
	8E/4	Std	2.94	1.78	1.35	1.0		
	8E/4	Wide	3.47	2.3	1.35	1.0		
	9E	Std	2.94	1.78	1.27	1.0		
	9E	Wide	3.6	2.4	1.34	1.0		
	9E	Special Wide	3.6	2.18	1.34	1.0		
	9E	Close	2.55	1.78	1.27	1.0		
	31A	Std	3.6	2.18	1.56	1.0		
	32A	Std	2.94	1.78	1.27	1.0		
	32A	Wide	3.6	2.4	1.34	1.0		
	32A	Special Wide	3.6	2.18	1.34	1.0		
	34/36A	Close	2.55	1.78	1.27	1.0		
	34/36A	Special Close	2.55	1.73	1.25	1.0		
	36A	Silverstone	2.55	1.55	1.17	1.0		
	37A	Wide	3.6	2.4	1.56	1.0		
	2T/3T	Sports	3.06	1.9	1.32	1.0		
	2T/3T	Wide	3.6	2.02	1.4	1.0		
Albion	Anzani twins		2.93	1.82	1.35	1.0		
	Challenger 250		2.22	1.57	1.2	1.0		
	Challenger 360		1.94	1.52	1.17	1.0		
	Silverstone RBS		2.39	1.88	1.4	1.1	1.0	
	Silverstone RCG		2.39	1.88	1.4	1.1	1.0	
	Silverstone RDS		1.96	1.52	1.29	1.09	1.0	
	Silverstone RES		1.96	1.52	1.29	1.09	1.0	
	Oulton RFS		1.96	1.52	1.29	1.09	1.0	
Greeves	Griffon 250/380		1.97	1.52	1.18	1.0		
Puch	Pathfinder		4.01	2.65	1.95	1.52	1.17	1.0

Bultaco-Greeves drag racer—still competitive in 1984. It had an air-cooled 250 kart engine in a Silverstone road-racer frame with a Honda 2LS front stopper

48
SKG 55

A VENDRE

Anglo-Japanese trials iron—a Honda CD175-powered Anglian, seen in Belgium during 1969

Model identification and changes

1954

Range introduction

1955

5 in. brake drums	20R3/4
Armstrong rear spring/damper units	R and S
Sealed ball-bearing wheel hubs Front wheel axle keeper plates Cast-alloy tank badge Front brake cable rerouted	All
One-piece headlamp brackets	All roadsters
Anzani 322 motor introduced Twin 6 in. front brake drum 7 in. rear brake drum	32D

1956

Villiers 9E motor introduced	D, S and T
Steel engine cradle plates	D, S and T
Armstrong rear spring/damper units	D and T
New dualseat in light blue	All roadsters
New seat	S
New Dunlop rubber saddle	T
Twin seat-pillar/frame ties	S and T
Redesigned exhaust system	T
$3\frac{1}{2}$-gallon fuel tank New tool box, number plate and chain guard	All roadsters
New top fork shrouds	32D
Larger cylinder finning and higher cr	25D/R, 32D

1957

Girling damper units for front forks	All
Tool box and tanks in blue/grey	All roadsters
Tanks in light blue/grey	S and T
New dualseat in small blue check	All roadsters
Flat handlebar 20 in. front wheel Twin 6 in. front brake	32D

1958

New frame with stiffer cast beam Single-tube seat-pillar/frame tie	S and T
Narrow rear fork and subframe New dualseat Open megaphone	S
New high-level exhaust system	T
Alloy tank badge with model name	All
Dull-chrome fuel tank	SAS–TAS
Introduction of Villiers 2T motor	25D
19 in. front wheel	All roadsters

1959

Introduction of Villiers 31A motor	24DB/SAS/TAS
Rear-fork chain oiler	S and T
Radial-finned brake drums	24SAS
Dull-chrome fuel tank	S and T
Siamezed exhaust system	25DB
$2\frac{1}{2}$-gallon fuel tank in Essex grey/Moorland blue Alloy mudguards 18 in. rear wheel New tool box New dualseat in grey check	All roadsters

1960

Introduction of Villiers 32A motor	24TCS/DB
Introduction of Villiers 34A motor	24SCS
Introduction of Villiers 3T motor	32DB
New frame with taper head bearings	D and S
One-piece rear subframe New moulded seat	S
4 in. rear tyre	S and T
Large-flange rear hub	24SCS
New frame with shorter wheelbase Increased steering lock Shortened chain guard	T

1961

New frame with taper head bearings	T
One-piece rear subframe	D and T
New engine plates	T
Alloy square cylinder Alloy fuel tank Garda air filter	24MCS
Fuel tank in blue with gold lining	D

1962

New frame with extended top tube Square-section rear fork	MS and T
Redesigned forks	All
Full-width alloy hubs	M and DCX

<table>
<tr><td>Alloy square cylinder</td><td rowspan="2">24TES</td></tr>
<tr><td>Alloy fuel tank</td></tr>
<tr><td>One-piece engine cradle</td><td>24TES and MDS</td></tr>
<tr><td>New exhaust system</td><td>24TES</td></tr>
<tr><td>Fibreglass fairings</td><td rowspan="5">DCX</td></tr>
<tr><td>Recessed fuel tank</td></tr>
<tr><td>Rear-mounted footrests</td></tr>
<tr><td>Twin exhaust system</td></tr>
<tr><td>Pale turquoise blue with yellow flash finish</td></tr>
</table>

1963

<table>
<tr><td>Launch of the Silverstone road racer</td><td>24RAS</td></tr>
<tr><td>Introduction of the Villiers Starmaker motor</td><td>24ME</td></tr>
<tr><td>New exhaust system</td><td>24ME/TES</td></tr>
<tr><td>Fibreglass mudguards</td><td>24TES</td></tr>
<tr><td>Fibreglass fuel tank</td><td>25DD</td></tr>
<tr><td>36A primary-chain case</td><td rowspan="2">24TES</td></tr>
<tr><td>New seat</td></tr>
<tr><td>Full-width alloy hubs</td><td>24TES/25DD</td></tr>
<tr><td>Twin exhaust system</td><td rowspan="2">25DD</td></tr>
<tr><td>Deep-valance plastic mudguards</td></tr>
</table>

1964

<table>
<tr><td>Introduction of Villiers 4T motor</td><td>25DD/DCX</td></tr>
<tr><td>Introduction of Challenger motor</td><td>MX1, 24RBS</td></tr>
<tr><td>Revised one-piece frame</td><td rowspan="2">24RBS</td></tr>
<tr><td>Albion five-speed gearbox</td></tr>
<tr><td>Revised expansion chamber</td><td>MX1, 24RBS</td></tr>
<tr><td>Revised gear-change lever</td><td rowspan="3">24RBS</td></tr>
<tr><td>Revised tacho drive</td></tr>
<tr><td>275 × 18 rear tyre</td></tr>
<tr><td>Plastic mudguards</td><td rowspan="2">MX1</td></tr>
<tr><td>Fibreglass fuel tank in white</td></tr>
<tr><td>Peacock blue finish with light/dark blue tank</td><td>25DD</td></tr>
</table>

1965

<table>
<tr><td>Introduction of Villiers 4T motor</td><td>25DC</td></tr>
<tr><td>Duplex primary chain</td><td>24RCS, MX2</td></tr>
<tr><td>Improved gear-selector barrel</td><td>MX2</td></tr>
<tr><td>Challenger cylinder</td><td>24TFS</td></tr>
<tr><td>Full-width alloy hubs</td><td>All roadsters</td></tr>
<tr><td>7 in. twin-leading-shoe front brake</td><td>24RCS</td></tr>
<tr><td>Plastic front mudguard</td><td rowspan="4">24TFS</td></tr>
<tr><td>Alloy speedometer cowling</td></tr>
<tr><td>Cable-operated rear brake</td></tr>
<tr><td>Repositioned footrests</td></tr>
<tr><td>Revised expansion chamber</td><td>24RCS–24TFS</td></tr>
<tr><td>Restyled fuel tank</td><td rowspan="2">MX2</td></tr>
<tr><td>Mid-green frame finish</td></tr>
<tr><td>Black frame finish</td><td>25DC</td></tr>
<tr><td>New tank logo</td><td rowspan="2">24RCS</td></tr>
<tr><td>Full fairing with perspex nose</td></tr>
</table>

1966

<table>
<tr><td>Introduction of Villiers 37A motor</td><td>24TGS</td></tr>
<tr><td>New Albion five-speed gearbox</td><td rowspan="2">24RDS</td></tr>
<tr><td>Remote gear-change lever</td></tr>
<tr><td>Redesigned primary-drive case</td><td>MX3</td></tr>
<tr><td>Monobloc carburettor</td><td>24TGS</td></tr>
<tr><td>Larger air filter</td><td>MX3</td></tr>
<tr><td>Banana forks</td><td>24TGS, MX3</td></tr>
<tr><td>Alloy mudguards</td><td rowspan="5">24TGS</td></tr>
<tr><td>19 in. rear wheel</td></tr>
<tr><td>Plain, pressed-steel front hub</td></tr>
<tr><td>Redesigned one-piece frame in grey</td></tr>
<tr><td>Fibreglass fuel tank in red</td></tr>
<tr><td>New fairing</td><td>24RDS</td></tr>
</table>

1967

<table>
<tr><td>Introduction of short-stroke Challenger motor</td><td>24MX5</td></tr>
<tr><td>Introduction of 360 Challenger motor</td><td>36MX4</td></tr>
<tr><td>Concentric carburettor</td><td>24MX5, 36MX4, 24THS</td></tr>
<tr><td>New conical wheel hubs</td><td>36MX4</td></tr>
<tr><td>Improved gearbox</td><td>24MX5</td></tr>
<tr><td>New primary-drive case</td><td>MX</td></tr>
<tr><td rowspan="2">Lengthened frame</td><td>in silver: 36MX4</td></tr>
<tr><td>in dark green: 24MX5</td></tr>
<tr><td>Frame finished in silver</td><td>24THS</td></tr>
<tr><td>Rod-operated rear brake</td><td>24THS, MX</td></tr>
<tr><td>Ceriani forks</td><td>24MX5</td></tr>
<tr><td>Restyled fuel tank</td><td>MX</td></tr>
<tr><td>Silver frame finish with red tank</td><td>24RES</td></tr>
<tr><td>Alloy mudguards</td><td>MX</td></tr>
</table>

1968

<table>
<tr><td>Introduction of Oulton motor</td><td rowspan="4">35RFS</td></tr>
<tr><td>$1\frac{1}{2}$ in. GP carburettor</td></tr>
<tr><td>Twin expansion chambers</td></tr>
<tr><td>5-gallon tank</td></tr>
<tr><td>Steel fuel tank</td><td>24TJ</td></tr>
<tr><td>Conical hubs</td><td>24MX4</td></tr>
<tr><td>Ceriani forks</td><td>24TJS</td></tr>
<tr><td>Cast-iron cylinder barrel</td><td rowspan="2">24TJ</td></tr>
<tr><td>Villiers S25 carburettor</td></tr>
<tr><td>300 × 18 tyres</td><td rowspan="2">35RFS</td></tr>
<tr><td>Red finish</td></tr>
</table>

1969

Introduction of 380 Griffon motor		380
New Greeves gearbox		All
New Greeves clutch assembly		All
Introduction of all-tubular frame		All
Restyled dualseat		All
Restyled fuel tank		All
Fibreglass components	Moorland blue	250
	red	380
Redesigned high-level expansion chambers		All

1970

Introduction of Puch 175 motor	Pathfinder
Alloy fuel tank	Pathfinder
Purpose-designed expansion chamber	Pathfinder

1971

Single-port, high-level expansion chamber	380QUB
Telesco forks	380QUB
Motoplat ignition system	380QUB
Frame finished in black	380QUB
Fibreglass components in gold	380QUB

1975

Restyled fuel tank	380QUB

1976

Repositioned rear shock absorbers	380QUB Mk II

A real shoehorn job—a 499 cc Velocette engine-gearbox in a Hawkstone chassis, seen in 1963

Original equipment suppliers

Engine units		Villiers Engineering Company, Wolverhampton.
		British Anzani Engineering Company, Hampton Hill, Middlesex.
		Puch, Graz, Austria.
Frame tubing	531	Reynolds Tube Company, Birmingham.
	Truweld	Le Bas Tube Company, London.
General steel supplies		MacReady's Metal Company, London.
Petrol tanks, chain and mudguards		Speedwell Gearcases Company, Birmingham.
Seats	Luxuride	H. E. Halford, Birmingham.
Tyres, wheel rims, rubber saddles		Dunlop, Birmingham.
Tyres (roadsters)		Avon, Wiltshire.
Hubs	Motobrake Motoloy	British Hub Company, Birmingham.
Brake linings		Ferodo, Stockport.
Paint		Pinchin & Johnson.
Chain	Mark 10	Renold Chain, Manchester.
Plugs		Lodge Plugs, Rugby.
		Champion, Feltham, Middlesex.
Dampers		Girling, Birmingham
		Armstrong Patents Company, Beverley, Yorks.
Suspension rubbers		Metalastik, Leicester.

Control cables		S. J. Clark, Birmingham.
Levers		Doherty, Birmingham.
		Amal, Birmingham.
Carburettors		Amal, Birmingham/Spain.
Speedometers/ rev counters		Smiths Industries, London.
Crankshafts		Alpha Bearings, Dudley.
Front forks		Ceriani, Italy.
		Telesco S.A., Spain.
		Metal Profile, Dudley, Worcs.
Magnetos		Stefa, Sweden.
		Motoplat, Spain.
Kickstart and gear levers		Motor Cycle Equipment, Birmingham.
Lubricants		Shell Oils.
Gearboxes		Albion, Birmingham.
Pistons	Hepolite	Hepworth & Grandage, Bradford.
Lighting equipment		Miller, Birmingham.

36
AVON - RACING

A BSA B40 mounted in a Silverstone chassis, pictured at Mallory Park in March 1965

Model chart

	1954	1955	1956	1957	1958	1959	1960	1961	1962	1963	1964	1965	1966	1967	1968	1969	1970	1971	1972	1973	1974	1975	1976	1977
Road racing																								
24RAS										×														
24RBS											×													
24RCS												×												
24RDS													×											
24RES														×										
35RFS															×									
Roadsters																								
20D	×	×	×	×	×																			
25D	×	×	×	×	×																			
32D		×	×	×																				
20R	×																							
20R3		×	×																					
20R4		×	×	×																				
25R		×	×	×																				
24DB						×	×	×																
25DB						×	×																	
32DB							×																	
20DB								×																
20DC								×	×		×	×												
24DC								×	×															
25DC								×	×	×	×	×												
25DC Mk II												×												
32DC								×	×	×														
25DCX									×	×	×													
32DCX									×	×														
25DD										×	×	×												
32DD										×														

Model chart

	1954	1955	1956	1957	1958	1959	1960	1961	1962	1963	1964	1965	1966	1967	1968	1969	1970	1971	1972	1973	1974	1975	1976	1977
Scrambles/Motocross																								
20S	×	×	×	×																				
20SA					×																			
20SAS					×	×																		
24SAS						×																		
25SA					×																			
20SC									×	×														
20SCS							×	×																
24SC									×															
24SCS							×	×																
24MCS								×																
24MD										×														
24MDS									×		×	×												
24ME										×														
24MX1											×													
24MX2												×												
24MX3													×											
24MX4															×									
24MX5														×										
36MX4														×	×									
Griffon 250																×	×	×				×	×	×
Griffon 380																×	×	×						
QUB380																		×				×		
QUB380 MkII																							×	×
Trials																								
20T	×	×	×	×																				
20TA					×	×																		
20TAS						×																		
24TAS						×																		
25TA					×																			
20TC							×																	
20TCS							×																	
24TCS							×																	
20TD								×	×															
24TD									×															
24TDS								×																
20TE									×	×	×	×												
24TE									×	×	×	×												
24TES									×	×	×													
24TFS												×												
24TGS													×											
24THS														×										
24TJ															×									
24TJS															×									
Pathfinder																	×	×						

Machines on show to the public

Beaulieu Motor Museum 1960 motocross replica, to the same specification as the 1960 Bickers European winner and featuring a detachable-port cylinder. No frame number is shown, but the engine has been declared as 203F 3814, which is out of sequence for the machine's age. The machine was actually built at the Greeves factory, from spare parts, and presented to the museum as an example of British craftsmanship and expertise. The frame is stamped with a single 'E' to denote that it is for exhibition only.

National Motorcycle Museum 1955 trials 20T, restored to the original specification.
1963 International 250, restored to original ISDT specification. This machine, frame number 24 IN 146, is shown on the factory records as 458 J00 and was ridden by Peter Stirland in the 1963 Czech event.

Sammy Miller Museum 1955 trials 20T, frame number 5018T, restored to original specification.
1964 24TES, frame number 24TES 352, refurbished, but bearing many non-standard parts from the era.
1965 24RCS, frame number 24RCS153, in original, unrestored condition—straight from the race track.

Other motorcycle titles from Osprey

Osprey Collector's Library

AJS and Matchless—The Postwar Models
Roy Bacon 0 85045 536 7

Ariel—The Postwar Models
Roy Bacon 0 85045 537 5

BMW Twins and Singles
Roy Bacon 0 85045 699 1

BSA Gold Star and Other Singles
Roy Bacon 0 85045 447 6

BSA Twins & Triples
Roy Bacon 0 85045 368 2

Classic British Scramblers
Don Morley 0 85045 649 5

Classic British Trials Bikes
Don Morley 0 85045 545 6

Classic British Two-Stroke Trials Bikes
Don Morley 0 85045 745 9

Classic Motorcycle Racer Tests
Alan Cathcart 0 85045 589 8

Ducati Singles
Mick Walker 0 85045 605 3

Ducati Twins
Mick Walker 0 85045 634 7

Gilera Road Racers
Raymond Ainscoe 0 85045 675 4

Honda—The Early Classic Motorcycles
Roy Bacon 0 85045 596 0

Kawasaki—Sunrise to Z1
Roy Bacon 0 85045 544 8

Moto Guzzi Singles
Mick Walker 0 85045 712 2

Moto Guzzi Twins
Mick Walker 0 85045 650 9

MV Agusta
Mick Walker 0 85045 711 4

Norton Singles
Roy Bacon 0 85045 485 9

Norton Twins
Roy Bacon 0 85045 423 9

Royal Enfield—The Postwar Models
Roy Bacon 0 85045 459 X

Spanish Post-war Road and Racing Motorcycles
Mick Walker 0 85045 705 X

Spanish Trials Bikes
Don Morley 0 85045 663 0

Suzuki Two-Strokes
Roy Bacon 0 85045 588 X

Triumph Twins & Triples
Roy Bacon 0 85045 700 9

Velocette Flat Twins
Roy Bacon 0 85045 632 0

Villiers Singles & Twins
Roy Bacon 0 85045 486 7

Vincent Vee Twins
Roy Harper 0 85045 435 2

Yamaha Dirtbikes
Colin MacKellar 0 85045 660 6

Yamaha Two-Stroke Twins
Colin MacKellar 0 85045 582 0

Osprey Colour Series

Fast Bikes
Colin Schiller 0 85045 761 0

Japanese 100hp/11 sec./150 mph Motorcycles
Tim Parker 0 85045 647 9

Road Racers Revealed
Alan Cathcart 0 85045 762 9

Restoration Series

BSA Singles Restoration
Roy Bacon 0 85045 709 2

BSA Twin Restoration
Roy Bacon 0 85045 699 X

Norton Twin Restoration
Roy Bacon 0 85045 708 4

Triumph Twin Restoration
Roy Bacon 0 85045 635 5

General

British Motorcycles of the 1930s
Roy Bacon 0 85045 657 6

British Motorcycles of the 1960s
Roy Bacon 0 85045 785 8

Café Racers
Mike Clay 0 85045 677 0

Ducati Motorcycles
Alan Cathcart 0 85045 510 3

Ducati—The Untold Story
Alan Cathcart 0 85045 789 0

German Post-war Road & Racing Motorcycles
Mick Walker 0 85045 759 9

Honda Gold Wing
Peter Rae 0 85045 567 7

In Pursuit of Perfection
Geoff Duke 0 85045 838 2

Motorcycle Chassis Design: the theory and practice
Tony Foale and Vic Willoughby 0 85045 560 X

Track Secrets of Champion Road Racers
Alan Cathcart 0 85045 774 2